A Strange Goodness?

Stephen Ames

For
Ella, Lara, Thomas, Oliver, Eva, Gabriel

A Strange Goodness?

God and Natural Evil

Stephen Ames

Adelaide
2023

Text copyright © 2022 remains with the Anthony J Kelly and the CSsR, Australia, and for the collection with ATF Theology. All rights reserved. Except for any fair dealing permitted under the Copyright Act, no part of the publication may be reproduced by any means without prior permission. Inquiries should be made in the first instance with the publisher.

A Forum for Theology in the World
Volume 11, Issue 1, 2024

A Forum for Theology in the World is an academic refereed journal aimed at engaging with issues in the contemporary world, a world which is pluralist and ecumenical in nature. The journal reflects this pluralism and ecumenism. Each edition is theme specific and has its own editor responsible for the production. The journal aims to elicit and encourage dialogue on topics and issues in contemporary society and within a variety of religious traditions. The Editor in Chief welcomes submissions of manuscripts, collections of articles, for review from individuals or institutions, which may be from seminars or conferences or written specifically for the journal. An internal peer review is expected before submitting the manuscript. It is the expectation of the publisher that, once a manuscript has been accepted for publication, it will be submitted according to the house style to be found at the back of this volume. All submissions to the Editor in Chief are to be sent to: hdregan@atf. org.au.

Each edition is available as a journal subscription, or as a book in print, pdf or epub, through the ATF Press web site — www.atfpress.com. Journal subscriptions are also available through EBSCO and other library suppliers.

Editor in Chief
Hilary Regan, ATF Press

A Forum for Theology in the World is published by ATF Theology and imprint of ATF (Australia) Ltd (ABN 90 116 359 963) and
is published twice or three times a year.

Cover design: original design by Sarannie Tong created from two AI generated images.

ISBN: 978-1-923006-62-1 soft
        978-1-923006-63-8 hard
        978-1-923006-64-5 epub
        978-1-923006-65-2 pdf

Published by

THEOLOGY

Making a lasting impact

An imprint of the ATF Press Publishing Group
owned by ATF (Australia) Ltd.
PO Box 234
Brompton, SA 5007
Australia
ABN 90 116 359 963
www.atfpress.com
Making a lasting impact

A Forum for Theology in the World Vol 11 No 1/2024

Table of Contents

Preface   ix
Acknowledgments   xiii

Part 1
What is the Problem in the Problem of Natural Evil?

I. What is The 'Problem' in The Problem of Natural Evil?
   1a. The logical problem of evil   2
   1b. A theological demand on the natural evil argument   7
   1c. Students meet the requirement   9

Part 2
A Solution to the Logical Problem of Natural Evil

II. A Start to a Solution the Problem of Natural Evil
   1. Introduction   13
   2. The kind of world we should expect God to create   13
      2a. Drawing on Aquinas   16
      2b. Is this cherry picking the Bible?   22
         (1) Historical background   22
         (2) Galileo's 'Two Books' principle   23
      2c. A too open-ended approach?   32
      2d. Does God create the best of all possible worlds?   33

III. The Divine Purpose for The Created Universe
   1a. The divine purpose in creation   35
   1b. Persons   36
   1c. Revelation   38
   1d. The ultimate order of the universe   39
   1e. Preliminary conclusion #1   41

IV. Locating This Theology of Creation
   1a. In relation to the natural sciences 45
       Natural Science is not Scientific Naturalism 45
       Human inquiry and theology 53
       Identifying the penultimate order 55
       Preliminary conclusion #2 61
   1b. Locating this theology of creation within
       Christian tradition 62
       Created in the 'image of God' 63
       Christ, the image of the invisible God 69
       The divine economy for the whole created universe 71
       The trinitarian understanding of God 73
       The biblical revolution: The fundamental order is
       personal 78
       preliminary conclusion #3 80

Part 3
Reality Checks

V. Reality Checks
   Introduction 83
   1. The 'Dead End' universe 84
   2. Destruction of the earth by asteroid collision 88
   3. A contradiction within the theology of creation? 94
   4. Colleagues' objections 98
       1a. Superlative power of God must be moral not
           just functional 98
       1b. The 'only way' argument 101
       1c. A good God indistinguishable from an evil God 102
           Where next? 106
       1d. God is reckless and cruel in creating this
           universe 107
   5. Stephen Fry's tirade against God 110
   6. The evidential problem of natural evil (William Rowe) 115
   7. JL Schellenberg—The new logical problem of evil 123
   8. Conclusion—The strange goodness of God 130

Appendix: Clarification of the Idea of God in the Problem of
       Natural Evil 135
   1. Clarifying a high-profile and widespread confusion
       about the idea of God 136
   2. Alternative Concepts of God 139

3.	Classical Theism—A Common Core of Beliefs	144
	3a. Historical Threads	144
	3b. More on Motivation	149
4.	Clarifications in the light of Criticisms	154
	4a. Philosophical incoherence	155
	4b. Is God complex or simple?	158
	4c. Criticisms of God existing necessarily	160
	Are there many necessary existents?	160
	Necessary divinity and contingent creation.	
	Is this incoherent?	160
	4d. Is God immutable?	164
	Is God 'eternal' or 'everlasting'?	165
	Is God static or dynamic?	168
	Does God suffer or is God beyond all suffering?	171

Bibliography   175

A Forum for Theology in the World Vol 11 No 1/2024

Preface

This book comes from lecturing for twenty years in the subject, 'God and the Natural Sciences', a second-year subject in the History and Philosophy of Science (HPS) programme at The University of Melbourne, Australia. For the last eight of those years I have been working with my colleague, Dr Kristian Camilleri, in the HPS programme. We were joined by Dr John Wilkins in 2016. Previously I have worked with Dr Neil Thomason and with Dr Keith Hutchison also from the HPS programme, with whom I co-designed the subject, which was initially funded by a grant from the John Templeton Foundation. Kristian, John, Neil, and Keith are atheists, and I am a Christian, a priest in the Anglican Church, at St Paul's Cathedral, Melbourne. I am a fellow of ISCAST, Christians in Science and Technology. I have a PhD in physics and a PhD in philosophy of science, both from The University of Melbourne.

In designing and improving this university subject, we wanted to show that an intelligent, public conversation about science and religion is possible and illuminating for all. Such seems to be the case because between sixty and one hundred students enrol each year. Generally, about forty percent are committed atheists, forty percent are committed to a religious tradition, mainly Christian with some Muslim, Jewish, and Buddhist students, and twenty percent are agnostics.

One important feature of all the years working together is that there has been complete agreement on affirming the results of the natural sciences. There has been clear disagreement on the philosophy of science concerning naturalism, especially the claim that the natural sciences reveal or will one day reveal all of reality. We have had almost no disagreement on the history of science. There have been fundamental disagreements about God. It is also worth saying that while we are immersed in a culture saturated with science, technology, and the economy all deeply interwoven, this has not become a theme either in our discussions or in our lectures. I think of this as rightly part of a third or fourth year HPS subject.

Some Christian students have asked what kind of Anglican I am. I regard myself as a theologically orthodox Christian. For example, as part of the Christian community I recite the Nicene Creed on Sunday mornings at the celebration of the Eucharist. As a Christian, I live from the 'good news' of the vulnerable, yet invincible Triune God revealed through Christ. This revelation of God includes the good news of the divine economy for the whole universe, from creation to consummation. As well, this understanding of the good news is critically formed from Scripture, tradition, reason, and experience available within the Anglican Church and from the testimony of the wider Christian tradition, as well as from the diversity of scripts, traditions, reasoning, and experiences available to me within and beyond Australian society. Like everyone else, I stand in a position critically formed by and in response to particular traditions.[1]

The book is written from this theological standpoint. It is written for students and for the wider public interested in an intelligent and constructive conversation about science and religion, in particular Christianity. I hope that many, who are looking for something more substantial, even more subtle, than the mutual dismissal between 'new atheists' and fundamentalists, find here something of what they are looking for.

In my opinion one of the things many students and others are looking for is a large 'frame' or 'worldview' or 'grand narrative' or simply a 'way' in which to locate and hold together the many

---

1. One stream of theological thinking that informs me is the Radical Orthodoxy movement, yet another is the work of Rowan Williams, and a third is the work of Jesuit philosopher Bernard Lonergan. I have been greatly helped by the work of the Centre for Theology and Natural Sciences in Berkley California and its founder Robert J. Russell, http://www.ctns.org/; the work of the Ian Ramsey Centre for Science and Religion, in Oxford, http://www.ianramseycentre.info/; The Ordered Universe Project at Durham University, https://ordered-universe.com/nd; The Faraday Institute for Science and Religion, https://www.faraday.st-edmunds.cam.ac.uk/; and the work of ISCAST here in Australia, http://www.ianramseycentre.info/.

different aspects of their thinking and living. They sense that sorting out questions about 'science and God' is important for finding what they seek, whatever shape it may eventually take. All this without mentioning any postmodern problems with 'grand narratives'.[2]

For many people, the problem of natural evil is a very significant obstacle to identifying with the God Christians worship and so they cannot find in Christian faith and theology such a 'framing'.

As an introduction to the book, I want to say it is about the problem of natural evil meaning all the suffering and death brought about by natural processes. These natural processes are judged to be a problem for the belief that they are the creation of a God who is all-powerful, all-knowing, and all-good, who created the world *ex-nihilo* for some purpose. Many people find the actual world contradicts the kind of world they expect an omni-God to create. This contradiction gives them strong grounds for choosing not to believe in such a God. The book aims to give people good reason to revisit that decision.

My first step in Chapter I provided a critique of the standard argument from natural evil to rejecting belief in God. The critique is that describing natural processes as 'evil' and using that to argue against the existence of God the creator of the actual world, presupposes that these natural evils contradict the kind of world a wholly good God is expected to create.

The critique is that no proper basis is provided for that expectation. The proper basis required is to argue *from* the idea of the omni-God *to* the kind of world we should expect that God to create. Without such an argument, there is no basis for speaking about natural processes as 'natural evils', which contradict the existence of God. I have not found this critique stated anywhere else. On the other hand, students claimed to meet this requirement and still have good grounds for rejecting belief in the omni-God. Their statements s(a) to s(d), in Chapter I claim to meet this requirement and to do so obviously.

Chapter II examines whether s(a) to s(d) does follow from the idea of the omni-God which together show that the actual world is not what we should expect if this idea of God were true. I will argue that s(a) to s(d) does not necessarily follow from the idea of the omni-

---

2. J Lyotard, *The Postmodern Condition: A Report on Knowledge*, translated by G Bennington (Minneapolis, University of Minnesota Press, 1984 [*La Condition postmoderne: Rapport sur le savoir*. Paris: Éditions de Minuit, 1979].

God. I also argue *from* the idea of the omni-God *to* a different account of the kind of world we should expect this God to create and that it is a *better* kind of creation than that represented by s(a)–s(d).

Initially I do this without using any idea of the purpose of God in creating. I then argue *from* the idea of God as perfectly good *to* how we should identify the divine purpose in creating and show what impact this has on the kind of universe we should expect this God to create. There follow two sections where I place this theology of creation in relation to the natural sciences and then in relation to the Christian tradition. I then address in Chapter V eight objections or reality checks against my argument.

Acknowledgments

I want to thank the many people for the conversations that have helped me in developing the ideas in this book, especially my colleagues at The University of Melbourne, Dr Neil Thomason, Dr Keith Hutchison, Dr Kristian Camilleri, Dr John Wilkinson, especially Dr Bruce Langtry, Dr Paul Carter and the many students who engaged with me in God and the Natural Sciences from 2001 to 2020; from the University of Divinity, Professor Mark Brett, Rev Dr Robyn Whitaker, Dr Call Ledsham, Rev Dr Mark Lindsay, Rev Dr Bob Derrenbacker, and from ISCAST, Rev Dr Chris Mulherin, Professor emeritus John Pilbrow and the members of the Melbourne Lonergan Group, especially the late Fr Tom Daly SJ. I accept complete responsibility for any errors in the book.

PART 1

WHAT IS THE PROBLEM IN THE PROBLEM OF NATURAL EVIL?

Chapter I
What is The 'Problem' in The Problem of Natural Evil?

In engaging students and my colleagues, I find it important to take the time to come to an agreement on what is the 'problem' in the problem of natural evil. Otherwise, we might just be talking past each other. One way of identifying the problem in the problem of natural evil came from an atheist student who said, 'Looking around the world, both the natural world and the human world, and remembering that people say this world was created by a perfectly good God, I think it would have to be a very strange goodness'. I commended the student for allowing this possibility. My atheist colleague Kristian said, 'If it is too strange, we might not want to call it 'good''. Another question is, what is it compared to, to which the goodness of God would be so strange? In the end I will return to this claim about the 'strange goodness' God would have to be for this world to be created by such a God, and whether it is so strange that we would not want to call it good.

The problem of natural evil traditionally takes two forms: the logical problem and the evidential problem. The latter is the evidence of dreadful pointless suffering in the world which challenges belief in God. William Rowe[1] is widely seen to have presented this problem in sharpest form, which I will discuss later when the ground has been prepared. The logical problem is the presence of evil in the world as logically contradicting the claim that God exists and that God is said

---

1. William Rowe IX, 'The Problems of Evil and Some Varieties of Atheism', in *American Philosophical Quarterly*, 16/4 (1979): 335–341 and 'The Evidential Argument from Evil: A Second Look', in D Howard-Snyder, *The Evidential Argument from Evil* (Indiana University Press, 1996).

to be all powerful, all knowing and wholly good, the omni-God.[2] I begin by responding to this form of the problem.

1a. The logical problem of evil

This is the claim that the idea of the omni-God is logically contradicted by the presence of evil in the world. It is common for students to present some version of the logical problem. For example, they cite the following statement by Michael Tooley.[3]

Thus, if we focus on a conception of God as all-powerful, all-knowing, and perfectly good, one very concise way of formulating such an argument is as follows:

1. If God exists, then God is omnipotent, omniscient, and morally perfect.
2. If God is omnipotent, then God has the power to eliminate all evil.
3. If God is omniscient, then God knows when evil exists.
4. If God is morally perfect, then God has the desire to eliminate all evil.
5. Evil exists.
6. If evil exists and God exists, then either God doesn't have the power to eliminate all evil, or doesn't know when evil exists, or doesn't have the desire to eliminate all evil.
7. Therefore, God doesn't exist.

This as a logically valid argument, meaning necessarily if the premises are true the conclusion is true. A response to this logical problem of evil, widely recognised as successful, is Alvin Plantinga's free

---

2. Philosophers of theism have long distinguished between defences and theodicies. A defence purports to show that some truth involving evil is compatible with the existence of God. A theodicy aims to show that God is in fact justified in causing or permitting this or that specific kind, or amount of evil. I am preparing the ground to work out a theodicy, which is presented in Chapter III.
3. Michael Tooley, 'Problem of Evil', in *Stanford Encyclopaedia of Philosophy*. Section 1. (Original, 2001. Substantially revised 2015). For a critique of Tooley's 'The Argument from Evil', in *Philosophical Perspectives*, 5 (1991): 89–134, see B Langtry, *God, The Best, And Evil* (Oxford: Oxford University Press, 2008). Langtry's work offers a formal philosophical response to the problem of evil in defence of God.

will defence[4] showing that the existence of evil in the world is not necessarily a contradiction of the idea of the omni-God.

Tooley's argument obviously holds for the problem of 'natural evil' as a particular form of evil. As noted above, 'natural evil' is taken to refer to the dreadful suffering and death of living things due to natural processes like tsunamis, extreme weather events, genetic disorders, and all the suffering and death in the evolution of life, which natural processes God has freely created and sustains in existence. We have a contradiction between the understanding of God as creator and what God has created. The conclusion (7) to Tooley's argument remains: 'Therefore God does not exist.' I have been greatly helped by Plantinga's defence, to resist the critique of many people that any instance of evil in the world contradicts belief in the omni-God. However, I do not find it helpful regarding the problem of natural evil, in which it is God freely creating the circumstances and events widely recognised as natural evil.

This is argument against the existence of God arising from a contradiction between this understanding of God and the lack of any recognisable divine activity in response to natural evil.[5] Atheist students and colleagues regard this as a strong argument. The point is pressed to me, 'If *you* had the knowledge and power to help someone in terrible need, you would of course help them. Not to do so could also be said to fail to follow God's second commandment to love your neighbour as yourself.' Students make the point that by not intervening in the myriad of situations of terrible pain and suffering God fails to lead by example, by not keeping God's own commandment. (Certainly, their points express 'attitude', but how is that surprising?) In some quarters, theology would not accept the idea of God being subject to the laws that God commands human beings to keep. But I regard that as too defensive of God and hardly meeting the challenge.

---

4. Alvin Plantinga, 'The Free Will Defence', in Max Black, *editor, Philosophy in America (Ithaca, NY: Cornell University Press, 1965); God, Freedom, and Evil (Grand Rapids, MI: Eerdmans, 1977).*
5. This argument could charitably be taken to mean God should have eliminated natural evils as an option. Evil should not have been allowed to arise in the first place. I take this to mean God should have created a different kind of universe in which natural evils do not arise. See below, where this option is proposed by students.

The point being made by students is that such natural processes are rightly said to be 'evil' because they can and do blindly undermine the 'good' of life through an overwhelming pain and suffering, or premature death, which, we as moral agents would ordinarily try to prevent in order to preserve this good. It seems obvious that while such natural processes are crucial in bringing about the good for living things, they can go against the value of this good and therefore these 'disvalues' should be the concern of the omni-God to prevent or redress. Notice that students appeal to a common sense understanding of 'good', which they believe applies to such a God as (supposedly) the wholly good moral agent.

Tooley's valid argument presents the problem of natural evil, concluding that God does not exist. The conclusion can be resisted by denying the idea of God in (1), for example by denying that God is all-powerful or all-knowing.[6] Also, Tooley's statement in (6) is open to challenge. Could there be circumstances where suffering and death are required to bring about some greater good or to prevent some greater evil? If so, then (6) is not true. The omni-God could be understood as permitting suffering in these circumstances.

Of special interest is Murray's question, 'what would it take to have a morally sufficient reason for permitting an evil?' Murray argues three conditions must be met.[7]

- (A) The Necessity Condition: the good secured by the permission of the evil, E, could not have been secured without permitting either E or some other evils morally equivalent to or worse than E.
- (B) The Outweighing Condition: the good secured by the permission of evil is sufficiently outweighing.
- (C) The Rights Condition: it is within the rights of the one permitting evil to permit it.

(A) allows us to see a particular line of argument against the existence of God. Is there evidence of suffering due to natural processes that cannot be understood as required to bring about some greater good or prevent some greater evil? If so, this would contradict (A) and so

---

6. For example, DR Griffin, *Evil Revisited: Responses and Reconsiderations* (Albany, NY: State University of New York Press, 1977).
7. MJ Murray, *Nature Red in Tooth and Claw* (Oxford, Oxford University Press, 2008), including Murray's defense of these conditions, 14–16.

argue against the existence of God. An argument for such evidence against God is known as the 'evidential argument'.

Another response to Tooley's valid argument is to ask whether it is it sound. I explain to students that I have two concerns. One is whether one accepts the understanding of God used in Tooley's argument and the other is the understanding of 'natural evil'. Tooley uses an understanding of God that does not mention God as the creator of the universe. I am at least working with the idea that God is all-powerful, all-knowing, perfectly good, who creates the universe *ex nihilo*[8] and sustains it in existence for some purpose.[9] What effect does this have on understanding the 'problem' in the problem of natural evil?

Tooley's argument would lead us to expect an omni-God would be intervening everywhere to correct or prevent natural processes producing so much natural evil. But if God is the creator of the universe, then God intervening that way would mean God was good but deeply irrational, since God is supposedly the creator of these natural processes! Not intervening would mean God was rational and cruel, not good. This idea of God as the all-powerful, all-knowing,

---

8. This says that God creates the universe from 'nothing' meaning not from prior existing 'stuff', as if God were like an architect and builder ordering prior existing material to manufacture the universe. This *ex-nihilo* prevents any answer to the problem of natural evil along the lines of blaming poor materials for God to work with in forming a world. God is wholly responsible for bringing the universe into existence and sustaining it in existence. God creates the universe *ex nihilo* means all that God brings into existence is good. Thus, evil is traditionally understood as not existing in its own right, that is, not created by God. Evil is the corruption or privation of some created good that properly belongs to the created world. See J Hick, *Evil and The Love of God* (London: MacMillan, 1966), 65.
9. This difference and a certain vagueness about the idea of God in the problem of natural evil has prompted me to prepare Appendix 1 as a clarification of the idea of God in the problem of natural evil. It may help to add that in the early centuries of our common era the Christian Church had a sustained argument with the various schools of Gnosticism who held to a view of the true God as the redeemer of the elect from this world, who was definitely not the creator of this garbage heap of a world. Theologians of the Church maintained that the creator and redeemer are one. The difference was important then in the attitude to the world. While I don't regard Tooley as a latter-day Gnostic I do want to be explicit about including in the argument the idea of God as the creator of the world. It helps make explicit a requirement noted above on those who affirm and those who deny the problem of natural evil.

and perfectly good Creator of our universe would be contradicted either by God's *action* or *inaction*. Therefore, we should not expect such a God to create a universe like ours with the pain, suffering, and death involved in the evolution of life and other natural processes. Again, students regard this as a strong argument against the idea that our universe is the creation of such a God.

A third argument—the evidential argument noted above and to which I return in detail in Chapter V, section 6—highlights instances of pointless suffering, and death in the natural world, for example the excruciating death of a fawn in a forest fire, started by natural causes. According to the argument, there is no greater good for the sake of which these examples of pointless suffering are permitted by God. Such suffering contradicts the kind of world we should expect to be created by a wholly good God. It counts as a 'natural evil' and so the actual universe is very different from what we would expect a wholly good God to create and sustain in existence. Therefore, we ought to reject this idea of God. I read the following comment from Richard Dawkins as making this point.[10]

> In a universe of blind physical forces and genetic replication, some people are going to get hurt, other people are going to get lucky, and you won't find any rhyme or reason in it, nor any justice. The universe we observe has precisely the properties we should expect if there is, at bottom, no design, no purpose, no evil, no good, nothing but blind, pitiless indifference.

The first argument was from God's inactivity in the face of natural evils. The second argument is that both divine activity and inactivity would contradict the idea of such a God creating our universe. Our universe is very different from what we should expect such a God to create. The third argument is that natural processes involve pointless suffering and death and are rightly called 'natural evils' because they contradict the kind of world you would expect a wholly good God to create and maintain. Atheist students think these are good arguments for denying the existence of God.

---

10. R Dawkins, *River Out of Eden: A Darwinian View of Life* (London, Phoenix, 1996), 133.

1b. A theological demand on the natural evil argument

In the face of these strong arguments against God, where does one begin to respond? I would not begin with some religious students, who in the face of this denial of God ask where atheists get their idea of the good, as if, without God, atheists had undermined their own argument by having no idea of good. But this is not so for two reasons.

One was noted earlier. Atheist students appeal to a common-sense understanding of the good. Natural processes are said to be 'evil' because they can and do blindly undermine the 'good' of living things by overwhelming suffering, or premature death, which, morally, we as moral agents would ordinarily try to prevent in order to preserve this good and count the effort itself as good. If religious students respond by saying 'who says that is "good"?', atheist students think they can simply 'rest their case' for it seems that religious students are kicking an 'own goal' by appearing to deny an obvious good. If God is perfectly good, it seems to atheist students that the 'good of life' and the effort to sustain it should come within the active concern of such a God. Secondly, and perhaps more importantly, the natural evil argument is made in response to the claim by people of *faith* that the world is created good by a wholly good God.[11]

The 'natural evil' argument makes the claim that the actual universe contradicts the kind of universe we should expect the omni-God to create. For the argument to work we need to have an idea of what kind of world we should expect such a God to create. Otherwise, we could not say that the *actual world* contradicts the *expected world* and so contradicts this idea of God. Therefore, without this argument, we could not fairly say that some processes or events, in the actual universe are natural evils in the sense that they contradict the idea of

---

11. McGrath rightly says, 'the judgment that any natural process is 'evil' is unsustainable from an evolutionary point of view' because such 'a moral evaluation is not based on natural criteria, but on the position of a human moral framework'. He is wrong to use this as a basis for describing the discussion concerning 'natural evil' as 'sterile'. The talk of 'natural evil' is not within an evolutionary viewpoint but draws on faith's claim that the world is created good (as atheist students and colleagues have pointed out). A McGrath, *Darwinism and the Divine, Evolutionary Thought and Natural Theology*, The 2009 Hulsean Lectures, University of Cambridge (Malden, Mass: Wiley-Blackwell, 2011), 202.

this universe being created by a perfectly good God and so provide a basis for rejecting the existence of God.[12]

It might well be asked how the conclusion would be changed by proceeding *from* the idea of God *to* the kind of world we should expect such a God to create? Well, it may not. However, I want a moment for theology to explicitly consider proceeding *from* the idea of omni-God *to* the kind of world we should expect such a God to create. This is a different starting point from that of seeing some instance of human or animal suffering that could be prevented or ameliorated and deciding to act accordingly, which the supposedly all good omni-God does not do. Rather, we are asked to somehow envisage a perfectly good God creating a whole world for some purpose. What bearing would the idea of perfect divine goodness have on our understanding of this act? What kind of world should we expect such a God to create? Does theology have anything to say here?

We can see that this change of standpoint might make a difference. For example, if we concluded that the actual universe is indeed the kind of universe we should expect such a perfectly good God to create, we could not say that divine inactivity was a problem for belief in such a God. It would be deeply irrational to expect such a God to be intervening in our universe to prevent/correct natural processes that are in accord with what we should expect from a wholly good God. But what understanding of the 'good' (if any) would allow us to argue along those lines? Would it involve some special pleading on behalf of God? Would it have to reject the common-sense understanding of the good held by atheist students? Would it be a very "strange" goodness and what would that be? Might it be so strange that we would not call it good?

I see the need for a 'theological moment' which develops an argument *from* this idea of God *to* the kind of world we should expect such a God to create and so to compare the actual world and the expected world. Such an argument should be provided to support the claim that there are natural evils and therefore this universe is not created by a perfectly good God. Likewise, such an argument should be provided to support the claim by those arguing that the suffering and death due to the natural processes in our universe are *not* 'natural

---

12. Recall that the negative expectation (Rowe, Tooley) that a wholly good God would create a universe without any undesirable states is mistaken, where this God is the creator of a universe that includes persons with freedom for good but which may be used otherwise.

evils' because they do not contradict the kind of universe we should expect a perfectly good God to create. Both atheists and theists need to variously engage in such a 'theological moment' that can support their different positions. The 'theological moment' will trace a path of reflection from the understanding of God as all powerful, all knowing, and all good, to the kind of universe we should expect such a God to create, *ex nihilo*, for whatever purpose God may have in mind. Atheists would thereby make explicit their thinking about the God they do not believe in, and theists would thereby make explicit their thinking about the God they do believe in. This may seem like a daunting task, but it correctly brings to the fore an important part of the 'problem' in the problem of natural evil.[13]

Atheist colleagues and students accept the requirement. This is important as indicating a condition for the conversation to continue. Note also, this is to be a theological argument that is independent of a scientific account of the actual universe. This approach will require the further statement of how the theological view of the kind of universe we should expect God to create compares to the scientific view of the actual universe. I discuss that matter in Chapter IV, section 1a.

1c. Students meet the requirement

In response and with some irony, atheist students have provided just such a 'theological moment', arguing that,

> s(a) a perfectly good God would create a perfectly good universe;
> s(b) the universe would therefore be created in its 'end state' thereby perfectly fulfilling the divine purpose in creation;
> s(c) the perfectly good 'end state' would not include any pain, suffering, or death;
> s(d) there would be no process leading to the fulfilment of the purpose.

---

13. Compare, A McGrath, 'A Wider Teleology' in A Mc Grath, *Darwinism and the Divine*, 203, 4. 'We cannot produce another universe against which to evaluate the one we know; we can only assert that we believe a better universe is possible. We are not in a position to demonstrate that there is or could be a superior way of constructing this world, or bringing life in general, and humanity in particular, into being. We may complain about the existence of pain and suffering. But that hardly amounts to a disconfirmation of the goodness of the world.'

The 'end state' was not formulated beyond being whatever fulfilled the divine purpose in creation. The atheist students did not clarify this purpose. With much left unsaid, s(a) and s(b) positively characterise the kind of creation we should expect of God, and this provides the basis for saying in s(c) and s(d) what would not characterise the created universe.

Assuming this argument is correct, the evidence from the natural sciences concerning our universe strongly supports the conclusion that our universe has not been created by such a perfectly good God. For example, s(d) is contradicted by the long process of evolution leading to human beings. Anyone disputing this conclusion would have to provide good theological reasons for not accepting statements s(a)—s(d) about the kind of world a perfectly good God should be expected to create. Some other account of the move from the idea of a 'perfectly good' God to the kind of world we should expect such a God to create would need to be presented and appropriately supported.

Atheist students and colleagues have pointed out that the Christian Bible presents the biblical God as creating the world but not in its 'end state', for it presents visions of the 'end state' (for example Isa 11:6–9; Rev 21) that this God will finally bring about. The possibility of identifying the biblical God as perfectly good, at least requires there to be good reasons for not accepting one or more of statements s(a)—s(d) about a perfectly good God. Again, some other account of the move from the idea of a 'perfectly good' God to the kind of world we should expect such a God to create would need to be presented and appropriately supported.

I take all this to set out the 'problem' in the logical problem of natural evil.[14] On the one hand, there needs to be a 'theological moment' presenting an argument from the idea of God to the kind of world you would expect such a God to create. Without it, there is no basis for speaking of 'natural evils' that can then serve to contradict the idea of the actual universe being created for some purpose by an omni-God. On the other hand, statements s(a)—s(d) are claimed

---

14. Later I discuss the view of the atheist JL Schellenberger in his chapter 'A New Logical Problem of Evil', in D Howard-Snyder, and P McBrayer, editors, *The Blackwell Companion to the Problem of Evil* (West Sussex: John Wiley and Sons, 2013), Chapter 3. I regard it as a much more sophisticated argument supporting the students' claim s(a), that God should be expected to create a perfectly good world.

to meet this requirement and to do so obviously. Both the scientific account of the evolution of life and the different biblical story of the creation of the world contradict s(a)—s(d). The conclusion is that this world has not been created by a wholly good God nor by the biblical God. End of story.

Is it possible to reasonably open up a different 'theological moment' leading from this idea of God to a different idea of the kind of world we should expect such a God to create and thereby show that s(a)—s(d) is not obvious and so is not 'End of Story'?

PART 2

A SOLUTION TO THE LOGICAL PROBLEM OF NATURAL EVIL

Chapter II
A Start to a Solution the Problem of Natural Evil

1. Introduction

This book is about the problem of natural evil meaning all the suffering and death brought about by natural processes. These natural processes are judged to be a problem for the belief that they are the creation of a God who is all-powerful, all-knowing, and all-good, who created the world *ex-nihilo* for some purpose. Many people find the actual world contradicts the kind of world they expect an omni-God to create. This contradiction gives them strong grounds for choosing not to believe in such a God. The book aims to give people good reason to revisit that decision.

2. The kind of world we should expect God to create

I aim to say what kind of world we should expect God to create based on the idea of God presented to me by colleagues and students in raising the problem of natural evil. In Chapter I, the students' argument s(a) to s(d) is a theological argument expounding the kind of universe we should expect a perfectly good God would create and concluding that it is contradicted by what we know scientifically of the actual universe. They conclude it cannot be the creation of such a God. My argument parallels but differs from the students' argument. I will claim this difference undermines the students' argument, while supporting my claim that this universe is the creation of an all-knowing, all-powerful, wholly good God.

In this chapter I make a start to a solution to the logical problem of natural evil. The argument continues in Chapters III and IV. Only at the end of Chapter IV, section 1a do I claim that there is good reason to think the actual universe does not contradict the kind of universe we should expect the omni-God to create.

I will be referring to the theology of Thomas Aquinas, from the thirteenth century[1] because of the value Aquinas has for our thinking through the implications of the idea of the omni-God.[2] I have earlier asked for a 'moment' to consider what theology might say about the created world in which we live and what impact this might have for thinking about the problem of natural evil. I am therefore attempting to offer an account of God as creator based on the idea of the omni-God, *without* using the scientific understanding of the universe and without concocting a theology to suit the scientific, especially post-Darwin view of our universe. It is not at all that I discount the scientific view of the universe, but if it is to be engaged theologically, it is surely appropriate to hear what if anything theology as such proposes about the world it says God created.[3]

While there are things that can be said about the kind of world we should expect such a God to create, there will be an inescapable limit, not just due to mere human limitations. If creation is a free act of divine will, the creation would be contingent on divine freedom. There will be much about the detail of this contingent creation which we will not be able to derive as a necessary consequence from the idea of God. You might think this undermines the project of saying how the actual world, (which we here assume is created by God, and known through the natural sciences), compares with the kind of world we should expect God to create. It turns out not to be so, as we shall see.

---

1. Many people have trod this path before me and have done so far more deeply. Among Anglican theologians I especially acknowledge, Austin Farrer, *Finite and Infinite, A Philosophical Essay*, (Westminster: Dacre Press, 1943); *Love almighty and ills unlimited: an essay on providence and evil containing the Nathaniel Taylor lectures for 1961*, (London: Collins, 1962); and Eric Mascall, for example, Eric Mascall, 1966, *Existence and analogy: a sequel to 'He who is'*, London: Darton, Longman & Todd.
2. The idea of the omni-God presented in the problem of natural evil is standardly recognised as part of classical theism and Aquinas is widely recognised as giving the best exposition of this form of theism. See the Appendix for a discussion of criticisms of this idea of God and an introduction to other ideas of God in circulation.
3. Two examples of elaborating a Christian doctrine of creation without using the results of the natural sciences are, Norman Young, *Creator, Creation and Faith*, London: Collins, 1974, and, Colin Gunton, *The Triune Creator, A Historical and Systematic Study* (Grand Rapids: Eerdmans, 1998).

I intend to take up Aquinas' thinking on just two matters, but without taking over the cosmology and philosophy of his day.[4] I will be looking at Aquinas' discussion of two pertinent questions in his *Summa Theologiae*: *whether all things are governed by God immediately?*[5] and, *whether God is active in every agent cause?*[6] Would God create a universe in which things have their own real powers or would God create a universe in which God is the only power at work? Before getting into this discussion, I think a very brief indication of the context of these questions is useful.

David Lindberg[7] tells us that the intellectual life of Europe in the 13th century was dominated by the organisation and assimilation of the new learning, Greek and Arabic in origin, made available through the activity of the translation movement in Islam.[8] The central figure in the new learning was Aristotle (384–322 BCE). 'Tensions between this new learning and the blend of Platonic philosophy and Christian theology that had come to dominate European thought over the previous millennium set an agenda that would challenge many of the best of European minds.'[9]

The writings of St Augustine (354–430 CE) had provided the dominant version of this blend but Augustinian views were displaced by Aristotelianism and by the new blend of Aristotelianism and Christian theology known as 'scholasticism' that was brought to an exquisite formulation by Aquinas. Later, Augustinian views were revived by the Reformers, Luther, and Calvin. Later still, they were revived within the Catholic Church in a movement known

---

4. For example, I have no basis for assuming a hierarchical cosmology. Two contemporary versions of Thomistic thinking are, Bernard Lonergan, *Insight, A Study of Human Understanding*, (London: Darton, Longman and Todd, 1958); and Michael J Dodds, OP, *Unlocking Divine Action, Contemporary Science and Thomas Aquinas* (Washington DC: Catholic University of America Press, 2012).
5. Q. 1a, 103, art. 6, St Thomas Aquinas, *Summa Theologiae [ST], Volume 14, Divine Government*, translated by TC Obrien (Spottiswoode: Blackfriars), 1975, 25–27.
6. Aquinas, ST, q. 1a, 105, art. 5, 75–79.
7. David Lindberg, 'Medieval Science and Religion', in GB Ferngren, *Science and Religion, A Historical Introduction* (Baltimore: Johns Hopkins University Press, 2002), 65.
8. Iqbal Muzaffar, *Islam and Science* (Ashgate, Hampshire: Ahmad Dallal, 2002), 'Science, Medicine and Technology', in J Esposito, editor, *The Oxford History of Islam* (Oxford: Oxford, 2000).
9. Lindberg, *Medieval Science and Religion*, 65.

as 'Jansenism'. Today the Radical Orthodoxy movement is one contemporary retrieval of Augustinian and Platonic thinking in Christian theology.[10]

Al Ghazali, a great 11th-century Muslim scholar in the school founded by al-Ash'ari in the 9th century, wrote 70 books on philosophy and Sufism, most famously *The Incoherence of the Philosophers*. He rejected Aristotle and Plato. *The Incoherence* was directed against Islamic scholars drawing on Greek philosophy. His resolution of the tensions between reason and revelation was accepted by later Muslim theologians. Among the many topics he treated, al Ghazali is generally understood as teaching 'occasionalism'—the view that causal events are not necessary material conjunctions in which effects necessarily follow from causes, but rather from the immediate and present will of God.

Later, Luther and Calvin, the leading lights of the Protestant Reformation in Europe, held that God is the only power at work in the universe.[11] The causal powers we believe are at work in the world, like the warmth of the sun's light melting snow or the campfire warming us, or the destruction produced by a volcano, are mere appearances. On this view, it is God in the fire or God in the sun's rays that is the power at work bringing about the effects we observe.

2a. Drawing on Aquinas

For Aquinas, God is the primary cause, creating from nothing and sustaining in existence the secondary causes we see operating in the world. Thomas' view of 'secondary causes' is often mentioned in the 'science and theology' scene but what is not sufficiently noted is the strictly *theological* reasoning that drives Thomas' argument.

---

10. John Milbank, *Theology and Social Theory: Beyond Secular Reason* (Oxford: Blackwell, 1990); John Milbank, *Beyond Secular Order: The Representation of Being and the Representation of People* (Chichester: Wiley-Blackwell, 2014); Paul Tyson, *Returning to Reality, Christian Platonism for Our Times* (Eugene OR: Cascade Books, 2014).
11. Garry B Deason, 'Reformation Theology and the Mechanistic Conception of Nature', in David L Lindberg and Ronald L Numbers, editors, *God and Nature, Historical Essays on the Encounter between Christianity and Science* (Berkeley, University of California Press, 1986), 175–178.

According to Aquinas, God is the very essence of goodness: that than which none greater can be conceived. Therefore, we should allow this superlative to serve as a criterion informing our thinking and speaking of God.[12] So we should prefer to say, and so assert, that God creates things with real causal powers rather than with no real powers. This is because it is a greater exercise of power, which creates things that are not only good in themselves but the cause of good in others. A saying from our own day makes the point: feeding hungry people with fish is good but teaching them how to fish and so feed themselves is better.

Aquinas also argues that if creatures did not exercise the powers we observe at work in the world they would appear to have a pointless existence.[13] Also, 'God would appear to prefer the lesser excellence of a thing being good in itself rather than the greater excellence of a thing being good in itself and a cause of good in others'.[14] Such a view implies a lack of power in their creator to create things with their own powers and we should not attribute such lack to God.[15] God acting as the first cause brings all things into existence with their own real causal powers. On the one hand, this in no way makes the activity of the secondary causes superfluous—at least not on this understanding of God. For Aquinas, God creates things in such a way that things have the dignity of also being causes,[16] rather than, so I would add, the indignity of not being causes. Notice that the argument is not yet saying what things with their real power we should expect God to create. It is only establishing grounds for saying that God creates things with their own real powers. See 2c. below on whether this is too open, too vague an approach to what we should expect God to create.

Does God create things with their own real powers in a way analogous to a 'collage' of things or should we say God would create things analogous to parts of an ordered whole, in which created things

---

12. Aquinas, 1975, ST 1a. 105.5, art. 6. Here and elsewhere, I use the locution 'so we should prefer to say. . .' to indicate that I am allowing Aquinas's point about the superlative as fitting for speech about God to inform what I thereby assert about God.
13. Aquinas, 1975, ST 1a. 105.5, art. 5.
14. Aquinas, 1975, ST 1a. 103.6.
15. Aquinas, 1975, ST 1a. 105.5, art. 5.
16. Aquinas, 1975, ST 1a. 22.3.

hold together? It seems clear that the latter would be a greater exercise of God's power, and even more so for a beautiful whole, which is to say a 'cosmos'. Thus, we should prefer to say that God creates things that are parts of an ordered cosmos, or universe, though we cannot yet say what is that order.

By the same reasoning we should expect that God would maximize these features of creation—creatures each with their own real powers, creatures as co-creators bringing new things into existence, even living things, even intelligent life, a diversity of creatures in a life-producing universe. Following Aquinas, we may envisage the creation as a wholly participatory universe. There are no 'wall flowers'. On the other hand, nor is God rendered superfluous by creating secondary causes, as if created things were now detached from God. Rather, God sustains them in existence at every moment, or they 'would at once cease to be, and their nature would collapse.'[17] God also imparts to things their distinctive powers and is the end of all their action. Recall Aquinas' point that God creates things that are not only good in themselves but also good for other things. The last point is that every action takes place for some true or seeming good and nothing is good in fact or in appearance unless it is similar in some degree to the supreme good that God is. Ultimately, all action, including causes and their effects, takes place for the sake of God.[18]

In this theology of creation, God creates things with their own real powers, things that are not only good in themselves but also the cause of good in others. As befits God' superlative knowledge, power, and goodness, new things, even living things, are brought into existence, not as a 'collage' but as a 'cosmos', that is a life-producing universe. This life-producing universe represents at least one thing of value to God, distinct but not separate, from the divine purpose in creation (see below).

By the same theological reasoning, we should expect God would maximise the realisation of the value of creatures with their own real powers, leading to creatures as co-creators. Thus, cooperation between creatures is expected at every level of complexity leading to a life producing universe. The maximising of this value is also expected to lead to conflict as well as cooperation, as some creatures with their

---

17. Aquinas, 1975, ST 1a. 104.1.
18. Aquinas, 1975, ST 1a. 105.5.

own real powers cut across other processes, including life-producing processes, leading to the death of living things. It is easy to see that these contrary outcomes are in opposition,[19] but also to some extent aligned, in that the basic constituents remaining from the destruction of new things could be available for their repeated production, as well as possibly, the production of unprecedented new things, actualising more of the possibilities (full potential) for the co-creation of new things. The maximising of what is of value to God is expected to lead to conflict as well as cooperation, to the interplay of life-producing and life-destroying processes. If what is of value to God is that all creatures are co-creators in a life-producing universe then we should expect the life-producing processes should in some sense exceed the death-dealing processes.

This leaves open how to think about God maximizing these features of the created universe. For example, it could be that God creates a small number of types of basic things each with their own powers that by their interaction bring new things into existence with new powers, leading to new interactions, bringing yet new things into existence. So, transformations would be included in the created world. These transformations would mean creatures together participate in God's work as Creator in bringing new things into existence—again, new things not just good in themselves but for the good of others.[20] The greater the transformations, the more fittingly they manifest the superlative excellence of God's knowledge, power, and goodness; for example, transformations from simple to complex things and from non-living to living things. This greatly deepens the meaning of saying that God creates in such a way that things also have the dignity of being causes.

We should therefore prefer to say that in this way God creates a life-producing universe, which is better than only producing an inert universe, or a merely mechanically interactive universe or a chaotic universe. Therefore, we should expect that things make other

---

19. Students immediately raise this question in response to this account of God creating in this way. The question is addressed later in section 3 Chapter V. 'Reality Checks'.
20. This does not blur the distinction between Creator and creature, for creatures as co-creators do not bring new things into existence *ex nihilo*. Also, all creatures ultimately remain ontologically dependent on God for their existence.

things and overall creation makes itself[21] as much as possible as a life-producing universe for the sake of the good, which God is and is reflected in the created world.

A student wanted to know on what basis I claimed that for God to create things with their own powers and to maximize this feature of creation was a better type of creation. There was a suspicion that I was projecting my own values onto God. It is a 'better' type of creation because compared to other possible types of creation (such as an inert or chaotic or mechanically interactive universe) the creation of a life-producing universe is more like the life-giving God who brings into being what does not exist, who is not only good in God's self but the cause of good in others.

This understanding of God claims to express at least one thing that is of value to God as creator: creatures with their own real powers, creatures as co-creators, in a life producing universe. Furthermore, this value is distinguishable from whatever God's purpose may be in creation for we have reached these conclusions by only *mentioning*

---

21. This phrase 'creation makes itself' was used by Charles Kingsley, original edition 1863, in his *The Water Babies* (London: Hodder & Stoughton, 1930), 248: 'Tom to the mother of creation "I heard you were always making new beasts out of old." 'So people fancy' she said, 'I make things make themselves.' Cited by Charles Birch, 'Neo-Darwinism, Self-Organisation and Divine Action in Evolution', in *Evolutionary and Molecular Biology, Scientific Perspectives on Divine Action*, edited by Robert J. Russell, W. R. Stoeger, SJ, and F Ayala, 1998, Vatican City: Vatican Observatory and Berkeley: Center for Theology and the Natural Sciences, 1988), 225. Birch writes, 'Four years after Charles Darwin published *The Origin of Species* the Church of England vicar and novelist, Charles Kingsley wrote for his children the evolutionary fairy tale *The Water Babies*. Kingsley was convinced that the Darwinian theory of evolution was the context within which it was possible to find the working of 'a living, immanent, ever-working God'. The concept of God immanent in creation was understood by Kingsley as a creation in which 'God makes things make themselves'. As far as I can see Kingsley was inspired by Darwinian theory but gave no independent theological basis and exposition of this term. Darwin quoted Kingsley's letter to him in the second edition of *Origin* (1860, 481): 'A celebrated author and divine has written to me that "he has gradually learnt to see that it is just as noble a conception of the Deity to believe that He created a few original forms capable of self-development into other and needful forms, as to believe that He required a fresh act of creation to supply the voids caused by the action of His laws"'.

that God has some purpose in creating but not *using* any idea of what is that purpose.[22]

There is more to say about the kind of universe we might expect such a God to create. For example, the need for order sufficient for living things to live and be sustained by the universe that produces them. A disordered universe could not embody the value of creatures as co-creators. Therefore, we should expect a sufficiently ordered universe, though at this stage of this discussion we cannot say theologically what that order would be.

Several clarifications are in order. We can wonder if the previous talk of creatures as co-creators being of value to God entails the idea of an 'end' being realised through the operation of the universe. This wondering would be appropriate only while appreciating that God is not viewed here as a micro-manager of the realisation of this end. The value being realised by God in the operation of the created universe is not 'efficiency' but creatures as co-creators. This would also be appropriate without confusing that 'end' with the divine purpose in creation. Recall that I have only *mentioned* God's purpose in creation but have not *used* this idea in the discussion. I will soon introduce the theme of God's purpose in creation.

The argument is claiming that the conditions for realising the *value* of creatures as co-creators, are immediately available as created things come into existence. This is not saying the conditions for producing life are immediately available. Rather, the immediately available conditions are oriented to eventually producing *life* however that occurs.

Another question might concern my theological reserve about the kind of world we should expect God to create, for example, about the kind of powers at work or the kind of order embodied in such a life-producing universe. I regard this reserve as a guard against claiming to know more than is possible about what kind of world we should expect to be created by God, *based on* this idea of God. Nevertheless, there is more to say. For example, let us suppose that God creates

---

22. The distinction can be noticed in discussion of organizational purpose, indicating the organisation's reason for its existence and direction of its life. Whereas an organization's values characterise the ethos of the organization, the preferred ways of its members behaving in any aspect of the organisation's life. On this analogy, the divine purpose in creation points to the reason for which creation exists and that at least one thing of value to God, which is exhibited in all its operations is that creatures are co-creators.

such a universe. How should we say God would do this? Here are two possible ways. Firstly, God says, 'Let there be X!', where X is just such a life-producing universe, with living things, including intelligent life, specially created, as Genesis 1 is commonly interpreted. Imagine the same world, which God creates by a different means. That is, by saying 'Let there be X!' where X is a created universe of different types of basic things all with their own specific, limited, powers in an ordered whole, so that the universe by its own God-given powers produces many more kinds of things including living things, including intelligent life, namely a life-producing universe. Given Aquinas' argument we should prefer to say that God creates a life-producing universe, according to the second approach.

2b. Is this cherry picking the Bible?

This conclusion may awaken various concerns. It may seem that I am dismissing the Bible where it doesn't fit my view. The 'new atheists' might say I am another Christian 'cherry picking' the Bible because I am *quietly* being guided by the natural sciences, without admitting it. So this section represents a pause in my saying what kind of universe we should expect the omni-God to create while I show these concerns are mistaken by referring: (1) to relevant historical background concerning the interpretation of Genesis in the light of Darwinian evolution; (2) Galileo's Two Books principle; and in (3) below I will offer independent support for identifying the actual universe with the kind of universe we should expect the omni-God to create. This pause in my exposition will return us directly to the problem of natural evil.

(1) Historical background

There is a relevant historical note concerning the interpretation of Genesis in the light of Darwinian evolution. Dr Aubrey Moore, a 19th-century Anglican scholar at Oxford and public defender of Darwin, pointed out that the theory of evolution was consistent with orthodox Christian theology at least since St Augustine (354–430 CE) (*De Genesis ad literam*). St Thomas Aquinas (1225–1274 CE) followed Augustine: 'As to the production of plants ... some expositors say that, on the third day (of creation), plants were actually produced each in its own kind—a view which is favoured by a superficial reading of the letter of Scripture. But Augustine says that the earth is then said to have brought forth grass and trees *causaliter*—that is, it then received the power to produce them. This view he confirms with the authority of Scripture, which says, 'These are the generations of the heaven and the earth, when they were created in the day that the Lord made the earth and the heavens, and every plant of the field before it was in the earth, and every herb of the field, before it grew.' [Genesis 2:4] Before, then, they came into being on the earth they were made causally in the earth. And this is confirmed by reason. For in those first days God made creatures primarily or *causaliter*, and then rested from His work, and yet after that, by His superintendence of things created, He works even to this day in the work of propagation.' (Aquinas, *ST* 1, 69, 2).

According to Moore, orthodox Christian theology was under no obligation to think in terms of the widely approved work of W Paley, *Natural Theology: Or Evidence of the Existence and Attributes of the Deity. Collected from the Appearances of Nature* (London: R Faulder, 1802). Paley proposed that each animal was specially designed and created by God for the place in which it lived. AL Moore, *Science and the Faith* (London: Keagan Paul, Trench, and Co, 1898), 162–180. The theological story I am telling about God as primary cause creating secondary causes is very close to orthodox theology in the West from Augustine! This is not 'cherry picking'.

(2) Galileo's 'Two Books' principle

My approach to the Bible is principled, not ad-hoc. Of the several principles I use I refer here only to the first and most important which is Galileo's 'Two Books' principle. Galileo, the most famous natural philosopher of his day, did get into trouble with the Church. The Church responded to him with a very heavy hand in an extremely tense context of the Reformation, and the thirty-year, war-torn strife between Catholics and Protestants that ensued (1618–1648).

The Galileo Affair remains a focus of lively scholarly research. I will briefly comment on some aspects of the interaction in Galileo's writings between the Bible and Galileo's new natural philosophy. I will say nothing about Galileo's role as a courtesan in the Court of Cosimo

II de Medici.[23] Nor anything about the role of different factions within the Catholic Church of his day, and I will barely touch on the impact of the Protestant Reformation and Catholic Counter Reformation on all involved in the Galileo Affair. The details of Galileo's 'trials' in 1615 and 1633[24] will not be discussed and almost nothing will be said about his famous *Dialogue*, published in 1632, which precipitated the trial of 1633. Against certain claims I have encountered I will say Galileo was not burned at the stake, nor tortured, nor was it the case that church authorities thought the earth was flat, nor did they object to Galileo's telescopic observations. These had been reproduced by the Jesuit astronomers.

Nevertheless, did Galileo's view get into trouble with theology? Was Copernicanism a problem for theology? Initially yes,[25] but ultimately no. We can see this from the care taken by Galileo about his theological argument in his *Letter to the Grand Duchess Christina*, drawing strongly on St Augustine as an acknowledged theological authority. This is underlined when in 1893 Pope Leo XIII issued *Providentissimus Deus*, an encyclical letter on the relation between science and biblical exegesis, which corresponds to Galileo's position in the *Letter to Christina*!

The Grand Duchess Christina who asked how Galileo reconciled his sun-centred Copernican view of the world with the completely different biblical view which had the sun circling a stationary earth. Here is a summary of Galileo's 'two books' principle.[26]

- God is the author of two books, the book of nature and the book of Scripture.
- The book of nature is written in the language of mathematics.
- The book of Scripture is written in the common language of the day (181, 182, 201).

---

23. Biaglioi, M, (1990), pp. 1–62.
24. M Finocchiaro, translator and editor, *The Galileo Affair, A Documentary History* (Berkley: University of California Press, 1989). 1989)
25. A brief introduction is given in GB Ferngren editor, *Science and Religion, A Historical Introduction*, (Johns Hopkins University Press, Baltimore, 2002): Chapter 7, Owen Gingerich, 'The Copernican Revolution', and Chapter 8, Richard J Blackwell, 'Galileo Galilei'.
26. G Galileo, 'The Letter to the Grand Duchess Christina', in SDrake, *Discoveries and Opinions of Galileo* (New York: Doubleday, 1957). Page numbers above are from this edition of the *Letter*.

- The purpose of the Bible is to communicate 'faith and morals': 'how to go to heaven not how the heavens go' (186).
- Because God is its ultimate author the Bible cannot contain any error when it is correctly interpreted.
- The two books have one author and so cannot be in conflict if each is interpreted correctly.
- If there is a literal contradiction between the Bible and what the natural sciences tell us about some aspect of the natural world then, (following St Augustine) where the Bible is speaking about that same aspect of nature, we should retain what the natural sciences provide and interpret those passages of Scripture in terms of 'faith and morals'. They are to be given a theological and ethical interpretation (186, 194).[27]

Students have raised an objection to the principle: the principle seems to simply rule out any contradiction between science and the Bible when 'everyone knows' there are contradictions. But Galileo and the Church authorities were in no doubt there was a contradiction between the Copernican view and the literal interpretation of many biblical texts. Likewise, there is a literal contradiction between St Paul's claim (Romans 5) that death entered the world through the sin of Adam and the fossil evidence that death was in the world long before human beings showed up in the evolutionary process. Where such a contradiction exists, then the principle requires that we hold to the assured conclusion of natural science, since God is the creator of the world that the natural sciences show us much more accurately than common sense. Consequently, since the purpose of the Bible is to teach faith and morals, the portion of the Bible contradicted must be given a theological and or ethical interpretation—since God is the ultimate author of the Bible and the natural world.

This is a challenge to believers: can such an alternative interpretation be provided? Does it have any independent support or is it *ad-hoc*? Is it credible? The principle cannot be used as a 'magic wand' to sweep away any contradiction between the literal reading of

---

27. So too Fr Pereya (1535–1610), the most prominent Catholic Bible scholar in the second half of the sixteenth century; see, Blackwell, R., *Galileo, Bellarmine and the Bible: Including a Translation of Foscarini's Letter on the Motion of the Earth* (Notre Dame IN: Notre Dame University Press, 1991), 22.

the Bible and the natural sciences. On the contrary, the principle sets a powerful challenge to believers who hold the principle.[28]

We can better grasp this principle by seeing how it can inform the interpretation of Genesis 1 with its story of the creation of the universe in six days. Firstly, we are to retain the well-established scientific view of our 13.7-billion-year-old universe. (Thank you, St. Augustine.) Secondly, we are then to seek a theological and ethical interpretation of Genesis 1 and so of the universe God is said to have created. For help I draw on the work of J. H. Walton, Professor of Old Testament at Wheaton College, who refers to the 'cognitive environment' of the Ancient Near East, (ANE) which Israel shared with its neighbours.[29]

In the Hebrew Bible the only divine rest that occurs is the rest associated with God's presence in his temple. This, together with the data from the ANE about divinities resting in their temples, confirms for Walton 'the idea of deity resting, as on the seventh day in Genesis 1, is a clear indication to the reader that a temple metaphor underlies the understanding of the deity's status.'[30] This is further supported by the fact that this rest takes place on the seventh day. Examples of temple inaugurations 'show that these rites took place in the course of seven days and that the deity entered the temple to take up his rest on the seventh day.'[31]

Walton suggests further connections to other temple-inauguration accounts.

> For example, in the case of Gudea's temple inauguration, most of the ceremony was taken up with proclaiming the functions that the temple would have and installing the functionaries so that the deity could enter the temple (on the seventh day) to take up his rest, at which point the temple becomes functional.[32]

---

28. Of course unbelievers would not hold this *theological* principle, though it may help them critically consider the way believers approach the interpretation of the Bible in the light of the natural sciences.
29. John Walton, *Genesis 1 as Ancient Cosmology* (Winona Lake, Indiana: Eisenbrauns, 2011). I will be taking only a few 'threads' of Walton's detailed work.
30. Walton, *Genesis 1 as Ancient Cosmology*, 181.
31. Walton, *Genesis 1 as Ancient Cosmology* 181. Walton earlier discusses the evidence for this claim presented by EC Kingsbury, 'A Seven Day Ritual in the Old Babylonian Cult at, Larsa', in *Hebrew Union College Annual (journal) HUCA*, 34 (1963): 1–34. Kingsbury lists several other seven-day rituals. V Hurowitz, *I Have Built You an Exulted House*, in JSTOPSup 115; (Sheffield: JSDT, 1992).
32. Walton, *Genesis 1 as Ancient Cosmology*, 182.

Walton highlights how all of this 'resonates' with the Genesis account, as shown in the above discussion of Days 1–3, in which the functions of the cosmos are proclaimed, and the functionaries installed on Days 4–6.

> The biblical cosmic temple allows people to live and serve in the presence of deity; the functions of the cosmic temple are for their sake. This is a significant deviation from the Ancient Near Eastern cognitive environment, in which as Clifford notes, 'The world is not created for human beings but for "cult", the housing and feeding of the gods. In Genesis the focus of the cosmology is the support of the life of the people, not the life of the gods.'[33]
>
> The analysis presented in this chapter leads to the conclusion that the seven-day structure of Genesis 1 reflects the intention of the author to present the creation of the cosmos in terms of the inauguration of a cosmic temple . . . The entire cosmos is viewed as a temple designed to function on behalf of humanity[34]; and when God takes up his rest in this cosmic temple, it 'comes into functional existence' (real existence in ancient thinking) by virtue of his presence.[35]

Across the ANE, temples everywhere are for the worship of the gods. and temples everywhere are intimately connected to the cosmology. 'The temple was the hub of the cosmos and the rest of the deity in the temple was essential to his rule of the cosmos.' Temples were seen as 'models in miniature of the cosmos and were replete with cosmic symbolism.'[36] Genesis presents the radically different view that the created world is God's temple.

---

33. Walton, *Genesis 1 as Ancient Cosmology* 189. R Clifford, *Creation Accounts in The Ancient Near East and in the Bible*, *CBQMS* (Washington, DC: Catholic Biblical Association, 1994), 93.
34. Walton, *Genesis 1 as Ancient Cosmology*, 182, 'This is a significant differentiation from the Ancient Near Eastern cognitive environment, in which as Clifford notes, "The world is not created for human beings but for 'cult', the housing and feeding of the gods." Clifford, *Creation Accounts*, 65.
35. Walton, *Genesis 1 as Ancient Cosmology*, 190.
36. Walton *Genesis 1 as Ancient Cosmology*, 178.

The building of a temple is to be distinguished from its inauguration.[37] Across the ANE, temple inauguration is a seven-day process leading to the god taking up residence on the seventh day for 'rest', making the temple functional.[38] Here 'rest' means the god is enthroned and so rules from the temple.[39] Only when the functions are named, the functionaries installed, and the god enters to 'rest' in the temple, on the seventh day, is the temple functioning i.e., actually exists. This suggests the idea of the cosmos as the temple of God. This is not stated in Genesis, but the evidence suggests this is the idea: seven-day building/inauguration; functions named (days 1–3) and functionaries installed (days 4–6); God 'rests' on the seventh day. Only then does the temple, that is, the cosmos, really exist. People in the ANE context would grasp what the story is saying and how radical it was, for this idea that the cosmos is the temple of God is not found elsewhere in the ANE.

This part of Genesis is a recognisable 'creation myth' which, following John Walton, we can compare to other creation myths in the ANE.[40] The comparison with other ANE cultures includes some other important matters, for example, the role of humankind and not worshiping of the sun, moon, and stars. In contrast to Mesopotamian literature, where people are the slaves of the gods, in Genesis, humanity is a partner in the work of ruling. This includes the functional role of men and women, both made in the image of God. Including women as equal partners with men is radically counter to the ANE but is essential to the first aspect of the original blessing. Humanity has the status vis-à-vis the non-human creation that is analogous to the status and role of kings in the ANE. 'The task and trappings of royalty and cult have been transferred to humanity.'[41] I would be more cautious. The sovereign power associated with royalty has been transferred to

---

37. Walton, *Genesis 1 as Ancient Cosmology*, 183.
38. Walton, *Genesis 1 as Ancient Cosmology*, 178–181.
39. See Isa 66:1–2, Ps 132.
40. I am treating Genesis 1, not a historical report of what God supposedly did a few thousand years ago, but as an ANE creation myth declaring something of the theological meaning of our universe according to Genesis. I take the further step of regarding this as inspired by God. In the next chapter, the claim that the created universe is God's temple, based on this reading of Genesis, will find support from the New Testament. For example, see, NT Wright, *History and Eschatology, Jesus, and the Promise of Natural Theology* (London: SPCK, 2019), Chapters 5, 6.
41. Walton, *Genesis 1 as Ancient Cosmology*, 175, 175–178.

humanity but not 'the trappings of royalty and the cult', nor the status and role of kings in the ANE. The sovereignty given to human beings is to be exercised in the image and likeness of this God, not like the idols, the other gods, worshipped in the cult.

The attempt to reconcile Genesis with the scientific account of the universe has often popularly been by accepting the science but 'stretching' the biblical text over the science by exploiting various features of the text. For example, some people say that the 'days' in Genesis 1 represent vastly longer periods and this supposedly accommodates developments in science to do with the age of the earth or the solar system or the 'big bang'.[42] Or some people say that the order of vegetation and animals in Genesis 1 is the same as in the story told by evolution. These moves are aimed at producing a concord between the natural sciences and the Bible by using the science to say what the text means. There are problems with this approach. It is using whatever the latest science happens to be to say what the text means. What if the science moves on to new theories? Then this approach to reconciling the Bible and science simply fails. After all it is *ad hoc*. A second problem is that this approach gives authority to the sciences to interpret a text that is not a scientific text, nor even an ancient scientific text. This approach might be quite appropriate for a critique of Copernicus', *On the Revolutions of the Celestial Spheres*, in the light of our current scientific view of the universe. After all, it really is an ancient scientific text!

In relation to the opening chapters of Genesis, however, this approach ignores the evidence of the literary genre and details of the text, and ignores questions concerning the community for which it was written and for what purpose. It ignores what Walton calls the 'cognitive environment' of the ANE.[43] In this way the message of the text is in effect ignored. Instead, a way of trying to reconcile the Bible and the natural sciences commandeers our attention, as if reconciliation with natural sciences was the only priority for

---

42. One example is A Guyot, a Swiss physical geographer, who came to the United States in 1848. He was a follower of *naturphilosphie*; nature an ever-developing organism, following the same pattern in all its aspects. Late in life he arrived at a new interpretation of Genesis to accommodate Laplace's nebula hypothesis to explain the origins of the solar system. See R.Numbers, *Creation by Natural Law*, 88–94.
43. Walton, *Genesis 1 as Ancient Cosmology*. I will be taking only a few 'threads' of Walton's detailed work.

readers of the Bible. For my part, I will use the above principle to introduce an interpretation of Genesis.[44] Note that I am not giving a full exposition of this passage. The scale of such a task is indicated by critical commentaries on the book of Genesis[45] and by Walton's whole book just on Genesis 1! Nevertheless, my aim is to show the intelligibility and plausibility of this principled approach hopefully on the road to becoming persuasive.

The main point is that this application of Galileo's Two-Books Principle leads back to considering the interpretation of the Bible using contemporary scholarly study of Genesis 1 in its ANE context. This has shown that Genesis is offering distinctive wisdom,[46] theological and ethical: the created world is God's temple, in which God is present and all creatures are to worship of God. The 'seven days' are not about how long it literally took God to create the universe, supposedly 6,000–10,000 years ago.[47] The story of God creating a functioning universe is cast in the form of the familiar rites of temple inauguration over seven days with God resting on the seventh day. This is to make the distinctive theological point that the created universe is God's temple. This interpretive approach shows there is no requirement to take the ancient cosmology, common across the ANE, as what is being revealed through the text of Genesis 1.[48] Theologically, we may take this distinctive claim from Genesis

---

44. Among many good discussions, I mention, CS Barton, and D Wilkinson, *Reading Genesis After Darwin* (Oxford: Oxford University Press, 2009); D Alexander, *Creation or Evolution, Do we have to Choose?* (Oxford: Monarch Books, 2008).
45. A famous three-volume work by Claus Westerman, translated by John Scullion SJ, *Genesis 1–11* (1984); *Genesis 12–25* (1985); *Genesis 26–37* (1986); (Minneapolis: Augsburg Publishing House). More manageable, by another eminent Old Testament Scholar is W Brueggemann, *Genesis* (Atlanta: John Knox Press, 1982).
46. Here I mention again, T McLeish, *Faith and Wisdom in Science* (Oxford: Oxford University Press, 2014). Tom McLeish, FRS, is Professor of Physics at York University.
47. The dating of the age of the universe comes from Archbishop Ussher based on adding up the genealogies in the Bible. But there is no good reason for us to follow that approach.
48. The structure of the cosmos we find in Genesis is common across the ANE. On the principle that anything said to be specifically and distinctively revealed by God in Genesis cannot be common knowledge widely known by other means. It is not the structure of the cosmos that is being revealed in Genesis. Rather the text may be using the common structure to reveal something otherwise unknown, and here this is the idea of the cosmos as God's temple.

1 as applying to the created universe now, with the natural sciences showing us so much more about its history and operation on so many levels. After all, Genesis 1 does refer to our universe.

This leaves for reflection just how this theological theme connects in any way with the scientific picture of the universe. Can the universe shown us by the natural sciences be said to worship God? Note that the natural sciences are unable to affirm or deny this claim. It is simply not part of the natural sciences. The question is rather how theology can say of the universe that it is for the worship God. A clarification may help. We may fairly understand 'worship' as 'worthship'. That is, those acts by which the worth of something or someone is declared. Can theology say that the universe, as disclosed by the natural sciences, declares the worth of God? Do its structures and operations declare God's worth or value or glory or excellence?

Again, we note that this is a theological, not a scientific, question. This question might be taken to refer to the intelligibility of the universe, the lawfulness of its operation, the beauty of the physical laws and of the life forms that are produced. Theologically, they all testify to their creator—just as Psalm 19:1 says, 'the heavens declare the glory of God and the firmament tells his handiwork.' So too does Wisdom of Solomon 11:20, 'You have arranged all things by measure, and number and weight.'[49] Many religious people also look to the fact that the physical laws and constants of our universe are fine-tuned for life. To them this suggests the handiwork of God. The main alternative view is the multiverse proposal, which says there are a myriad of universes in a more abstract space, each with different laws and constants. On this alternative, there is then nothing special about our universe being 'fine-tuned' for life; it just turned out to have laws and constants that are 'just right' for producing life.[50] This is a contentious matter, since there is no way of directly testing the multiverse proposal

---

49. This informed the great polymath Nichola of Cusa (1401–1464), who taught that that in the use of the mathematical disciplines the human mind was demonstrating its likeness to the divine mind. For Nicholas, God, who created all things in number, weight, and measure arranged the elements in an admirable order. (Number pertains to arithmetic, weight to music, measure to geometry). See his *On Learned Ignorance*.
50. P Davies, *The Goldilocks Enigma, Why Is the Universe Just Right for Life?* (London: Allan Lane, 2006).

empirically.[51] Also, not all scientists are persuaded by the multiverse proposal, even if they reject any theistic interpretation.[52]

'Worship' may well seem odd as something for all creatures, especially for twenty-first-century human beings immersed in a culture saturated by science, technology, and the economy.[53] I am taking the theme of 'worshipping God', with its counter theme about the meaning and consequences of worshipping idols, as the guide to the central ethical wisdom offered by Genesis and indeed the whole Bible. It is common, theologically, to think of the natural world fulfilling God's commands, even glorifying the Creator and so worshipping God. Here we confront the theme of this book: the problem of natural evil in its claim that the natural world has not been created by a wholly good God.

2c. A too open-ended approach?

Here I return to the exposition of the kind of universe we should expect to be created by the omni-God.

It might be thought that this whole approach is rather open-ended, even sloppy. What if someone came up with a still richer idea of creaturely power, wouldn't that have to be added into the overall idea of a life-producing universe? The answer is that we are not obliged to take up any idea of creaturely power, but more importantly, nor is God. For not just any conceived power might cohere with all the other powers in the operation of a life-producing universe.

---

51. For the possibility of indirect testing see, W Stoeger, 'God, Physics and the Big Bang', *Cambridge Companion to Science and Religion*, edited by P Harrison (Cambridge: Cambridge University Press, 2010), 183–186.
52. P Davies, *The Goldilocks Enigma*; 'Universe from bit', in Davies and Gregersen, *Information and the Nature of Reality: From Physics to Metaphysics* (Cambridge: Cambridge University Press, 2010); L Smolin, in R Unger, and L Smolin, *The Singular Universe, and The Reality of Time: A Proposal in Natural Philosophy* (Cambridge: Cambridge University Press, 2015). For an excellent discussion of these matters, see, KJ Kray, editor, *God and the Multiverse: Scientific, Philosophical and Theological Perspectives* (New York: Routledge, 2015); GF Lewis and LA Barnes, *A Fortunate Universe: Life in a Finely Tuned Cosmos* (Cambridge: Cambridge University Press, 2016).
53. On the other hand, a text by Scott Hamilton and Stuart Kells, *Sold Down the River, How Robber Barons and Wall Street Traders Cornered* (Text Publishing, Melbourne Australia 2019) shows the devastating power of worshipping the golden rule—those who have the gold make the rules and the first rule is make more gold whatever it takes.

Secondly, there is no pretence to know ahead of inquiring just what powers have been given by God. For example, according to Abrahamic traditions, the power given to humankind is 'sovereign' power (Genesis 1:28), only a 'little less than the gods' (Psalm 8:5). We are still discovering the range of the God-given powers open to human beings, including the power to engage all the natural powers inscribed by God in created things. There is no need to prematurely finalise what the powers given to humankind may be.

2d. Does God create the best of all possible worlds?

So far, the criterion of speaking of God in terms of superlatives has functioned to move us to prefer the 'better' of which we have some inkling (e.g., thinking of God having power to create things with their own real powers), rather than the 'best' which we do not know. Shouldn't this criterion lead us to think of this superlative God as creating the 'best of all possible worlds' as proposed by the students in s(a) above? The idea of God creating the best of all possible worlds was famously proposed by Leibniz but not by Aquinas. The criterion moves us to avoid a lesser idea of God and prefer the better without presuming to know what the 'best' might be for God or whether any definite notion of the 'best' is sustainable given the inexhaustible goodness, power, and knowledge of God. But I am brought to a halt if I try to think of the 'best of all possible worlds' such an inexhaustible God would create. The form of theological reasoning I am following makes no pretence to know what is the 'best' God could do in creating a universe. Hopefully, this reasoning is moved by a discontent: not to be content with envisaging a lesser God and not to be content with a premature finality and even a premature closure as to what is the 'best' God might create.

Now this bears upon the students' argument. Their argument s(a) to s(d) appeals to God creating a world *in* the divinely intended end state—whatever that may be. It does not presume to know what is the 'best' God may have in mind, only that God's purpose would be the best and therefore that it would not include pain, suffering, and death. Again, the students meet my theological requirement. But my discussion claims the good that God is includes God valuing creatures as co-creators and that this type of creation is better than one where creatures are not co-creators, which includes not only the inert, mechanical, and chaotic universes already mentioned, but also the creation envisaged by the students in its perfect end state. It is a 'better' type of creation because creatures so created are more like the God who brings into being what does not exist, who is not only good in God's self but the cause of good in others.

The difference between the students and myself is partly due to a difference about the term 'good' and to this we will return, for my account of 'good' and 'better' is contested by students and colleagues in particular ways. It is also partly due to the students talking about God's purpose negatively—whatever it is it won't include pain, suffering and death. When I discuss God's purpose it will be positively. So far, I have been speaking of what is of value to God and this is distinct but not separated from God's purpose.

Chapter III
The divine purpose for the created universe

I have argued for (something of) the kind of universe we should expect God to create, without using any idea of divine purpose. The inclusion of the idea of God's purpose leads to at least three new developments of this expectation that are related to each other: the creation of what I will call 'persons', the revelation of God, and, thirdly, the ultimate ordering of the created universe.

1a. The divine purpose in creation

Informed by Aquinas' discussion of God's governing the universe in which created things have their own God-given powers, I begin to explore the idea of divine purpose for the whole creation. Aquinas tells us[1] that governing is for the sake of the governed, to bring them to their perfection. That form of government is better which communicates a higher perfection. I take it that a higher purpose in government aims at a higher perfection. Therefore, we are asked to think that God's government of creation is for the sake of creation as the life producing universe and finally to bring created things to their perfection. Since a higher purpose brings a higher perfection, what might that higher purpose and perfection be?[2]

A wholly good God is an all-loving God whom we should prefer to say loves the created universe and seeks to bring all created things

---

1. Aquinas, 1975, ST 105.5 article 6.
2. This view of ultimate governance is both radically top-down and radically bottom-up, for the sake of the 'bottom-up'. Does human governance have a better model?

into a loving, just relationship with this God.[3] No greater perfection is possible for created things that did not include this. Therefore, we should prefer to ascribe this purpose to God rather than any lesser purpose. God's governance of creation is for this end and all God's action is ordered to this one end. Again, this form of theological reasoning makes no claim to know what is the 'best' purpose God would have in creating this universe.

Since the divine purpose includes calling all creatures into a loving and just relationship with God, we have been correct to think of this diversity of creatures as a universe rather than as a 'collage' of things. The theologian Karl Rahner speaks for the tradition thus,

> if everything exists only by having its origins in God, then this means not only that all things in their variety proceed from one cause which, because it is infinite and all-powerful, can create the most varied things. It also means that this variety manifests an inner similarity and commonality, and that this variety or differentiation forms a unity in its origin, its self-realisation and its determination—that is, it forms a single world.[4]

1b. Persons

A wholly good God is an all-loving God whom we should prefer to say, and thereby assert, would seek to bring all things into a loving, just relationship with this God. Several things follow. Firstly, we should prefer to think of God as personal or even supra-personal, (rather than as impersonal or sub-personal), as befits the idea of the

---

3. Here I am drawing on the ordinary experience of love as part of the good I encounter in my life, and this as typical of human beings at their best. This is taken as the basis for speaking by analogy that 'a wholly good God is an all-loving God whom we should prefer to say loves the created universe and seeks to bring all created things into a loving, just relationship with this God.' I take this as an initial step to the idea that human beings are, in some minimalist sense, like God, though, beyond enabling us to begin thinking and speaking of God, the 'sense' of this likeness, is left open for the present.
4. Karl Rahner, *Foundations of Christian Faith* (London: Darton Longman & Todd, 1978), 181–182. A note in Appendix 1 responds to a deconstructive critique of such theology due to its rejection of a single origin or realisation of presence or of telos. See also, Dennis Edwards, *The God of Evolution, A Trinitarian Theology* (New York, Paulist Press, 1999), Chapter 6, with a discussion of Karl Rahner, Teilhard de Chardin, and Jurgen Moltmann.

perfectly good God creating the world for the purpose of inviting all created things into a loving and just relationship with God.

Second, not all created things would necessarily have the capacity to enter such a relationship, nor even know what such a relationship might involve. For this reason, we should prefer to think that a created universe must be such as to produce not only intelligent life, but intelligent life that has the capacity to enter such a relationship with this God, both on its own behalf and as eventually leading all other things into a form of life that has as its horizon this loving and just relation with God. I am calling that form of life 'persons', who are an integral part of this universe, embedded and embodied in this universe and so dependent on it for their life. We should prefer to say that God creates a life-producing universe, which produces all kinds of living things as good in themselves and good for others yet needing this personal form of life as an integral part of the universe created for and ordered to the fulfilment of this purpose.

Third, recall that this is a manifestation of God's sovereign choice of the purpose of the whole creation, and so this invitation is a 'call', a 'command'—'come!'—to enter such a relationship as and when God initiates this call.[5] Since all persons are to be called into such a relationship with God it follows that all are to be called to regard each other in that light and respect the dignity every person has in virtue of the powers with which they have been created and the end to which all are called.

Fourth, on this understanding, persons are brought into existence by a life-producing universe, with the capacity to enter a loving and just relationship with God. Nevertheless, as we shall see in a moment, we have reason to think that persons so created would not immediately exercise this capacity, nor even recognise God nor recognise themselves or each other in relation to God, nor recognize their situation in life as something of *value* to God. Rather, I envisage this recognition being acquired.[6]

---

5. Whether love can be commanded has long been discussed. Likewise, the question whether love can be promised. Much depends on what is meant by 'love'. One famous discussion of the commandment to love one's neighbour the question came down to having mercy shown by actions responding to obvious need. Such action was then commanded (Lk 10: 25–37).
6. In this account of created persons coming into existence I am not using the sophisticated perception of life in the 'immanent frame' as proposed by Charles

1c. Revelation

For persons, embodied and embedded in the life of the created universe, to enter such a relationship, we must assume that God makes God known to these creatures in ways appropriate to such a personal relationship; that these creatures are capable of knowing God in ways appropriate to such a relationship; and that these creatures do so freely and therefore that they may accept or refuse such a relationship. We now have a principled reason for thinking that the kind of universe God creates would be open to the divine initiative to reveal God for the purpose of inviting persons, representing, and leading everything else, into a loving and just relationship with God.

Let's examine the first of these points: that God makes God known to these creatures in ways appropriate to such a personal relationship. We should expect that the universe created by God would be open to God personally revealing God to each person, as an invitation, calling each and all to enter a loving and just relationship with God, however that may take place. For this invitation to be intelligible it must be possible for persons to come to know something of God from their living in a universe created by God. We should expect this universe created by God to mediate a general revelation of God to all persons, which would include the existence of God as the creator, the transcendent source of all that is, and something of the value to God of this life-producing universe and their place within it.[7]

Nothing in the argument ensures that persons so created would necessarily come to such knowledge. Indeed, given this account of God's purpose in creation it must be possible for this knowledge to be ignored, resisted, or even rejected. There needs to be some kind

---

Taylor in his *A Secular Age*. Nor am I assuming an absent deist God. Rather, I am holding together the idea of persons being brought into existence with God given capacities, with a God given role in relation to other creatures, all oriented to the divine purpose for the whole creation, and yet having to discover these things in the presence of God initially unrecognised.

7. For example, see Stephen Ames, 'Can we "live in but not of" the Immanent Frame?', in, *Religion in a Secular Age, The Struggle for Meaning in an Abstracted World*, ARENA *journal,* New Serie, 49/50 (2018): 169–203. Stephen Ames, 'The value given and presupposed in person centered dementia care, *OBM Geriatrics*, 3/3 Doi: 10.21926/obm.geriatr.1903068. 2019

of 'epistemic distance',[8] between God and created persons where this choice can come to be recognised and made one way or another without creatures being overwhelmed by the unmediated presence of God. It must be possible for persons to fashion a life without God.

In this context, we should also expect there would be the special revelation (however that might take place) of God personally inviting each and all persons to enter into a loving and just relationship with God, as the purpose for which the life-producing universe exists and for which they exist. This leaves open how well and how diversely this general and special revelation would be received or not, by each person.

1d. The ultimate order of the universe

As touched on already, such a universe must be ordered to produce and sustain life, but now the argument will clarify three forms of order: *ultimate, penultimate* and *dis-order*. It must be fundamentally and so *ultimately* ordered to serve God's purpose, which is for the whole creation to enter a loving and just relationship with God. The universe in all its parts, including embodied persons, must be ordered to this end so that this end is integral, not alien, to the created universe and every part of it, when and by whatever means God brings this purpose to fulfilment.

We should think that the universe is created by God with all that is needed ontologically (whatever that may turn out to be) and operationally for its own operation to bring living persons into existence oriented to this purpose for the whole creation. This means that the way the universe is ordered to produce and sustain life as a life-producing universe is not the deepest or *ultimate* ordering of the

---

8. This theme was introduced by John Hick, in *Evil and the God of Love*, revised edition (New York: HarperCollins, 1977), 372–73. For a critique, see Nick Trakakis, 'An Epistemically Distant God? A Critique of John Hick's Response to the Problem of Divine Hiddenness'. *Heythrop Journal* XLVIII (2007): 214–226. My argument above does not require Hick's conclusion that 'the world must be to man, to some extent at least, *etsi deus non daretur*, "as if there were no God"', Hick, *Evil and the God of Love*, 373. Nor is my view that of the 'skeptical theists' 'who emphasize the inscrutability of God's ways,—they are likely to hold that, just as we cannot be expected to discern God's reasons for permitting the evil and suffering we observe in the world, so too we cannot be expected to discern God's reasons for remaining hidden.' (Trakakis, 'An Epistemically Distant God', 223)

universe. Rather, it is the *penultimate order* and is to be understood as 'situated' within, in accord with, and to be fulfilled by, this *ultimate* order, which, on the above argument, starts to come to light as the life-producing universe produces persons. On this view, the general revelation of God does not have to 'break into' in the sense of 'go against the grain' of the created world in its being or its operation as a life-producing universe. It may be, however, that God must go against the grain of the forms of life that persons construct without God, whether not known or rejected, in order to fulfill the divine purpose in creating the universe.

The universe in all its parts, including embodied persons, must be ordered to this end. We should expect that created things, in virtue of their being, are orientated to this end as natural to them. This holds for embodied persons, who in their *being the creatures they are*, have built into them an orientation and inclination to God as their true end and true value, and their true interest, to which they owe their lives. In whatever ways this 'orientation', 'inclination', and 'owing' is recognised as persons respond to the general revelation of God, its being grasped is an acknowledgment (if limited and precarious) of the worth of God to them and of the intelligibility of their lives in the created universe. We should expect all this would be intensified, clarified, and brought home to each person by the special revelation of God, as and whenever it is initiated by God and received by each person.

This 'orientation', 'inclination', and 'owing' to God may instead be misrecognised. Given the divine purpose, this *ultimate* order must be thought to allow for this personal form of life to have the capacity to align with or go against God's purpose, including acquiring distorted understandings of God, the world and themselves, and so go with or against the ordering of their own being as persons. The *ultimate* ordering of the universe must allow persons to use the *penultimate* order to establish their lives, with or against the purpose of God. This requires a capacity to know and understand the world in which their lives are embedded and embodied, as a practical know-how to use the world, and a growing knowledge of the universe as amazing, with both mediating a general revelation of God that may be received with more or less distortion.

This means that the *ultimate* order cannot be so written into the operation of this universe and impose itself on life and on this personal form of life that no other order can be established on top of or against the *ultimate* order created by God. It must be possible for persons so created to establish their own (dis)order of living (against God's valuing of a life-producing universe[9] and against God's purpose for this universe and against their own true interests as persons) with whatever disturbance of them as persons and of the *penultimate order* follows from their *dis-ordering* of it. Also, this *dis-order* has no ultimate future, since it has no place in the purpose of God. On this view the only future[10] that is finally coming is the one that comes from God as God brings about the fulfilment of God's purpose in and for whole creation

Finally, this *dis-order* is to be understood as not preventing God initiating the personal revelation of God's ultimate purpose, which includes the personal revelation of God, however and whenever that may take place. Again, the *dis-order* established by persons may nevertheless withstand the revelation of God through not recognising it due to blindness acquired by the *dis-ordering* or recognising but rejecting the revelation due to a misplaced loyalty to a lesser good and so constituting themselves as 'children of a lesser god'. The recognition of the worth of God to persons and their living accordingly, or the worth of the misplaced loyalties and living accordingly, are each a form of 'worth-ship' or worship.

This account of the divine purpose in creation and the ultimate order of the universe, will be taken further in the light of section 1 of Chapter V Reality Checks, confronting this theology of creation with the scientific view of the expanding acceleration of the universe leading to what may be called a 'dead end' universe.

1e. Preliminary conclusion #1

The story I have briefly presented works from the idea of God that atheist students and colleagues bring to the discussion of natural

---

9. The personal form of intelligent life on planet earth has deployed its power to develop and establish forms of life in a great variety of cultures and societies. In a subset of these cultures and societies, this power has been deployed to the point of threatening the conditions under which it continues to exist (climate change and weapons of mass destruction). Theologically, this is an example of a tension between an *ultimate order* established by God for life, with created things being co-creators, and another *(dis)order* that people choose for their lives.
10. Eschatology (reflection on the 'eschaton': the 'end') is certainly part of this theology of creation. More will be said in response to the 'Dead End Universe' objection.

evil. I believe I have begun to answer the question as to the kind of universe we should expect such a God to create. Theologically it is a life-producing universe created *ex nihilo*, in which at least one thing of value to God is that all creatures are co-creators. God maximizes the realization of this value in this universe. The purpose of God in creating such a universe is for the whole creation to enter into a loving and just relation with God. We should expect the universe to produce creatures with capacities to enter such a relationship with God and these creatures are here called 'persons', who are embodied and embedded in the life-producing universe. We should expect there to be a general revelation of God made possible by the created world and a special personal revelation of God calling each and all persons into a loving and just relation with God. This universe is *ultimately* ordered to this purpose and *penultimately* ordered to this value. We should expect this universe to allow for a possible *dis-order* as and when persons choose not to accept this calling and form another way of life for themselves drawing on the resources of the *penultimate* order. This disordering would go against the grain of their being persons, oriented in their being to God as their true end and value, even while God remains to them *incognito*.

I have argued that this is a better type of creation than any which does not include creatures as co-creators on the grounds that, by comparison, in its being it is more like God who brings things into existence *ex nihilo* and is not only intrinsically good but also good for others. Consequently, I set aside the students' claims s(a)–s(d) namely,

> s(a) a perfectly good God would create a perfectly good universe;
> s(b) the universe would therefore be created in its 'end state' thereby perfectly fulfilling the divine purpose in creation;
> s(c) the perfectly good 'end state' would not include any pain, suffering, or death;
> s(d) there would be no process leading to the fulfilment of the purpose.

The universe as envisaged in my discussion is created by God *for* but not *in* its 'end state'. The powerful operation of creatures as co-creators leading to a life-producing universe entails some kind of process. There is likewise another process, so we may suppose, involved in the revelation of God and the reception of the revelation by persons entering a loving and just relationship with God oriented to the fulfillment of God's purpose in creation.

We are thinking that God creates a universe with the stated purpose. We note that any alternative that did not include this purpose would be a lesser good and so would not be chosen by God. On the other hand, this carries no suggestion of it being the 'best' because of the impossibility of envisaging the 'best' with respect to the inexhaustible goodness of God.

The students' argument is that compared to what the natural sciences show us about the actual universe, it is clearly not the creation of a perfectly good God as set out in s(a)–s(d). Likewise, students argue that the Christian Bible presents the biblical God as creating the world but not in its 'end state' for it presents visions of the 'end state' (e.g., Isaiah 11:6–9; Revelation 21) that this God will finally bring about. From s(a)–s(d) the biblical God is not the perfectly good God as understood by the students. As argued in this chapter, however, we should expect the universe created by the omni-God would not be created in its 'end state'. Therefore on that basis, s(a)–s(d) does not hold, nor, does the claim hold that the actual universe is not created by this God, and nor does it hold that the biblical God is not the perfectly good God we have been discussing.

These conclusions remove *that* barrier to assuming the actual universe is created by the omni-God. There are, however, further serious objections to be considered under Reality Checks, in Chapter V. Before engaging these objections, I want to locate this theology of creation in relation to what the natural sciences tell us about the actual universe and then in relation to the Christian tradition. I address these two matters in the next chapter.

Chapter IV
Locating this theology of creation

1a. In relation to the natural sciences

I want to locate this theology of creation in relation to what the natural sciences say about the actual universe.[1] The earlier account of 'the problem' in the problem of natural evil, concluded with the students' argument based on their theology of creation—a perfectly good, all powerful, all knowing God would create a world in its perfect end state concluded that science shows our universe could not have been created by such a God. This presents a powerful disjunction between their theology and the natural sciences. While I have argued against the students' theology of creation, I need to examine how the theology of creation I am proposing stands in relation to the natural sciences. A good place to start is by clarifying where I think there is a significant challenge to this theology that draws on the natural sciences. Strictly, it turns out to be a philosophical rather than a scientific challenge.

Natural Science is not Scientific Naturalism

There is a mistaken widespread belief of an inherent conflict (even 'warfare') between the natural sciences and Christian theology.[2]

---

1. For an excellent introduction to this topic see Alister McGrath, *Science and Religion, A New Introduction*, 2nd edition (Malden MA: Wiley-Blackwell, 2010), and Garry Ferngren, *Science & Religion: A Historical Introduction* (Baltimore: The Johns Hopkins University Press, 2002). The theology of creation I have been pursuing offers those holding this conflict view an alternative. A lot of work has been done by Christians who are theologians and/or scientists in the last century, but especially the last forty years. This is largely unknown to the wider public and poorly known in the churches. It is timely to recall the websites listed in the Preface that can help interested inquirers.
2. Chris Mulherin, *Science and Christianity, The Conflict Myth* (Melbourne: Garratt Publishing 2019).

However, there *is* an inherent conflict between theology and the philosophy of 'scientific naturalism'. Scientific naturalism is the conjunction of naturalism—the claim that nature is all there is and so there is no supernatural order above nature—with the claim that all objects, processes, truths, and facts about nature fall within the scope of the scientific method.'[3]

The most powerful form of scientific naturalism is physicalism.[4] It is the default position in English-speaking philosophy of science and philosophy of mind. It has several key ideas. One says that the only way to reliably find out about the world is to use the methods and epistemic standards that are used in the natural sciences. This is methodological and epistemic naturalism. The second is a metaphysical thesis which says that all there is, is what physics says there is, or complex configurations of the same. Physics makes no mention of God in its account of the world and so *physicalism* as a philosophy is in direct disagreement with theology. It is very common to find people taking for granted that by espousing the natural sciences they are thereby espousing scientific naturalism. The natural sciences are being confused with a philosophical position. This becomes clearer from the philosophical critique of scientific naturalism (see below) and of physicalism in particular.[5]

Four hundred and fifty years of the natural sciences shows the power of naturalistic explanations, and this is the basis for a positive induction that eventually everything will yield to a naturalistic

---

3. For a good introduction to scientific naturalism see B Edward and Robin Collins, 'Scientific Naturalism' in Ferngren, *Science & Religion*, 322–334.
4. David Stoljar, 'Physicalism', in *Stanford Encyclopedia of Philosophy*, substantive revision 9 March 2015, http://plato. standford. edu/entries/physicalism/; David Papineau, 2000, 'The Rise of Physicalism', in WF Martin Stone, and Jonathan Wolff editors, *The Proper Ambition of Science* (London: Routledge 2000); David Papineau,'Naturalism', in *Stanford Encyclopedia of Philosophy*, substantive revision in March 2015, https://plato. stanford. edu/entries/naturalism/ . Kelly J Clarke, editor *Blackwell Companion to Naturalism* (Malden MA, USA: John Wiley and Sons Inc, 2016).
5. This confusion is not attributed to theologians espousing a physicalist view of the universe and doing so for theological reasons, for example, Nancey Murphy who rejects dualism in favour of the biblical belief in the resurrection of the dead. See Nancey Murphy, *Bodies and Souls, or Spirited Bodies* (Cambridge: Cambridge University Press, 2006). The critique of physicalism still applies, notwithstanding Nancey Murphy, and Warren S Brown, *Did My Neurons Make Me Do It?* (Oxford: Oxford University Press, 2009).

explanation. For example, here is Jack Smart a famous Australian philosopher and atheist:

> There does seem to be, so far as science is concerned, nothing in the world but increasingly complex arrangements of physical constituents. All except for one place: in consciousness . . . That everything should be explicable in terms of physics . . . except the occurrence of sensations seems to me to be frankly unbelievable.[6]

On the other hand, see various philosophical critiques of physicalism.[7] Firstly, there is Hempel's dilemma,[8] which objects that no one thinks present physics is complete and who knows whether a future physics might include the mental. Secondly, in response to the metaphysical thesis, that 'all there is, is what physics says there is or complex configurations of the same', there is the open question 'is that all there is?' This cannot be answered by the natural sciences, since each particular science has its own field of phenomena and theories, and even all the natural sciences considered together cannot support a claim, 'this is all there is'.

Thirdly, an exception to there being only increasingly complex arrangements of physical constituents is unbelievable to Smart.[9] For him, consciousness doesn't provide the weighty grounds needed to support the claim that it is an exception. However, increasing

---

6. John JC Smart, 'Sensations and Brain Processes', *Philosophical Review*, 68 (1959): 141–156; 143.
7. John Haught, *Is Nature Enough?* (Cambridge: Cambridge University Press, 2006); Colin Cunningham, *Darwin's Pious Idea, Why the Ultradarwinists and Creationists Both get it Wrong*, Grand Rapids Mich Eerdmans, 2010) Thomas Nagel, *Mind and Cosmos: Why the materialist, neo-Darwinian Conception of Nature is Almost Certainly False* (Oxford: Oxford University Press, 2012); Stephen Ames, 'The Rise, Critiques and Consequences of Scientific Naturalism', in R Horner, P McArdle, and D Kirchhoffer, editors *Being Human, Groundwork For A Theological Anthropology For The 21st Century*, (Preston, Mosaic Press, 2013), 264–268.
8. Carl Hempel, 'Reduction: Ontological and Linguistic Facets', in Sidney Morgenbesser, Patrick Suppes, and Morton White editors *Philosophy, science, and method; essays in Honor of Ernest Nagel* (New York: St Martin's Press, 1969).
9. Smart, *Sensations*, 143, acknowledges that this is 'largely a confession of faith'.

physical complexity logically cannot explain at least one strand of consciousness that shows up in human inquiry.[10]

To see this, I first take Quine's point that an ontology is a theory of what there is.[11] I then argue that any ontology must meet the following general requirement. Any ontology, when combined with appropriate scientific theories, must yield an explanation of how inquirers have come into existence on this planet. If it could be shown that logically an ontology prevented this requirement being met, it would fail as an ontology because it would undermine its own claim to be known. It would also fail because as a theory of what there is it disallowed the inclusion of what any such theory must include, namely human inquirers, and how they have come into existence on this planet.

Many will judge the above requirement can be met via the many examples of emergence in the 13.7-billion-year-old story of evolutionary cosmology.[12] Human inquiry represents a stunning example of such emergence. For many it is a matter of 'case closed'. But this judgement is made without any account of human inquiry. As a matter of principle: something to be explained (explanandum) needs to be well articulated if a proposed explanation (explanans) is to be properly tested.

I argue that human inquiry has, among other things, a normative dimension with two aspects: *evaluative* (it concerns good arguments/good experiments) and *regulative* (inquirers ought to take on board the good arguments/experiments relevant to their inquiries).[13] Physicalism's metaphysical thesis can support a scientific view of what is or is likely to happen but that scientific view logically cannot

---

10. This failure in explaining is not a 'gaps' argument by which a current failure to explain would later be redressed by more scientific study. I now point out what it is about human inquiry that cannot be explained on physicalist assumptions and how it is logical matter, not a temporary gap in scientific knowledge.
11. VO Willard Quine, 'What there is', *Metaphysical Review*, 2/s (1948): 21–38.
12. Howard J Morowitz, *The Emergence of Everything: How the World Became Complex* (New York: Oxford University Press, 2002); Holmes Rolston III, *The Emergence of Everything: How the world became complex: Matter-Energy, Life, Mind* (New York: Columbia University Press 2012).
13. This normative dimension is acknowledged by naturalists such as WV Quine, B Ellis, W Lycan, D Papineau, M Smith. For my critique of their accounts of normativity see Ames, 'The Rise, Critiques and Consequences of Scientific Naturalism', 260–268. See also Patrick Rysiew 'Naturalism in Epistemology', in *Stanford Encyclopaedia of Philosophy*.

account for what ought to happen, including in human inquiry. Physicalists acknowledge the regulative as well as the evaluative aspect of normativity, but introduce an 'ought', by borrowing a hypothetical imperative. This may be found in Ellis,[14] Lycan[15], and Papineau. Papineau says, "[w]hen I first started work on this paper, I assumed that these hypothetical 'oughts' at least could be taken for granted by naturalism." He discovered, however, that this move is not available to naturalists.

> I assumed there was a sense in which
> (i) 'A ought to X' is an analytic consequence of
> (ii) 'A wants Y', and,
> (iii) 'X is necessary to [achieve] Y'. . . .
>
> I have been persuaded by a paper by John Broome that no special non-moral 'ought' can be analytically derived from (ii) and (iii) because no 'ought' of any kind can be so derived . . . This leaves us with the task of explaining the unreduced 'ought' which govern this prescriptive conditional.[16]

Michael Smith gave a 'consequentialist' reading[17] of the 'ought' as follows: 'You ought to do W iff W is the better means to achieve your goal G, compared to doing X, Y, Z.' The 'iff' symbol means it should be possible to read the claim in the reverse direction.

> (i) I have goal G.
> (ii) W is the better means to achieve G compared to X, Y and Z.

But logically, there is no entailment to what I ought to do as Papineau indicated in (2). For more on this question of normativity, see both

---

14. Brian Ellis, *Truth and Objectivity* (Oxford: Blackwell, 1988), 50, 52.
15. William Lycan, *Judgment and Justification* (Cambridge: Cambridge University Press, 1988), 128. See also, William Lycan, "'Is' and 'Ought' in Cognitive Science", in *Behavioural and Brain Sciences*, 4 (1981): 344–345.
16. David Papineau, 1999, 'Normativity and Judgement', *Aristotelian Society Supp*, 77 (1999): 18, fn.3.
17. Private communication after a lecture in Sydney. For more on these claims regarding normativity and a richer ontology, see, Ames, 'The Rise, Critiques and Consequences of Scientific Naturalism', 260–268. I have pursued the conversation with Michael Smith, which is included in my Stephen Ames 'Critique of Daniel Dennett's, *From Bacteria to Bach and Back, the Evolution of Minds*', in *Journal of Biomedical Engineering and Innovations*, 2022, 3/1 (2022): 3–4

Smith's response to this critique referring me to his constitutivism[18] and my reply.[19]

Physicalism fails to meet the requirement on any ontology to explain how inquirers have come into existence on planet earth.[20] A richer ontology is needed to account for human inquiry, even for

---

18. M Smith, 'Constitutivism', in, T McPherson and D Plunkett, *The Routledge Handbook of Metaethics* (New York: Routledge, 2018), .372.
19. S Ames, 'Critique of Daniel Dennett's, *From Bacteria to Bach and Back, the Evolution of Minds*, in, *Journal of Biomedical Engineering and Innovations*, 2022, 3/1 (2022): 1–7, especially 4.
20. This also remains a problem for Daniel Dennett, *From Bacteria to Bach and Back, The Evolution of Minds* (New York: WW Norton, 2017). See Ames, 'Critique of Daniel Dennett's, *From Bacteria to Bach and Back*, 1–7. The evolved modules of competence that compose our brain produce a 'user illusion' (so Dennett) enabling the human interaction of asking each other to justify our choices and actions, identified as "the logical space of reasons" (Dennett (41). Dennett cites Wilfred Sellars *Science, Perception and Reality*, (London: Routledge, and Kegan Paul, 1962). This space is bounded by norms, by mutual recognition of how things *ought* to go—the right way, not the wrong way to play the reason giving game. 'Wherever there are reasons, then, there is room for, and a need for, some kind of *justification* and the possibility of *correction* when something goes wrong . . . This normativity is the foundations of ethics: the ability to appreciate how reason giving *ought* to go is a prerequisite for appreciating how life ought to go in society.' (Dennett, 41). I would add that this logical space of reasons, with normativity and justification, is also manifest in human inquiry, especially epistemology, though not mentioned by Dennett, not even in his paradigms of top-down inquiry and comprehension—Picasso, Bach, Gaudi, Turing, Einstein, Dennett, 311. However, my critique of physicalism, shows it is logically impossible to claim that the brain produces such a 'user illusion' with its regulative 'ought'. A further problem for Dennett is that from Sellars (Wilfred Sellars, *Minnesota Studies in the Philosophy of Science*, 1 (1956): 253–329).and later McDowell (John McDowell, 2004, 'Naturalism in the Philosophy of Mind', in M De Caro and D Macarthur, editors *Naturalism in Question* (Cambridge Ma: Harvard University Press, 2004), 91–105. We need to recognise the distinct, logical space of 'subsumption under natural law'. The logical space of reasons is logically different from the logical space of explanation in terms of subsumption under natural law. It follows that explanations proceeding along the lines of subsumption under natural law (Dennett's 'competence') will logically be unable to reach explanations in terms of the logical space of reasons (Dennett's 'comprehension'). This distinction between the distinct 'logical spaces' from Sellars and McDowell is not mentioned by Dennett. For some of the subtleties in Sellars views see James R O'Shea, 'Normativity and Scientific Naturalism in Sellars' 'Janus-Faced' Space of Reasons', in *International Journal of Philosophical Studies*, 18/3 (2010): 459–471; Dyonisis Christias, 'Towards a Reformed Liberal *and* Scientific Naturalism', in *Dialectica*, 73/4 (2019): 507–534.

the explanatory successes that ground the positive induction above. This has consequences for the doctrine of the 'closure of the physical' (COP): all physical effects are ultimately produced by only physical causes. On this view there are no vital, mental, divine or other kinds of forces at work in the world. But the normativity of human inquiry is integral to producing physical effects as people go about conducting experiments and producing and presenting arguments. Yet physicalism cannot account for this normativity. Consequently, the COP is to be set aside.[21] Note, even Papineau an international exponent of naturalism, says that the historical and empirical data for the COP does not provide a 'knock down' argument. All that physics requires is that the forces act conservatively. 'Clearly conservation of energy as such leaves open exactly what basic forces exist. It only requires that, whatever they are, they operate conservatively.'[22] These arguments against physicalism also rebut Rovelli's claim that,

> objections against the possibility of understanding our mental life in terms of known natural laws on closer inspection come down to a generic repetition of 'It seems implausible to me,' based on intuitions without supporting argument. Unless it is the sad hope of being constituted by some vaporous supernatural substance that remains alive after death; a prospect that, apart from being utterly implausible, strikes me as ghastly.[23]

---

21. This conclusion completely changes the discussion of divine action in the world that is not closed to other sources of physical effects. God does not have to be understood as a non-interventionist God out of scruples about the closure of the physical or about deterministic laws of physics. See Jeffery Koperski, *The Physics of Theism, God, Physics and the Philosophy of Science* (West Sussex, UK: Wiley Blackwell, 2015), 146–196. Papineau thought that the closure of the physical was a standard part of physics until colleagues pointed out it was not found in physics textbooks. Koperski's discussion also give several examples of how outcomes of some classical physical processes are not determined by initial conditions plus laws of classical physics. This indeterminism is without reference to quantum mechanics or chaos theory to provide a source of indeterminism. Theologians who hold to a non-interventionist God have 'misidentified the enemy'. Not determinism but COP. 'In the debate over divine action in the world determinism is a red herring.' (184, 185.)
22. *The Physics of Theism, God, Physics and the Philosophy of Science*, 196. For more on the COP see Ames, 'The Rise, Critiques and Consequences of Scientific. Naturalism', 257–263.
23. Carlo Rovelli, *Helgoland*, translated by, E Segre, and, S Carnell (Dublin: Allen Lane, 2021), 157. Rovelli significantly underplays the arguments against a fully naturalistic account of consciousness.

At least one important consequence follows from this discussion. A richer account of nature is needed that includes but goes beyond what the natural sciences tell us. All there is, is richer than what physicalism says. Thus, a richer ontology than metaphysical naturalism is needed. I will not now pursue this 'richer ontology' save for four points. Firstly, a principled starting point is needed. A clue to such a starting point is what resists being completely naturalised by physicalism and so is indicative of this richer ontology. It is human inquiry that offers such resistance and so points to the richer ontology. Secondly, that in conjunction with the natural sciences and the various life sciences, this richer ontology must enable us to explain how human inquirers have come into existence on planet earth. Thirdly, there are several entrées into that discussion. I especially mention John Haught[24] and Daniel Helminiak[25] who both draw on the magnum opus of Bernard Lonergan[26], and Simon Conway Morris[27], with various authors representing counter position, for example, Paul Davies[28], Lee Smolin[29] and Daniel Dennett.[30] Finally, we can look for a consilience between such a richer ontology and my theology of creation, according to which the *ultimate* order of the universe is expected to be intimated as the penultimate order of the life-producing universe produces persons.

---

24. John Haught, *Is Nature Enough: Meaning and Truth in an Age of Science*, (Cambridge: Cambridge University Press, 2006).
25. Daniel A Helminiak, *Brains, Consciousness and God, A Lonerganian Integration*, Albany, State University of New York Press, 2015).
26. Bernard Lonergan, 2000, fifth edition of 1957, *Insight: A Study of Human Understanding*, Frederick E Crowe and Robert M Doran, editors (Toronto: Lonergan Research Institute of Regis College, University of Toronto Press, 2000), Chapters 4, 15.
27. Simon Conway Morris, *From Extra-terrestrials to Animal Minds to Six Myths of Evolution*, (Templeton Press, 2022). See also, Sean Carroll's Mindscape, https://www.youtube.com/watch?v=bWowIh6Zjzo .
28. Paul Davies, 'Universe from bit', in Paul Davies, and Neil Gregersen, editors, *Information and the Nature of Reality, From Physics to Metaphysics* (Cambridge: Cambridge University Press, 2010).
29. Lee Smolin, *The Life of the Cosmos* (Oxford: Oxford University Press, 1997).
30. D Dennett, *From Bacteria to Bach and Back, The Evolution of Minds* (Dublin: Allen Lane, 2017).

Human inquiry and theology

Above, in Chapter III, section 1d, on the Ultimate Order of the Universe, it was argued that created persons would be equipped with capacities to know and understand the created universe. Let's pursue that point. I understand creation to be a free act of divine will and so, while there are things that can be said about the kind of universe we should expect such a God to create, there will be an inescapable limit, not due to mere human limitations. Since creation is the free act of divine will, the creation would be contingent on divine freedom. Therefore, much about the detail of this contingent creation will necessarily not be derivable from the idea of God using reason alone. This nuances but does not undermine the project of comparing the actual world, which I assume is created by God, with the kind of world we should expect God to create.

While it is possible to work out something of the kind of universe we should expect God to freely create, it is not possible by reason alone to work out all the particularities of this free creation. To know what God has freely created requires that we attend to the actual world in all its particularity, which means, attending with our senses. But knowing is not just "taking a look".[31] God is deeply rational, so we should also expect to find that the actual world we engage through our senses is intelligible and open to rational explanation, but of course without prejudice to the forms of intelligibility and the forms of rationality that might be called for in order to understand what God has created.[32] It befits the superlative excellence of God's knowledge, power, and goodness for us to keep open to the possibility of human inquiry bringing into view processes in the created world that sustain its operation yet are presently hidden from our understanding.

---

31. Bernard Lonergan, 'Theories of Inquiry', in WFJ Ryan SJ, and BJ Tyrrell SJ, editors, *A Second Collection* (Toronto: Lonergan Research Institute of Regis College, Toronto, University, of Toronto Press, 1974). Daniel A. Helminiak, *Brain, Consciousness and God, A Lonerganian Integration*, (State University of New York, 2016) Chapter 2.
32. This assumes we as human inquirers have the created capacities to discern such intelligibility and rationality that is embodied in the universe ultimately because it is created by God. And the above theology of creation includes saying why we as persons, with these capacities, are part of the created world.

This interplay of the sensory, the intelligible. and the rational in human inquiry shows up in various ways in common sense activity, in the empirical inquiries conducted in the natural sciences[33] and the social sciences, in philosophical inquiries. It also shows up in the rather different inquiries of poets and artists with their distinct sensory awareness and their drawing on still other forms of intelligibility and rationality in responding to the created world. While it is possible to work out something of the kind of universe we should expect God to freely create, it is not possible by reason alone to work out all the particularities of this free creation. However, it is possible to see how the theology of creation presented here provides a basis for the diversity of human inquiries yielding different kinds of knowledge, including that of the natural sciences.

On this basis, we should not expect an *inherent* conflict between theology and the natural sciences. New discoveries in the natural sciences and in other forms of human inquiry may well provide challenges to theology, calling theology to engage its own resources more fully to respond to the challenge. But this is quite different from saying there is an inherent conflict (even, 'warfare') between the natural sciences and theology. We have already seen an indication of how the 'Galileo Affair' does not promote the 'inherent conflict' thesis, though it has been incorrectly used to that end.

Nevertheless, the problem of natural evil is an example of a claim to an inherent conflict between theology and the natural sciences. One focus of this problem is Darwinian evolution and the kind of world it shows us because of all the suffering and death involved in producing life. Here, we are still working our way towards addressing that claim.

---

33. Peter Harrison, *The Fall of Man and the Foundations of Science* (Cambridge: Cambridge University Press, 2007), 12, has questioned the view that this was an historically important part of the rise of experimental philosophy. However, the claim I am making is not that historical claim. Rather, I am proposing it as a theologically relevant consideration. It assumes a rationalist and voluntarist account of God creating the universe, though not the extreme voluntarism that God could order creation in any way God chose or continue to do so from moment to moment. On the other hand, Harrison shows how belief in the fall of humankind led to regarding human reason as impaired (contra Aquinas) which needs to be regimented by the senses attending directly to God's creation.

Identifying the penultimate order

One form of empirical inquiry was pursued by Darwin in the five years on the HMS Beagle, bringing to light a vast number and variety of observations and specimens in some of the most challenging environments in the world. Thank you, Charles Darwin, naturalist *extraordinaire*! Subsequently, through exchanges with many people, Darwin gathered a still wider body of data. With this collection of data and with a lot of hard thinking, Darwin eventually proposed his theory of evolution, subsequently developed in many ways. Neo-Darwinism tells us that we live in a life-producing universe, where life, including intelligent life, evolves by natural selection and many other processes identified by biologists, all being the lawful operation of 'blind' causal processes, over an immense time.[34] These processes fit well under the theme of creatures as co-creators in a life producing universe.

Theologically, it may be that God has a variety of ways by which a life-producing universe might actually produce life. Whatever these might look like in any other life-producing universe possibly created by God, the above discussion gives us good reason to say that in our universe it takes the form of evolution by natural selection.

This helps us towards understanding why God would create the world *ex nihilo*, sustain it in existence, and use something like

---

34. Readers familiar with Richard Dawkins, *The Blind Watchmaker* (Harlow: Scientific and Technical, 1986), may have been wondering how his discussion of the operation of blind, purposeless natural processes that produce the appearances of design relates to the present discussion. It would have been premature to address this question before introducing the ideas of creatures as co-creators, realising a value important to God, and before introducing the idea of the divine purpose in creation. From the above discussion, there is reason to expect God's purpose in creation not to be evident in the operation of the *penultimate* order of creation, namely. the life-producing universe. It is expected to come to light only through the special revelation of God. It is also premature for another reason. We have many examples of technology operating with 'blind' natural processes that have been deployed by rational agents for valued ends, e.g., iPhones for communicating with others. Might it be that the blind natural laws are deployed by God for valued ends? This is not a question discussed in the literature, but the valued end identified here is that of creatures as co-creators at all levels of a life-producing universe. An indication of how the blind natural process described by the laws of physics may be thought to be deployed for this valued end is addressed below.

Darwinian evolution to bring life into existence.[35] It expresses the value to God of creating in this way, namely, ensuring creatures at all levels have their own distinctive powers operating in a universe that is a life producing universe, and that the realisation of this value is maximised by God. This is a better type of creation, (compared to other possible types of creation identified above) in which as much as possible, creatures are co-creators.[36] The operation of this type of creation should be expected to disclose this value, (creatures as co-creators), but not the purpose God has in mind for the whole life-producing universe. This is a theologically grounded view of creation, otherwise spoken of as a theology of nature,[37] which for *theological reasons* (see above) waits upon the natural sciences to tell us in detail what the *penultimate* order of the life-producing universe is. This view of creation is entirely welcoming of what poets and artists might also show us with their different sensitivity to the universe and awareness of a different intelligibility. An example of such difference is Gerard Manly Hopkins, poet *extraordinaire*!

Assuming our universe is created by God, we have set out something of theology's view of the *penultimate* order of the life-producing universe and identified it in terms of Darwinian evolution. On this basis we can go further on this identification in three ways.

---

35. See, S Ames 'Why would God use evolution?', in J Arnould, editor, *Darwin and Evolution, Interfaith Perspectives* (Adelaide: ATF Press, 2010), 105–128.
36. In lectures this has often evoked from students the question, 'would a truly good God do this given all the death and suffering involved in the evolution of life on the planet?' I accept this question and discuss it in Chapter V as part of several 'Reality Checks' challenging what I have presented.
37. There are many examples of a 'theology of nature': for example, Jesuit, palaeontologist, Pierre Teilhard de Chardin SJ 1881–1995, see his *The Phenomenon of Man* (New York: Harper and Rowe, 1955); Karl Rahner, 'Christology within an Evolutionary View of the World', in *Foundations of Christian Faith: An Introduction to the Idea of Christianity*, translated by William V Dych (New York: Crossroad, 1978), 178–203; Arthur Peacocke, *Evolution, The Disguised Friend of Faith?*, (West Conshohocken: Templeton Press, 2009); Denis Edwards, *How God Acts, Creation, Redemption, and Special Divine Action* (Hindmarsh: ATF Press, 2010; Elizabeth Johnson, *Ask The Beasts: Darwin and The God of Love* (London: Bloomsbury, 2014); John Haught, *God After Darwin, A Theology of Evolution* (Boulder, CO: Westview Press, 2008), and, *Resting on the Future, A Catholic Theology for an Unfinished Universe* (New York: Bloomsbury Academic, 2015). Notice that the atheist students are also providing an interpretation of our universe as *not* created by God. Their interpretation presupposes an idea of God, one that is rejected, and to that extent it is also a theological interpretation of nature.

Firstly, the idea of the penultimate order flowing from the theology of creation developed above, argued from the divine purpose in creation that the life-producing universe should be expected to include creatures distinctively capable of entering a loving and just relationship to God. I called these creatures 'persons' and now argue we should identify human beings as such 'persons' in the sense explained. This identification is based on human beings as the only known creature that prays and envisages an ultimate purpose for the universe. Interestingly, we can include some reasons from the side of evolutionary science for saying that human beings qualify as 'persons' in the sense of that term in the theology of creation, namely as creatures, produced by the life-producing universe who have the capacity for a loving and just relationship with God.

In fact, human beings produced by Darwinian evolution have variously understood themselves in relation to a transcendent reality. Indeed Daniel Dennett[38] has conjectured how evolution leads to the construct of 'God' and so of religion as an evolutionary adaptation. Dennett offers this plausible conjecture but not by amassing the results of anthropological and archaeological research. I am quite happy to accept this conjecture. For reasons discussed above, I do not accept Dennett's naturalistic presuppositions, which rule out any transcendent reality. Dennett's story, however, makes no *use* of premises from scientific naturalism for his conjecture. It fits well within the theme of 'revelation' discussed above, especially the claim that created persons can come to know of God through the mediation of the created universe, including their reflection on their own shared existence.

Human beings brought into existence by the life-producing universe are to be identified as persons as presented in the theology of creation. This leaves open whether the life-producing universe has brought into existence other creatures that would count as persons, elsewhere than on planet earth. Nothing in the discussion rules that

---

38. Danielle Dennett, *Breaking the Spell: Religion as a Natural Phenomenon* (New York: Viking, 2006). For other relevant work see Edward O Wilson, Sociobiology: *The New Synthesis*, Cambridge MA: Harvard University Press, 1975). Elliott Sober and David S Wilson, *Unto Others: The Evolution and Psychology of Unselfish Behaviour* (Cambridge MA: Harvard University Press, 1988); Pascal Boyer, *Religion Explained: The Evolutionary Origins of Religious Thought*, London: Vintage, 2002); Scott Atran, *In Gods We Trust: The Evolutionary Landscape of Religion* (Oxford: Oxford University Press, 2004)

out. On the contrary it is entirely consistent within this theology of creation.[39]

Secondly, based on the identification of the penultimate order of creation in this theology with our grasp of our evolving universe, we can extend the identification to include the great scientific story of the laws of physics, of cosmology, and particle physics, which are fine-tuned to the production of carbon-based life.[40] These also indicate something of the God-given penultimate order of this life-producing universe.[41]

Thirdly, my identifying the penultimate order of this universe in this way entails, consequently, the further claim that the fine-tuning of physical laws and constants, is the way it is, *in order* for the universe to be a life-producing universe. This theologically

---

39. It is convenient to anticipate that we can trace this part of the theology of creation in the fabric of Christian tradition. This is not widely appreciated by Christians, but see, Thomas F O'Meara, *The Vast Universe, Extraterrestrials and Christian Revelation* (Collegeville: Liturgical Press, 2012); see also, the review by William Stoeger SJ, in *Theology and Science*, 11/1 (2013): 77–83.
40. The fine-tuning idea is that even a very small change in the value of the physical constants that characterise the physical universe would block the production of life. Geraint F Lewis, and Luke A Barnes, *A Fortunate Universe, Life in a Finely Tuned Cosmos*, (Cambridge: Cambridge University Press, 2016). See also, Paul Davies, *The Goldilocks Enigma, Why is the Universe Just Right for Life?* (Dublin: Allen and Lane, 2006). Note that I am not here making a natural theology argument *from* the observed fine-tuning *to* God. That line of argument is challenged by the various multiverse proposals, whereby a myriad of universes with randomly formed properties naturally have a few that have properties that are 'just right' for producing life and so appear to be fine-tuned for life. (For more details, see the two references just mentioned.) At present there is no independent evidence for a multiverse and while theoretical considerations motivating the multiverse proposals attract support, the lack of evidence and what seem to be the giving up on the need for evidence has led some senior physicists to question whether this is still empirical science, for example, Lee Smolin, *The Trouble With Physics: The Rise of String Theory, The Fall of a Science, and What Comes Next* (Boston: Houghton Mifflin Harcourt, 2006).
41. See Stoeger on his caution about laws of nature as '"models" or approximate descriptions, albeit very accurate and detailed ones'. William Stoeger, SJ 'Contemporary Physics and the Ontological Status of The Laws of Nature', in Robert Russell, Nancey Murphy and Chris J Isham, eds., *Quantum Cosmology and The Laws of Nature: Scientific Perspectives on Divine Action*, Vatican City State: Vatican Observatory Publications and Berkeley, CA: The Centre for Theology and the Natural Science, 1999), 207–231.

based claim goes well beyond the established scientific conclusion that the universe is fine-tuned for carbon-based life. It is claiming that the laws of physics and physical constants can in principle be explained in terms of the universe being life-producing. This moves our discussion into the neighbourhood of the discussions by Lee Smolin[42] and Paul Davies[43] who in different ways are asking, 'why are the laws of physics the way they are?' and are seeking a naturalistic answer with no reference to God. My theology of creation is in a very challenging environment.

It also faces at least two further objections. One comes from the idea of the multiverse which is thought to show that this universe just happens to have the fine-tuned properties that lead to carbon-based life. A second objection comes from PCW. Davies and SI Walker.

> Expressed more succinctly if one insists on attributing the pathway from mundane chemistry to life as the outcome of fixed dynamical laws, then (as our analysis suggests) those laws must be selected with extraordinary care and precision, which is tantamount to intelligent design: it states that 'life' is written into the laws of physics *ab initio*. There is no evidence at all that the actual known laws of physics possess this almost miraculous property.[44]

I have taken the discussion to this point to show that this theology of creation, which is asking what kind of universe we should expect the omni-God to create, comes to a particularly challenging moment, namely, is it possible to argue that the laws of physics are the way they are *in order* for the universe to be a life-producing universe? This may be thought to be drawing a very long bow, indeed for Davies, a miraculous bow. It is a bold claim arising from my theology of creation. It turns out that other work I have pursued has independently yielded an argument that supports this bold claim. The argument concludes 'the universe is structured according to the laws of physics by God,

---

42. Robert Unger and Lee Smolin, *The Singular Universe and The Reality of Time* (Cambridge: Cambridge University Press, 2015).
43. Paul Davies, *The Goldilocks Enigma*, and Paul Davies, 'Universe from bit', in Paul Davies, and Neil Gregersen, editors *Information and the Nature of Reality, from Physics to Metaphysics* (Cambridge: Cambridge University Press, 2010).
44. Sara I Walker and Paul Davies, 'The Hard Problem of Life', arXiv:1606.07184v1 [q-bio. OT], 2016.

the creator of the universe *ex nihilo*, in order that the universe be knowable through empirical enquiry, by embodied rational agents, using the principle of point-of-view-invariance.'[45] The argument responds to Professor Brian Cox' claim that big questions like why is there anything at all? and why are we here? are scientific questions.[46] It also draws on the work of well-known physicist and atheist, the late Professor VJ Stenger, especially his 2006, *The Comprehensible Universe, Where Do The Laws of Physics Come From?* in which he explains the meaning of the principle-of-point-of-view-invariance, used by physicists.

Of course, my argument calls for more discussion and something of that is available in Ames (2022). Broadly, my argument is not a 'gaps' argument nor an argument from the analogy of design after Paley. Furthermore, this argument has nothing to do with arguments from the Intelligent Design movement, or from 'fine tuning', or from 'anthropic principles'. It cannot be used as a science stopper. More specifically, the conclusion is independent of the question of the multiverse. I can await physicists' decisions on that question, as on others, for example, to do with dark energy and dark matter.

I want to acknowledge that while I appeal to Professor Stenger's work on the laws of physics, I arrive at a different metaphysics from him, which goes against the naturalism and anti-theistic arguments for which Stenger is well known. My limited aim here has been to briefly indicate on what basis I support a striking consequence of my larger argument concerning the kind of universe we should expect the omni-God to create, namely that it is appropriate to identify the actual universe with the universe we should expect God to create.

Finally, I return to a theological account of the ultimate and penultimate ordering of creation by God. For good theological reasons, we could say little in detail about the penultimate order. A great deal of this detail for the penultimate order (beyond common sense but without prejudice thereto) is only available through the natural sciences. The ultimate order serves the realization of the divine purpose in creation and as explained, this purpose is only knowable through the special revelation of God. There is good

---

45. S Ames, 'From Physics to Metaphysics, a New Way', in, *Christian Perspectives on Science and Technology*, New Series, 1 (2022): 46–71.
46. Brian Cox, 2021, BBC series, *Universe*, at the end of the fifth episode.

theological reason for thinking that the ultimate purpose of God in creation would *not* be visible from or through the penultimate order. The penultimate order of creation serves the promotion of at least one thing that is of value to God, namely, creatures at all scales as co-creators, leading to a life-producing universe. The penultimate order is 'situated' within the still greater ultimate order and is to be drawn into the fulfilment of the divine purpose by the workings of the ultimate order of creation. Recall that in this theology of creation, the ultimate order in creation is intimated as the life-producing universe produces persons. This motivates reflection on human persons to see whether such intimations can be found and if so, how well. A positive answer is suggested by a variety of references,[47] a negative answer by others,[48] with one example of an author keeping the account of the human person distinct from his explicit theology.[49] I will pursue this reflection on another occasion.

Preliminary conclusion #2

In the theology of creation presented here, the life-producing universe produces persons with the capacities to know God and to know and understand something of the universe, both in common sense, in the arts, and in scientific inquiries, in order to appreciate the particularities of what God has created and to establish a form of life.[50] We have good reason to think that the Darwinian evolution of life on this planet, with the physical laws and constants fine-tuned

---

47. Charles Taylor, *Sources of the Self: The Making of Modern Identity* (Cambridge: Cambridge University Press, 1994(; Bernard Lonergan, *Method in Theology*, Chapter 4 (London: Darton Longman and Todd, 1972); S Ames, 'The value given, and the value presupposed in person centred dementia care', *OBM Geriatrics*; 3(3), doi: 10.21926/obm.geriatr.1903068, 2019
48. The many naturalistic accounts of the human person, including the evolutionary explanation of how humans came to the idea of God, (for example, D. Dennett *et. al.* just noted). Of course, these evolutionary narratives, but without the philosophical assumption of scientific naturalism can all be turned towards supporting the preceding footnote!
49. Helminiak, (2016).
50. This theology of creation points towards a theology of the natural sciences, in the sense of a theological interpretation of the natural sciences within the life-producing universe that God creates. For an articulated Christian theology of science see, Paul Tyson, *A Christian Theology of Science, Reimagining A Theological Vision of Natural Knowledge* (Grand Rapids, MI: Baker Academic, 2022).

for life and the grand cosmological story of the universe do show us something of the God-given penultimate order of the life-producing universe we should expect God to create. All this goes a good way to support the conclusion that the actual universe is not different from what we should expect to be created by an all-knowing, all-powerful, all-good God. In this light, I claim there is no basis for speaking about 'natural evils', as if the actual universe contradicted what we should expect such a God to create and so provided grounds for rejecting belief in such a God. This is my answer to the logical problem of natural evil. Of course, it must face challenges that arise in public presentations of my views. I will shortly engage these Reality Checks.

1b. Locating this theology of creation within Christian tradition

I now want to show the congruence between the above theology of creation (elaborated from the idea of the omni-God) and the fabric of the Christian tradition from which this idea of God has been taken.[51] Having argued *from* this idea of God *to* a view of God's purpose in creation, of persons, of revelation (general and special), and the ultimate order of the created universe, much else that might be said depends on what is believed about that special revelation of God, where and how it is believed to take place. The Abrahamic traditions have much in common but differ on what they identify as that special revelation of God.

The following briefly indicates what more has been said about the omni-God from within the Christian tradition. This will support the claim that the biblical God indeed gives a self-exposition, not of a different god but of the one 'omni-God' we have been considering so far.[52] This remains a contested claim. Jewish and Muslim communities would say that Christians have gone astray in their beliefs about God by not holding to the belief that there is only one God. Rather, their view is that the Christian belief in the Triune God, Father,

---

51. Other religious traditions will give their own elaboration of the omni-God and locate it in the fabric of their own tradition. A conversation between different traditions so expounded would be very welcome.
52. An example of this matter is the Gospel writers' efforts to make plain that the strangeness of Jesus, the God of which he spoke and in whose name he acted, is indeed the God of Abraham, Isaac, and Jacob, of Moses and all the prophets. This is most acute with regard to the Christian proclamation of a crucified Messiah.

Son, and Holy Spirit speaks of three gods. Though I won't discuss this difference further, I will say that Christians respectfully disagree following the resolution of this same issue *within* Christianity in the fourth century. We worship one God, Father, Son, and Holy Spirit as I hope to clarify. Finally, this makes available the tradition from which I wish to engage the 'Reality Checks' to my solution to the logical problem of natural evil.

created in the 'image of God'

Christian theology asserts humankind is created in the image and likeness of God.[53] This 'original blessing' has been understood in four ways: ontologically, relationally, functionally,[54] with the fourth being, christologically.[55] The 'ontological' understanding concerns *who* we are—persons—and *what* we are—the human nature we all share. In a Christian account of the being of human beings the person is ontologically prior. We are each unique, embodied persons, ontologically oriented for communion with God and with one another.[56] To be is to be in communion.[57] This orientation is the basis

---

53. Gen 1:26–28; Ps 8.
54. Stephen Garner, 'Image bearing Cyborgs?' in Stephen Garner editor, *Theology and the Body* (Adelaide: ATF Press, 2002), 19.
55. This may baffle some readers. To understand something Christologically means to understand it in terms of Christ. How to do this and especially how to do it with respect to the creation of human beings in the image of God is not a theme people would usually encounter, say in their local church. I trust this key claim will shortly become clearer as the discussion proceeds.
56. This embodiment is different from the idea of the person as an immortal soul imprisoned in the body, also, from any idea of the body as secondary to the person, and from the idea of the person reduced to being wholly a function of the body. In addition to the reference before the previous one, some other useful discussions of these matters are, Joel Green, and Stuart Palmer, eds, *In Search of the Soul: Four Views of the Mind Body Problem* (Illinois: Intervarsity Press, 2005); and Nancey Murphy, *Bodies and Souls or Spirited Bodies?* (New York: Cambridge University Press, 2006); Karl Rahner, *Foundations of Christian Faith, An Introduction to the Idea of Christianity*, translated by William V Dych (New York, Seabury Press, 1978), 178–187; Helminiak, *Brains, Consciousness and God*, Chapters 4, 5; Robert Spitzer SJ, *The Soul's Upward Yearning, Clues to Our Transcendent Nature from Experience and Reason* (San Francisco, Ignatius Press, 2015).
57. Jean Zizioulas, *Communion and Otherness: Further Studies in Personhood and the Church*, P McParland, editor (New York: T&T Clark, 2006).

for the claim made famous by Augustine, that our hearts are restless until they find their rest in God.[58]

The communion with one another may take many forms but of special importance is the assertion that humankind is created in the image of God as 'male and female'.[59] Together men and women share the 'original blessing', including the shared exercise of 'dominium'.[60] The assertion in Genesis 1:26–28, was remarkably counter-cultural in its day as it accords extraordinary power to 'male and female'. It still is. Notice that, for all the disorders of life that humankind produces, there is nowhere in the Bible that tells of this 'original blessing' being withdrawn by God.

The 'relational' understanding concerns our being drawn and called into personal communion with God and with one another, and into an analogous relationship with the earth by which we are dynamically embodied and embedded. Thus, our relationship with each other is to be in the 'image of God', which was earlier introduced as follows: Since all are called into such a relationship with God it follows that all are called to regard each other in that light and respect the dignity every creature has in virtue of the powers with which they have been created and the end to which all are called marked by otherness, diversity, equality, and a dynamic unity that is life-producing.

The 'functional' concerns *humankind* being given 'dominium', sovereign power to be used *together* as good stewards of the earth for

---

58. Augustine, *Confessions*, translated by Henry Chadwick (Oxford: Oxford University Press, 2008).
59. Implications for same-sex relationships is discussed in Ames, 2013, 'Being, Wellbeing and Globalisation' in Peter Price editor, *Christian Perspectives on Globalisation, A World United or Divided*, (Adelaide: ATF Press, 2014), 16–17.
60. This is in some tension with St Paul in 1 Cor 11:2–16, which denies that women are created in the image of God and the 'shame' in 1 Cor14:35 should a woman speak in church. The latter may be thought to also be in tension with Gal 3:28 where 'in Christ' there is no 'male and female'. The distinction is hardly denied, as indicated in Paul's discussion in 1 Corinthians 6, but rather the way of living out the distinctions is now set free for the new humanity inaugurated in Christ. What will this be? Surely it is not the continuation of the old cultural practices of placing the man over the woman. Surely the guide should be that in Christ God's intention from the beginning should now be enacted in the world, as we see in Jesus' discussion of divorce and marriage, quoting from Gen 2:24, where the latter has the further truly countercultural note that it is the man who would leave his father and mother and be joined to his wife.

all humankind now and into the future.[61] By this power we are to do justice to our being embodied persons, to our utter dependence on the life-giving earth and to the fair share in the blessings of the good earth God has given to *humankind*, which is thus the common good and right of access for all people. This is the wide ambit of divine justice for created life and human life in particular. Genesis is already a prophetic vision of the life of *humankind* and so of life in what we would call 'global' terms.[62]

Humankind exists to enjoy the original blessing of being made in the image of God, to hear God speaking in many ways, calling us all to seek our life with God, to live justly and graciously with each other, enjoying the 'original blessing' in exercising an awesome dominion

---

61. This is a radical theme since such power was attributed only to rulers, whether in Egypt or in Babylon or the other nations, which Israel eventually wanted to emulate (1 Samuel). It is also radical in that land does not belong by right to the 'crown' but to God and to the people as God's stewards of the land. This stewardship is not an exclusive ownership of land but a trust in which all have a share, exercised in particular communities. In the ordinary exchanges between communities and individuals the stewardship ought not be bought or sold outside the extended family (see the story of Naboth's Vineyard, 1 Kgs 21), nor redefined by force of arms or a legal fiction declaring a different kind of sovereignty as was done by Governor Philip on 26 January 1788 at Sydney Cove in the name of George III, King of England. This has many implications for a theological appreciation of indigenous communities in their relation to the land. See the account of 'sovereignty' by First Nations in Australia, in the *Statement from the Heart*, https://ulurustatement.org.

62. This is not to invoke our global economy, which is driven by the 'Golden Rule'— those who have the gold make the rules, and the first rule is: always make more gold. As time goes by this is no longer a common-sense drive to a better life but becomes and end in itself. This is what Aristotle describes as 'chrematistics' and was taken up much later by Karl Marx and Max Weber. (See the discussion in Michael Eldred. *Social Ontology, Recasting Political Philosophy through the Phenomenology of Whoness* [Frankfurt, ontos/verlag, 2008], 85–121). This is the art of gaining wealth for its own sake and so is without limits. It can thus function as a surrogate for God. Aristotle distinguishes this from 'economics' (*oikonomike*), the art of gaining wealth to manage a household and has its limits in maintaining the way of life of that household. Surely chrematistics finds its most powerful expression two and half thousand years later in the so-called global 'economy'. Hundreds of millions of people have been lifted out of poverty by the expansion of a global economy over the last forty years. This is a good, but it is much, much less than is possible. It is a 'trickle-down' effect, and hardly the main purpose of the economy. See Terry Eagleton, *Hope Without Optimism* (New Haven: Yale University Press, 2015), 14–38.

over the earth—though not over each other, according to Genesis 1:26–28, as stewards who are the image and likeness of the living God who created the world.[63] Furthermore, the whole created order is good, yet still incomplete, being destined by God for a still greater goodness.

In fact, however, it is another orientation, with other possibilities of life, to which we listen most carefully and are led by more persuasively, while maybe ensuring there is a 'place' for God or the gods, unless we have come to see ourselves in a godless world. In any of its forms, this other orientation of individual and social life eventually comes to be established as if having a life of its own, an encompassing 'fiction'[64] more living us than being lived by us; a surrogate of true life, with its own economy, ecology and even theology, that possesses, shapes, flavours, and directs our living, as if it had a life of its own. This surrogate of true life in effect comes to assume the role of 'divinity': it defines the taken-for-granted 'reality'; practically, it becomes that in which we live and move and have our being; it takes over and makes-over people, forming them in its own image, even from birth, even in the context of invaders, occupiers, and colonisers, who are the carriers of their own 'divinity'; it rewards those that fit in, but demeans those it does not recognise, those that oppose it or do not fit, those for whom there is no room.[65]

---

63. It is the distortion of this 'dominiun' (which according to the Bible has never been withdrawn) after the idolatrous counter-image of the living God that is the source of the runaway human ecology and economy with its destruction of species, pollution, and global warming. The answer is not to deny human powers but to direct them in the image of the living God.

64. In discussion, some people find this use of the term 'fiction' unsatisfactory. It fails to convey the reality to which it points. Patriarchy would surely count as 'fictions' but for some it is a distortion that is real and a lie and so a 'fiction'. I continue to use the term which for me has all the power of a lived reality that is a distortion and to the extent that it is, but not more, it is also a lie. For a similar use of the term 'fiction' see Frank Brennan's book, *Sharing the Country* (London: Penguin, 1991), 19. 'This legal fiction of *terra nullius* became firmly embedded in our history. Though a fiction, it has taken on a reality of its own that cannot be undone.' For a recent theological discussion of living a 'lie' see A. Shank. 1987, discussing V. Havel's parable of the grocer shop in Havel's essay, 'The Power of the Powerless' (English translation by P Wilson), in 1987, *Living in Truth*, edited by Jan Vladislav, London: Faber & Faber, 1987), 41. See Andrew Shanks, 2000, *God, and Modernity: A New and Better Way to Do Theology*, London: Routledge, 2000), 1.

65. See Pope Francis, *Laudato Si*, http://w2. vatican. va/content/francesco/en/encyclicals/documents/papa-francesco_20150524_enciclica-laudato-si. html;

In any of its forms, this (mis-) orientation of individual and social life establishes a field of *dissonances* and *resonances* between the 'fiction' within which life unfolds and the life to which everyone is called by God, yet all the while drawing on the good of the created universe to sustain and expand the 'fiction'. In any of its forms the 'fiction' is an idolatrous way of being human that, as a form of life, degrades our humanity[66] and has no ultimate future, because it has no place in the future that is finally coming from God. According to the Bible, idols are constructed to serve the interests of those with power, whose interests are opposed to God's justice and so to the true interests of those with little or no power. 'Idolatry' sums up the (dis)order discussed earlier, which human beings establish when they go against the penultimate and ultimate order—the divine economy for creation and its consummation. Producing and becoming a 'creature' of this surrogate 'divinity' continues to be humankind's own most original sin.[67]

The 'original blessing' of humans, with its new reality of 'persons'[68] (that realises itself in relationships in family and community, with the earth, and with God), with its powers and capacities (that enable them to survive and develop to acquire knowledge, skills, tools, technology) is being explored and exploited in a long, unfinished, historical process, from early evolutionary post-hominid ancestors right up to today.[69] In this long history, human beings continue to

---

and Harvey Cox, 'How the Market Became Divine', *Dialogue: A Journal of Theology*, 55/11 (2016): 18–24.

66. According to Ps 115, idols have eyes but cannot see, feet but cannot walk etc. and those who worship them become like them. They degrade their humanity. They acquire a way of being human in the image of a lesser god. Idolatry is worshipping 'the work of our own hands' (Isa 2:1; Jer 1:16, Micah 5:13) and so has wider range of meaning beyond setting up an image and performing rituals. The encompassing 'fictions' human beings produce are precisely the work of their own hands.

67. For another complementary account of original sin, see, James Allison, *The Joy of Being Wrong: Original Sin Through Easter Eyes* (New York: Crossroads, 1998).

68. John Haught, *God after Darwin: A Theology of Evolution* (Boulder, CO: Westview Press, 2008), 2nd edition; Robert Spaeman, *Persons: The difference between 'someone' and 'something'*, translated by O'Donovan (Oxford, Oxford University Press, 2006); Michael Welker, editor, *The Depth of the Human Person: A multidisciplinary Approach* (Grand Rapids, MI: Eerdmans, 2014).

69. I identify the rise of the new natural philosophy in 16th to18th centuries in Western Europe as an important example of the 'original blessing' being explored and exploited, generating new encompassing fictions, for example, the

produce a great variety of encompassing 'fictions' through which the 'original blessing', (however that is grasped and named) continues to be discovered and drawn out with whatever distortions due to the 'fictions'. This is an important consequence of the point that the 'original blessing' has never been withdrawn by God.

We see testimony to this contested human history in the Hebrew Bible in the stories of Cain's murder of Abel, of the violence of all against all in Noah's generation, in the Tower of Babel, and continued within the ambiguous order of Israel's life, with key figures remembered as called and empowered by God for special roles in the life of the people, but ultimately for all the nations. Abraham, the Patriarchs, Moses, Samuel and all the prophets. We see this testimony especially in the exile of Jews in Babylon, their learning to live faithfully without being seduced by the powerful 'fiction' of the Babylonian Empire, but rather from their own traditions concerning God, which eventually form the Hebrew Bible. We see this testimony in their return to the land of Judah and the continuing 'exile' due to the occupation of the land by foreign powers. These are pictured in Daniel[70] as the rise of monsters, especially the occupation by Antiochus IV, who styled himself as 'The Manifest', that is, 'the epiphany of God'. By contrast Daniel promises a time when the most humane reign of the living God would come, and all 'monstrous' human rule would be overcome.[71] This history continued with the Roman occupation of the land, their destruction of the city of Jerusalem and its temple, and the dispersion and oppression of the Jews as well as the 'fictions' produced by Jews, (like everyone else), most painfully by precipitating the war with Rome. Antiochus IV shows that the encompassing 'fictions' are driven by the desire for 'divinity', to have sovereign power, that power of which there is none greater.[72] This is the essence of empire. That history of oppression continues through the Holocaust to which Christianity in one way or another contributed.[73]

'clockwork universe'. See also S Ames 2004, 'Resonance and Dissonance between Church and Society, in Francis Sullivan and Sue Lippert, editors, *Church and Civil Society* (Adelaide, ATF Press, 2004), 142–185.
70. Dan 7:1–8; 23–25.
71. Dan 7:13–14; 26–27.
72. See, CK Barrett, *From First Adam to Last: A study in Pauline Theology*, London Adam & Charles Black, 1962), 17–21. For a contemporary expression of this desire for divinity, see, Yuval Noah Harari, *Homo Deus, A Brief History of Tomorrow* (London: Harvill Secker, 2016).
73. For example, the Nazis could publish Luther's tract, *The Jews and Their Lies*, without amendment.

Christ, the image of the invisible God[74]

The evangelists and seers of the church tell of the promise in Daniel being fulfilled in Jesus the Messiah in whom the 'new reality' of the most humane reign of the living God comes into the world. This 'arrival' provokes the most critical moment in the conflict between God and the human preference for encompassing 'fictions' whether religious, political, or domestic, all of which appear in relation to Jesus.

The Christian understanding of God came from the church's extended reflection on the new reality that had come into the world through Jesus, illuminated by and illuminating the Hebrew Bible which was then recognized as testifying to this 'new reality'. The God so revealed in Jesus was recognized by Christians as the God who had spoken in many and various ways through the Law and the Prophets of Israel,[75] whose reality was intimated in ordinary experience,[76] who now has spoken through his Son. This new reality is the foretaste and anticipation of the coming of the reign of God in glory, the only future that is coming—fullness of imperishable life which will flood the whole universe.[77] It shone through the Spirit-empowered person of the Son incarnate in Jesus, his teaching, his mighty works[78], his forgiving

---

74. Col 1:15.
75. Heb 1:1.
76. For example, Ps 19; Rom 1:19–20; Acts 17:28. This indicates the general revelation to all people.
77. Recall the story in the Gospel of Mark of the woman that breaks a flask of pure nard to wash Jesus' feet before he dies. The whole house was filled with the perfume from the broken flask (John 12:1–7). For Christians, it is a sign of what is to come, when God will be "all in all" (1 Corinthians 15:28.)
78. The 'mighty works' refers to the miracles of Jesus reported in the Gospels. Recalling the discussion in Chapter 1, 8, it may be wondered whether these acts should count as 'irrational' on the part of God the creator intervening to fix up the operation of the created world. My argument expects God to create a life-producing universe, in which all creatures are co-creators with God. This is one thing of value to God. It would be deeply irrational of God to create such a universe yet have to intervene to fix or repair some part of the operation of the universe. The purpose for which God creates such a universe cannot be reached by the operation of the created universe. It is the purpose *for* the whole created universe in all its parts. It is not to be understood on the venerable analogy of the acorn and oak tree. The action of God to reveal and fulfil this purpose are distinct from (but not split from or alien to) the operations of the penultimate order of the life producing universe. Recall section 3d. above, on the ultimate order of the created universe with all created things are in some sense oriented in their being

sins, and his fellowship with the spiritually outcast and marginalized. It shone through his being raised from the dead[79] and was only then seen in his crucifixion. It was received in the new experience of the Spirit[80] among his disciples following his death and resurrection. The heart of this new reality was indicated in Jesus' words, 'No one knows the Son except the Father, and no one knows the Father except the Son and those to whom the Son chooses to reveal him.'[81] It is this new reality being made known by the Son incarnate that led to God suffering. In a lecture, when asked by students why I am a Christian rather than something else, I explain there is no neutral space from which anyone could answer this question and went on to say that I could not worship a God who could not suffer. A student shouted out "Why should *God* suffer?" This is what I answered,

> Jesus the divine Son made flesh has come into the world and here God establishes in the world an opening into the life of God. Everyone is invited into this opening. It is for everyone. But amazingly this provokes very different reactions. His

---

to the ultimate order of the universe. Thus, it is fitting that in Psalms 96 and 98, the animals, trees, seas, mountains and forests are shown as ecstatic at the coming of God to judge the earth. The miracles of Jesus are signs of the coming of the Reign of God through Jesus, now in anticipation, finally in glory. In Matthew's Gospel (25:34) we learn that this Reign of God has been prepared from the foundation of the world. This is the divine purpose for the whole creation.

79. Likewise, I want to maintain that the historical investigation of the early Christian claims in their contemporary context, both Jewish and Hellenistic, concerning Jesus' resurrection from the dead, yields a rational belief in the resurrection as an inference to the best explanation given all available evidence. Here I depend especially on NT Wright, *Surprised by Hope* (London: SPCK, 2007). NT Wright *The Resurrection of the Son of God* (Minneapolis: Fortress Press, 2003). See especially Wright, *The Resurrection of the Son of God*, 717–718.

80. For a comparison of different usages of 'pneuma' and 'pneumatikos', especially in the Old and New Testaments, see Edward Schweizer, πνευμα, πνευματικοσ in Gerhard Kittel and Gerhard Friedrich eds, and Geoffrey W Bromley, translator, *Theological Dictionary of the New Testament*, (Grand Rapids, MI: Eerdmans), Volume VI, 332–455.

81. Matt 11:27. St John's Gospel is the extended reflection on this new reality. This is the special revelation of God to call all into a loving and just relation with God through Jesus. This relationship between Jesus and his Father, was unknown prior to Jesus. All the remarkable intimacies between God and human beings prior to and apart from this revelation, including for example, the prophet Jeremiah, have not included God revealed as the Father of the divine Son incarnate in Jesus.

> disciples don't understand what he is about, nor do the adoring crowds, nor do the authorities, who want to get rid of him. But Jesus keeps on; he keeps on keeping the opening open, right up to when he is crucified. But then God raised him from the dead. Thereby the opening remains open but is transformed and expanded by his resurrection because the whole created universe is going to be drawn into this opening. Everyone is called and invited to enter and live their life now in this opening. God suffered to keep the opening open.

The student's face lit up at this answer. The deepest demonstration of the worth to God of the whole creation and of humankind is the costly way God has shown in the incarnate Son an alternative way of being human, to redeem us from all idolatrous ways of being human, which together represent a path that has no future, because it has no place in the only future that is finally coming from God. Through the incarnate Son the new reality of this opening into the life of God has come into the world. The world could not bear this new reality, so it rejected Jesus, even to the point of crucifying him. But this was not the last word. Just when we had thereby seemingly slammed shut the door that God had opened, the new reality triumphed. Jesus remained open to his Father even in the extremity of his death as a victim of human violence. By the Spirit, the Father raised Jesus to glory, to vindicate him and so to keep open the possibility of everyone, indeed the whole creation, sharing the divine life. This is God's purpose in creation. This opening of the divine life to the whole creation is the costly, unbounded, love of the Triune God, a cost that God allows to enter the uttermost depths of God.[82]

The divine economy for the whole created universe

This revelation of God in Christ brought to light the 'mysteries of God', the divine *oikonomia*, (economy, hence, order, plan) for the whole world,[83] long hidden in God the creator, as God's eternal purpose for

---

82. 'This is the context for my understanding Jesus' death as a sacrifice for the life of the whole world, and for approaching the many biblical texts that bear on this theme, especially Isaiah 53:1–12, and 2 Corinthians 5:21.
83. 1 Cor 4:1; Eph 1:9–10; 3:9–11; Col 1:24–29; Rom 16:25; Matt 25:34. See also, Raymond Brown, *The Semitic Background to the Term 'Mystery' in the New Testament* (Philadelphia: Fortress, 1968).

the whole creation. (This accords well with the idea of divine purpose in the above elaboration of the theology of creation.) All things are created in and through the divine Word, and in this Word is that life that lightens every person.[84] This created order, that is 'flesh', is such that it is possible for the Word to become flesh and dwell among us.[85] This means that the creation is ontologically ordered to the Word become flesh, from the beginning. I take this to be the theological basis for the ontology of the created order, including human beings who are created in the image and likeness of the person of the Word, to exercise 'dominium'. Ontologically, the created universe as such is not alien to the Word and, even more importantly, the Word become flesh, is, without blurring the distinction between creator and creature, ontologically, not alien to us—even with the dreadful resonances and dissonances between the incarnate Word and the way human beings live. As mentioned earlier, this is the fourth Christological way of understanding the assertion that human beings are created in the image and likeness of God.[86]

God is everywhere at work to bring the created universe to the fullness of its life-producing capacity and to its consummation, when all things in heaven and earth will be transformed by being united 'in Christ',[87] when 'God will be all in all',[88] when the whole creation is drawn into the life of the Triune God. This is the end,

---

84. Jn 1:1–5.
85. Jn 1:14.
86. These reflections follow from Dr Barry Marshall who in 1962, my first year at Trinity College Theological School taught me to begin theology with creation not the fall and to understand the incarnation as God's eternal purpose in creation and so the inner meaning of creation. The latter theme was enhanced by reading a history of the opinion that the incarnation was a consequence of creation not the fall in BF Westcott, 1886, 'The Gospel of Creation', an appendix in his 1886, *The Epistles of St John: the Greek Text with Notes and Essays* (2nd edition. Cambridge & London: Macmillan. 1886), 285–328. A helpful discussion by Duncan Reid explains Westcott in the context of contemporary discussions of the relation between theology and the natural sciences, and as "an early venture into the ecological theology we are familiar with today." Reid concludes his paper by citing a line from 1892 sermon by Westcott, who now wanted to speak of "our debt to the future" which Reid paraphrases as our "commitment to the future of God's creation." Duncan Reid, 2013, 'A Reading of Westcott's Gospel of Creation: An Early Venture into Ecological Theology?', in *Journal of Anglican Studies* (2013): 1–18.
87. Eph 1:10; 3:11.
88. 1 Cor 15:28.

telos not terminus, to which human history is heading, through all the resonances and dissonances between this divine economy and human beings exploring and exploiting all the creative powers of the original blessing. These creative powers are being discovered and deployed, even in and through all the distortions due to the idolatrous encompassing fictions humans prefer, and just there the grace of God continues to meet us to bring us on our way in a turbulent history.[89]

This is good news because we are created in the image of God, who came in human form and at such a cost, to open an entrée into the life of God for which we were created and to do so from *within* our world. This is what we and the whole created universe are worth to God. These indications of the divine economy point us to the ultimate order of the universe introduced earlier in the elaboration of the theology of creation. Previously it was only the bare statement of the order by which the divine purpose is to be realised.

The trinitarian understanding of God

The distinctively Christian understanding of God is expressed in the two dogmas[90] of the Trinity, God is Father, Son and Holy Spirit, and of the Incarnation, the divine Son became flesh in Jesus Christ. A crucial matter in each dogma concerns the understanding of the term 'person'. It was Christian theologians who made an original and extended exploration of the meaning of this term.[91]

In the early centuries of our common era Christian theologians turned to Greek thought to help articulate the gospel of Jesus the

---

89. See, Bernard Lonergan, 'Healing and Creating in History', in *A Third Collection*, Frederick Crowe, editor (New York: Paulist Press, 1985).
90. Defined at the Councils of Nicaea (325) and Constantinople (381) leading to the 'Nicene Creed', with further refinement at the Council of Chalcedon (451). For the text of the Nicene Creed, see https://www. britannica. com/topic/Nicene-Creed. The term 'dogma' was used in a scientific context by Francis Crick in published form in 1958 and restated in 1970. 'The central dogma of molecular biology deals with the detailed residue-by-residue transfer of sequential information. It states that such information cannot be transferred back from protein to either protein or nucleic acid.' Francis Crick, in *Nature, 227/ 5258 (1970): 561–3.*
91. Philip A Rolnick, *Person, Grace, and God* (Grand Rapids: Eerdmans, 2007). A huge number of books and articles are published on the Trinity and Christology every year. I have referred to Rolnick because of his attention the historical and theological use of the term 'person'.

Messiah in ways that could make sense to their Hellenistic audience.[92] Platonism and Neo-Platonism initially seemed a most promising resource. Everyone involved was aware that various aspects of Christian belief were at risk of distortion by this medium. Charles Taylor identifies several points of tension as follows:[93]

1. In the pagan view the body was ruled by the soul, but in Palestine of Jesus' time this view, if present, was secondary to the question of the state and direction of the heart.
2. This leads to a new significance for history. 'The relation of the human heart to God was a story of falling away and returning.'[94] This was the central narrative of human history, which had an end. For Christians the end was a gathering of the whole story, of all the stories, not just the arrival at an end state.
3. The stories gathered into God's eternity entail the significance of individuals 'whose identities are worked out in these stories.'[95] By contrast, the different ways of access to the eternal for Plotinus and Aristotle means loss of individuality.
4. The stories that are the central narrative of the history give a new place to contingency. This includes responding to the neighbour who accidently crosses my path. History is not the implementation of the rigidly scripted divine plan of the Stoics but a resourceful responsiveness on God's part, come what may, to bring history to its end—which as noted I take to be a telos not a terminus, the fulfillment of divine purpose in creation not its termination.
5. With all these factors there is also the place of the emotions. For Christianity, rather than the highest human condition being purged of emotion, they are part of our relation to the highest being. Taylor[96] quotes Martha Nussbaum's discussion of Augustine:

   > We hear sighs of longing and groans of profound desolation. We hear love songs composed in anguish, as the singers' heart strains upward in desire. We hear of a hunger that cannot be

---

92. Charles Taylor, *A Secular Age* (Cambridge MA: Harvard University Press, 2007), 275.
93. Taylor, *A Secular Age*, 275–279.
94. Taylor, *A Secular Age*, 276.
95. Taylor, *A Secular Age*, 277.
96. Taylor, *A Secular Age*, 278.

satisfied, of a thirst that torments, of the taste of a lover's body that kindles inexpressible longing. We hear of an opening that longs for penetration, of a burning fire that ignites the body and the heart. All of these are images of profound erotic passion and all of them are images of Christian love.[97]

The problem was that the educated elite of Hellenism conceived of God as 'apatheia', beyond emotion. But this was in tension with the Christian identification of Christ with God and with the pain-filled death of Christ.[98]

6. According to Taylor, all these factors only make sense in the context of the Christian belief in the personal being of God, not just as agency, but as capable of communion. The theological struggle was to make sense of the scriptural witness to the divinity of the Father and of the Son and of the Spirit, and its equally powerful witness that God is one. What follows is an impossibly brief summary of some of key themes in the development of this understanding of God.

At its core the Arian controversy was about the understanding of God to be used in interpreting the Bible. Arius (256–336 CE), a Christian priest from Alexandria in Egypt took the understand the understanding of the being (*ousia*) of God from Greek thinking. This choice guided his interpretation of the Bible. God had no contact with creation and so Jesus could not be God incarnate. There had to be a difference in being between Jesus and God. Athanasius (298–373 CE), the bishop of Alexandria, allowed the Bible to inform his understanding of God, which led to a new understanding of being. The Father and the Son have the same being (*homoousios*). Likewise, the Spirit was of the same being as the Father and the Son. This understanding of God was set forth by the first ecumenical council of bishops from the across the Church in Nicaea in 325 and modified in the second ecumenical council in Constantinople in 381. It is set out in what is known as the Nicene Creed.

---

97. Martha Nussbaum, *Upheavals of Thought* (Cambridge: Cambridge University Press, 2000), 528.
98. See the discussion of this contested theme of the suffering of God in recent theology by Chris Mostert, 2011, 'God's Transcendence and Compassion', in *Pacifica*, 24/2 (2011): 172–189.

Following Athanasius, a crucial step was taken by the Cappadocian theologians.[99] Whereas *ousia* and *hypostasis* were synonyms in Greek philosophy for 'substance', 'essence', these theologians distinguished between *ousia* and *hypostasis*. 'God is one *ousia*, ('substance', 'essence', or 'being') equally and fully expressed in three *hypostasis*, the Father, Son, and Spirit.'[100] This innovation initiated Christianity's distinctive elaboration of the meaning of *hypostasis*, still an ontological term, to refer to 'person' (rather than 'prosopon' or 'persona' (for the face or, the mask used in the theatre, or a social role) and as an entirely new thought, was irreducible to *ousia*. The divine substance has no reality 'prior' to or apart from the distinctions between the three persons. These distinctions are eternal and are ontologically primary. While each *hypostasis* has 'common qualities, like infinity, being uncreated, . . . each *hypostasis* can also be distinguished by origin, relatedness, and how it is known by creatures.'[101] The three 'persons' are mutually defined in their uniqueness and otherness; they ontologically co-inhere in their dynamic unity, their perichoresis ('dance'), their communion. These themes mark out the distinctively Christian understanding of being: to be is to be in communion,[102] dynamic communion. Lastly, the sovereignty or 'monarche' of God is to be thought of as belonging not just to the Father (contra the Cappadocians) but to the Triune God (following Athanasius).[103]

This trinitarian understanding of God expresses what is new in Christianity, while maintaining that there is one God. We can recognise in it what talk of the omni-God says about God who freely creates the universe *ex nihilo* for some purpose. Yet it goes well beyond the idea of the omni-God, not by being derived from that idea, but because it draws on the revelation of that God in the history of Israel in which the divine Son becomes incarnate and the Holy Spirit is poured out on the Israelite followers of Jesus. Later, in the light of this

---

99. Basil (330–379 CE), Gregory of Nazianzus (329–389 CE) and Basil's younger brother Gregory of Nyssa (335–395 CE).
100. Rolnick, *Person, Grace and God*, 18.
101. Rolnick, *Person, Grace and God*, 19.
102. John D Zizioulas, *Communion and Otherness*, Pal McPartland, editor (New York: T&T Clark, 2006).
103. Kevin Giles, *The Trinity and Subordinationism: The Doctrine of God and the Contemporary Gender Debate* (Westmont: Illinois: Intervarsity Press, 2002), 40–43.

revelation the term 'person' was introduced (Cappadocian Fathers) and attempts were made to develop the understanding of 'person' and to explain why three persons in one God (e.g., St Augustine (354–430), Boethius (480–524), Richard of St Victor (d.1173), Thomas Aquinas (1225–1274).[104]

Briefly, here are four points about the term 'person' that came to the fore in a developing understanding through the work of theologians in the East and the Latin West building on and criticising earlier work. One is the agreement that there is something unique and untransferable about individual human beings. The incommunicable quality is picked out by the term 'person'. Secondly, there is the distinction between person and nature. A given nature is universal, person is particular. Human nature a substrate of person and person cannot be reduced to nature nor predicated apart from nature. We can think of a what without a who (nature without a person,), but not a who without a what (a person without a nature). Thirdly, persons are persons in relation, (a father/mother and his/her child) whereas natures are not defined relationally. Fourthly, person unites: in human persons the unification involves diverse components, such as body, emotions, soul, thoughts, commitment, action, and relationships; in the Chalcedon creed, human and divine natures are united in the person of the Son.[105]

Understanding this revelation of God in Christ was a contentious matter from the start and continued after the ecumenical councils. The Council of Chalcedon in 451 met to resolve controversies over understanding the incarnation of the Son. The solution known as the Chalcedon Definition declared that Christ had two natures (*physeis*) united in one person (*prosopon, hypostasis*). Hence described as 'hypostatic' union. The Son is consubstantial with the Father in divinity and consubstantial with us in humanity. "Therefore, the Son is a revelation of the divine nature and, in close association but not admixture with it, human nature is revealed in its greatest conceivable light." On this view, Christ assumed human nature not

---

104. Rolnick, *Person, Grace and God*, Chapter One.
105. This ancient discussion of person and nature has many resonances and dissonances with the contemporary discussion of person and nature where nature is understood in terms of the natural, sciences, including, neuroscience and of the life sciences. For constructive discussions, see Helminiak, *God, Brains and Consciousness*, and M Welker, *The Depth of the Human Person*.

a human person. "By understanding *hypostasis* as that which unites the two natures, we glimpse the ontological and axiological priority of person over nature."[106]

The biblical revolution: The fundamental order is personal

Taylor places this theological achievement in a context of a struggle:

> the whole package (1)—(6), arose out of a struggle, that of Patristic theology with earlier ideas of an impersonal order, be it that which identified the highest with an Idea . . . or with Plotinus' One or with a God whose defining characteristic was *apatheia*. Now in the modern era we see this package challenged by new understandings of order, running at one end of the spectrum from Deism to modern atheist materialism at the other.[107]

Taylor explains that the 'pull towards the impersonal pole of this continuum'[108] from the 18th century on, was due to the ways the human condition was understood in terms of an impersonal order that ultimately has its roots in the rise of modern science, both for deism and for modern atheistic materialism. This move was further understood as superseding the earlier idea of the fundamental personal order, which was then seen as belonging to a bygone era.[109]

Colin Gunton[110] points out the further move towards the impersonal in Descartes' defining the human person in terms of an individual non-spatial mind and a spatial body which 'it is very difficult, even for God, we might say, to join together.'[111] Cambridge Platonists were anxious about Descartes' philosophy which included reducing animals to machines. Given all that animals could do, it seemed to open the way to treating human beings as machines.

---

106. Welker, *The Depth of the Human Person*, p.34.
107. Taylor, *A Secular Age*, 279.
108. Taylor, *A Secular Age*, 280.
109. Especially helpful here is Paul Tyson, *De-fragmenting modernity, Reintegrating Knowledge with Wisdom, Belief with Truth, and Reality with Being* (Eugene Oregon, Cascade *Books*, 2017).
110. Colin Gunton, *The Promise of Trinitarian Theology* (Edinburgh, T&T Clark, 1991), Chapter 5.
111. Gunton, *The Promise of the Trinity*, 87.

This fear was fulfilled by de La Mettrie's (1709-1751) book, *Machine Man*,[112] and more latterly with evolution, cognitive sciences, and neuroscience proposing a completely naturalistic account of the human mind.

For Gunton, the Cartesian tradition, even in its naturalistic form is the dominant modern tradition about persons. However, he also points to a minor tradition represented by the Scottish philosopher John MacMurray's second volume of his 1953-1954 Gifford Lectures,[113] with a crucial link to this later development of the relational view of persons, possibly being 19th century Scottish philosopher Sir William Hamilton influenced by Calvin in the 16th century. What is also of interest is the parallel between MacMurray and the writings of Richard of St Victor in the 11th century who continues the Christian Trinitarian reflection on the understanding of 'person'. Gunton observes that here the idea of God does not fit Feuerbach's maxim: theology is really anthropology in disguise.[114]

Cartesian influences on theologians meant that the distinctively Christian view of 'person', both divine and human, receded. The recovery of Trinitarian understanding of God initiated in the twentieth century in Protestant (K. Barth) and Catholic theology (K. Rahner), and massively developed[115] subsequently, is a prerequisite for a Christian view of 'wellbeing'. This is also the recovery of the Patristic struggle for a fundamentally personal order rather than the prevailing view of a fundamentally impersonal order. One task for theology is to show how this fundamentally personal order, theologically understood, can robustly and convincingly incorporate

---

112. Julien Offrey de La Mettrie, *Machine Man and Other Writings*, translated and edited by Ann Thomson (Cambridge: Cambridge University Press, 1996).
113. John MacMurray, *Persons in Relation* (London: Faber & Faber, 1961).
114. Gunton, *The Promise of the Trinity*, 93.
115. Among many, many books I mention the following in addition to those already noted, Karl Bath, *Church Dogmatics*, Volume 1, G Bromiley, and TF Torrance, editors (London: T&T Clark, 2009); Karl Rahner, *The Trinity*, Joseph Donceel, translator, index and glossary by Catherine Laguna (New York: Crossroad, 1997); Catherine La Cugna, *God for Us, The Trinity and Christian Life* (San Francisco: Harper, 1993); Alan Torrance, *Persons in Communion: An essay in Trinitarian description and human participation, with special reference to volume one of Karl Barth's Church Dogmatics* (Edinburgh: T&T Clark, 1996); Colin Gunton, *Father, Son & Holy Spirit: Toward A Fully Trinitarian Theology* (Edinburgh: T&T Clark, 2003).

the large impersonal scientific story of the universe, including the evolution of life and human life in particular. A step in that direction is provided by the theology of creation in this chapter, sections 2 and 3, with its ultimate and penultimate orders, with the latter identified in section 4(a) in terms provided by the scientific account of the world.

preliminary conclusion #3

The theology of creation presented above proceeds *from* the idea of God as that than which non-greater can be conceived, the all-knowing, all-powerful, wholly good God, who freely creates the universe *ex nihilo*, for some purpose, *to* the idea of God creating creatures as co-creators in a life-producing universe. The divine purpose in creating was identified as God drawing all creatures into a loving and just relationship with God. From this idea of divine purpose in creating, the kind of universe we should expect God to create was further elaborated in three ways: the creation of persons, the revelation of God, and the ultimate order of the created universe.

The discussion gives an indication of how and how deeply this theology of creation can be traced within the fabric of Christian tradition.[116] The omni-God as understood and elaborated in this chapter can be recognised in the God Christians claim is revealed in Christ. The argument supports the acclamation that God is wholly good, whose created universe with all the suffering and death due to natural processes create by God, is indeed 'very good'. This denies

---

116. There is no claim that this idea of God is distinctive to Christianity. What I regard as distinctive of Christianity is the revelation of this God that has come into the world through Jesus Christ. W. Stoeger synthesises insights about God by late Medieval Jewish, Christian, and Muslim scholars such as Maimonides (1135-1204), Aquinas (1225-1274), Averroes (1126-1198), and Avicenna (980-1037). God is understood to be the supremely perfect, free, transcendent, and sovereign creator, who freely creates the world and on whom the world depends for its existence. See W Stoeger, 'God, physics and the Big Bang', in P Harrison, editor, *The Cambridge Companion to Science and Religion* (Cambridge: Cambridge University Press, 2010), 180ff. See also the papers in DB Burrell, C Cogliati, JM Soskice, and WR Stoeger, editors, *Creation and the God of Abraham*, (Cambridge: Cambridge University Press, 2010). See especially, DB Hart, *The Experience of God, Being, Consciousness, Bliss* (New Haven: Yale University Press, 2013), Chapter 3.

there are natural evils in the world that motivate the denial of God's existence. I do not feel this is a sufficient for inviting people to revisit their decision to deny God based on natural evils. Before I make that invitation, I want my position about God and creation to meet in Chapter V a set of Reality Checks that challenge the claim that the actual universe is indeed the universe we should expect the omni-God to create and so is not very good as the problem of natural evil for belief in that God has always maintained.

PART 3
REALITY CHECKS

Chapter V
Reality Checks

Introduction

Presenting this approach to the problem of natural evil in live discussions evokes objections testing the solution I offer to the logical problem of natural evil. This includes responses from my atheist colleagues who drew my attention to Stephen Fry's widely viewed tirade against God. I also take up William Rowe's evidential problem of natural evil because it is rightly renowned and because I think my response to the logical problem also provides a basis for an answer to the evidential problem. I discuss the new logical problem of evil from J.L. Schellenberg, which I consider to be a more sophisticated version of the student's argument in Chapter I. Here is the list of objections considered.

1. The 'dead end' universe.
2. Destruction of the earth by an asteroid collision.
3. A contradiction within the theology of creation.
4. Colleagues' objections
   a. The superlative power of God must be moral not just functional.
   b. The 'only way' argument.
   c. A good God indistinguishable from an evil God.
   d. God is reckless and cruel in creating this universe.
5. Stephen Fry's tirade against God.
6. The evidential problem of natural evil presented by William Rowe.
7. The new logical problem of evil presented by JL Schellenberg.
8. The strange goodness of God. I return to my opening in the first chapter, to the point made by the student who said that if this world was created by a wholly good God, it would be a very strange goodness and whether, if it is so strange, we might not be able to call it good.

1. The 'Dead End' universe

First, how can we theologically respond to the prospects of the universe heading for the 'big freeze'? The life-producing universe is heading for a dead end. The universe began with the big bang 13.7 billion years ago and it has gone on expanding according to the laws of nature, producing the amazing complexity of billions of galaxies. The universe began in a very low state of disorder and is slowly increasing in disorder. The common term for disorder is entropy.[1] As part of beginning in this low state of disorder the universe is very finely tuned to produce complex carbon-based life. The fine-tuning makes it a bio-friendly universe. The laws of nature and the physical parameters like the speed of light or the mass of an electron, to take just two examples, would only need to be varied by very tiny amounts for this to be a very different universe.[2] Remarkably, it is this increasing disorder that is integral to how complex systems are formed and maintain themselves over a long time before eventually breaking down. Complex chemical and biological systems are open systems. They take in energy from the environment, use it to repair and maintain themselves, and sometimes to elaborate themselves to a new level of complexity, against the tide of disorder, while expelling waste energy at a higher level of disorder than the energy taken in.[3]

Evolutionary theory says that complex chemical and biological systems evolved on planet earth and possibly elsewhere in the universe. Evolution is a blind causal process that has produced the amazing forms of life in prolific numbers and diversity. This has been a long, blind process involving suffering, pain, and death on a vast scale. Here 'blind' means that these biological processes do not

---

1. See, John Barrow, *The World Within the World* (Oxford: Clarendon Press, 1998), 122–127; J Victor Stenger, *The Comprehensible Universe, Where Do the Laws of Physics Come From?* (New York: Prometheus Books, 2006), index.
2. An excellent discussion of this matter is found in Lewis and Barnes, *A Fortunate Universe*.
3. For a fuller discussion of these matters recall Russell, 'The Groaning of Creation: Does God Suffer with All Life?', 30, 131; Ilya Prigogine, *From Being to Becoming: Time and Complexity in the Physical Sciences* (San Francisco: WH Freeman and Company, 1980). A non-technical introduction is Ilya Prigogine and Isabelle Stengers, *Order Out of Chaos: Man's New Dialogue with Nature* (New York: Bantam Books, 1984); A Peacocke, *An Introduction to Physical Chemistry of Biological Systems* (Oxford: Clarendon Press, 1983).

include any reference to God's purpose in creation and do not permit any inference to that purpose.

Evolution depends on the fact that the universe is everywhere increasing in disorder yet allowing for some local regions, such as planet earth, where the process of increasing disorder is, for a while, locally reversed by the self-organising capacities of matter, while increasing disorder overall continues.

It was an open question as to whether the universe would go on expanding into the 'big freeze' or collapse back into the 'big fry'. From discoveries reported in 1998, it became clear that some time back the universe began expanding at an accelerating rate, though no one really knows why. We are heading for the 'big freeze', billions and billions of years into the future: a cold, dark, undifferentiated sea of low-grade energy. Complete disorder. No distinctions. A dead universe, that goes on and on, without telos or terminus—apparently no point and no stopping. Is this, ironically, the divine purpose for the universe? (I do respond to this challenge below. But it is worth saying that the point of some process is not necessarily at the end of the process, though it may. For example, a birthday party may reach its telos, its 'point', halfway through the process—presents, speeches, and so on. The terminus of the event is switching off the lights, having cleaned up the remnants of the party after the guests have gone.)

There is a connection to be made between this 'reality check' and the earlier discussion of the value to God of creatures as co-creators in a life-producing universe. For we can now at least *begin* to see the increasing entropy and all that goes with it, including the very low entropy state in which the universe began, as the way God enables created things to be co-creators in this universe. My theology of creation allows us to theologically frame and thereby *begin* to make some theological sense of increasing entropy of the universe and its low entropy beginning.

Nevertheless, on the face of it, the prospect of a dead-end universe appears to contradict the idea of there being any purpose for the whole creation. Are we reduced to be 'bolting on' the divine purpose or pulling it like a rabbit out of the divine hat? Is there no inner link, no underlying intelligibility? God is the one author, working everywhere for the one purpose in both creation and its consummation, which includes 'redemption' from human beings pursuing a path that theologically has no ultimate future. Therefore, we may wonder if there is in the mind of God, and embodied in all God's works, an internal connection between creation, redemption, and consummation.

My response is to return to the discussion of God's purpose in creation to make a point I could easily have made earlier. The purpose of God in creating includes drawing created things into a loving and just relationship with this God. Should we say that relationship is a brief encounter, the equivalent of 'a one-night stand'? For a wholly good God, I would prefer to say that the relationship is one in which all created things explore the length, breadth, height, and depth— without limit—of their relationship with God.

Let us hold together the thought of this God creating co-creators via the means of increasing disorder[4] *and* creating with the purpose of the whole creation entering such a relationship with this God. Rationally, this would mean that the increasing disorder and all that goes with it, including the prospect of the dead-end future for the universe should not be thought of as having the last word. Those processes serve the value to God of creatures as co-creators. The purpose of God presupposes that value but goes beyond it to what is the divine purpose *for* that creation. This is the gift and invitation to what does have the last word, namely the still greater good of unending life with God for the whole created universe.

The big freeze ending of the universe according to the scientific view of the universe is not how the created universe will end according to the theology of creation pursued here. The increasing entropy begins to be understood theologically as at least a means to maximising the realisation of the value to God of creating a universe in which creatures are co-creators, even to producing life. This cannot contradict the divine purpose, in the first place because God's purpose is *for* the life-producing universe, created in this way! In the second place the divine purpose is distinct from this value and is pursued by God using other means.

According to this purpose, we should think that the physical conditions under which the life-producing universe evolved and produced life will be transformed by God. Rather than a dead end, we should think of the physical conditions of the universe being transformed in a way that allows this purpose to be fulfilled.

---

4. This use of 'disorder' when speaking of entropy should be distinguished from my speaking of (dis)order set up by human beings constructing their lives apart from God.

Traditionally, Christians have understood the bodily resurrection of Jesus as the 'first fruits', an anticipation, ahead of time, of the final transformation of the universe. The bodily resurrection of Jesus is the great sign that there is a future for our material universe not determined by the prospect of the big freeze, that God's goodness has the first and the last word for all the processes of creatures as co-creators. We have strengthened the inner link we found when we realized that we had a theological framework within which to begin to make some theological sense of the increasing entropy (disorder) of the universe. We now see that the same theological perspective rationally leads us to expect a transformation of present conditions, familiar from our best science, under which the whole universe operates. This is the theological perspective developed from Aquinas, within the context of the good news of Jesus the incarnate Son of God, who was crucified and yet was raised bodily from the dead, the definitive, but not the only, anticipation of the fulfilment of God's purpose, who will come again in glory.

This resurrection of the universe is what this theology of creations expects God to initiate, sometime before the universe reaches its 'dead end'. This is just a beginning of attempting to understanding how the scientific prospect of a 'dead end' universe and the divine purpose in creation are related. But at least the above line of thought means it is not an ad hoc matter, no rabbit out of the hat, no bolt-on solution. Much more needs to be said; for example, on why entropy marks the operation of the created universe. This mere beginning of understanding leads to more questions. What is God about now in the time between the life, death and resurrection of Jesus and the resurrection of the universe? What is God calling believers and unbelievers alike to be about in this time? How is all life that has perished in the evolving cosmos to be included within the resurrected universe? In principle the divine purpose for the whole creation and all its parts, with all living things that have perished are to be included in the fulfilment of the divine purpose. For humans who have died, see NT Wright's argument about 'life after life after death'.[5] For other animals see, C Southgate's *Groaning of Creation*.[6] The possibility of

---

5. NT Wright, *Surprised by Hope*, 52f.
6. See C Southgate, *The Groaning of Creation*, Chapter 5 for helpful discussion of various positions on this matter in the science and theology scene.

human beings making their way to other planets in the universe is indeed thinkable within this theology of creation but on its own does not address the challenge of the dead-end universe to the idea of divine purpose in creation nor how the divine purpose is able, in principle, to meet that challenge.

Long before this universe reaches its anticipated dead-end, our solar system will be greatly disturbed. Somewhere between five to eight billion years ahead, in the death throes of our sun becoming a red giant, it will so expand in size that it will absorb the earth, having first destroyed all life. The means of reconciling this destruction with the divine purpose in creation could be as above—beforehand, God initiates the resurrection of the universe. Alternatively, sometime before the sun gets to the red giant stage humankind (with animals?) may migrate to one or more exoplanets in the galaxy or beyond. This speculation briefly indicates ways the universe, as we find it to be, can begin to be understood within this theology of creation.

2. Destruction of the earth by asteroid collision

Approximately 66 million years (My) ago there was a mass extinction event (Cretaceous-Paleogene (K-Pg)).[7] In 1980 Nobel Laureate Louis Alverez[8] and his son Walter proposed that the K-Pg was caused by the impact of a massive comet or asteroid (10–15 km wide). This hypothesis was supported by the discovery of the 180km Chicxulub crater in the Gulf of Mexico' Yucatan Peninsula in the early 1990s.[9] In January 2020 scientists[10] reported new evidence that the extinction was due to asteroid impact not vulcanism. One estimate is that 75%

---

7. R Paul; Alan L Deino; Frederick J Hilgen; F Klaudia, F Kuiper; Mark, F Darren; William Mitchell; Leah E Morgan; Roland; Jan Smit Mundil, 'Time Scales of Critical Events Around the Cretaceous-Paleogene Boundary', in *Science*, 339/6120 (2013): 684–687.
8. LW *Alvarez, W Alvarez, F Asaro, HV Michel, 'Extraterrestial cause for the Cretaceous-Tertiary extinction', in Science, 208/4448 (1980): 1095–1108.*
9. AR Hildebrand, GT. Penfield, *et al*, 'Chicxulub crater: a possible Cretaceous/Tertiary boundary impact crater on the Yucatán peninsula, Mexico', in *Geology*. 19/9 (1991): 867–871.
10. Hull M Pincelli, Andrea Bornemann, Donald E. Penman, 'On impact and volcanism across the Cetaceous-Paleogene boundary, in Science, 367/6475 (17 January 2020): 266–272.

or more of all species on the earth vanished.[11] The disruptions due to asteroid impacts is one among several accounts of mass extinctions,[12] due to climate change, volcanic eruptions, and human beings as the super predator.

While acknowledging that claims of periodicity in impact cratering and biological extinction events are controversial, Michael Rampino et. al.[13] provide support for linking the age of craters with repeated mass extinctions over a 250million year (or 250 My period.

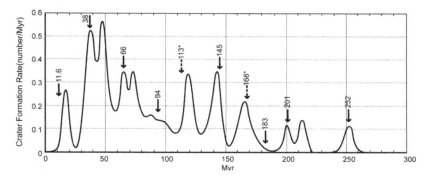

Figure 3 Probability distribution of crater-formation rate for the last 260 Myr. The probability distribution of 37 crater ages (with their 1σ errors) has been smoothed by a Gaussian window function of 3 Myr. Solid arrows indicate times of eight significant extinction events after Raup & Sepkoski (1986). Broken arrows with asterisks indicate two additional potential extinction events at 113 Myr ago and 168 Myr ago. The impact crater ages show 11 peaks over the last 260Myr, at least 5 of which correlate with significant extinctions events (6, if the potential extinction events in Table 2 are included).

---

11. D Jablonski, WG Chaloner, 'Extinctions in the fossil record (and discussion)', in *Philosophical Transactions of the Royal Society of London B*. 344/1307 (1994): 11–17.
12. A convenient over-view is provided by https://en.wikipedia.org/wiki/Holocene_extinction (accessed 22 July 2020).
13. M Rampino and K Caldeira, '**Periodic** impact **cratering and extinction events over the last 260 million years**', **in Monthly Notes of the Royal Astronomical** *Society*, 454 (2015): 3480–3484; M Rampino and K Caldeira, 'Comparison of the ages of large-body impacts, flood-basalt eruptions, ocean-anoxic events and extinctions over the last 260 million years: a statistical study', in *International Journal of Earth Sciences*, 107 (2015): 601–606; M Rampino, 'Relationship between impact-crater size and severity of related extinction episodes', in *Earth-Sciences Reviews*, 102990 (2020): 201.

> Our work, and the recent work of others (for example, Chang & Moon 2005; Lieberman & Melott 2007, 2012; Melott & Bambach 2010, 2013), support the idea that impacts and extinction events are periodic, with a period of ~26–27 Myr, and that the hypothesis of periodic extra-terrestrial impacts as a contributing cause of periodic extinctions of life, while controversial, is still viable (Randall & Reece 2014, Rampino 2015).[14]

The asteroid impacts and extinction events were correlated about every 26–30 My. These periodic phenomena were possibly correlated with another 30 My cycle as 'the solar system oscillates with respect to the midplane of the disc-shaped Milky Way Galaxy with a period of about 60 My. The sun and its family passes through this plane every 30 My or so. The solar system behaves like a horse on a carousel—as we go around the disk-shaped galaxy we bob up and down through the disk, passing through its densest part roughly every 30 million years.'[15] In 2014 physicists 'suggested that the largest gravitational perturbations of the Oort Cloud could be from an invisible disk of exotic dark matter.' The disturbance of the distant Oort comet cloud that surrounds the Sun would lead to periodic comet showers in the inner solar system, where some comets strike the Earth.

Rampino presents an overview in his 2017 *Cataclysms: A New Geology for The Twenty First Century* and concludes with this summary.

> We can no longer depend on the slow and gradual progression of geologic change or describe evolution as the history of life's continuing triumphs over the slow rhythms of geologic upheavals and climatic changes. In the new geology, life, though resilient, is bombarded from space, exposed to massive volcanic eruptions emanating from Earth's deep interior, and suffers periodic catastrophic environmental changes and mass extinctions. These events change the course of evolution. All this activity may be merely side effects of encounters with dark matter during the rhythmic motion of the stars around and through the great cosmic wheel of the

---

14. Rampino and Caldeira, 'Periodic impact cratering and extinction events', 3484. Illustration credit, 3482: M. Rampino / New York University
15. M Rampino, 'Dark Matter's Shadowy Effect on Earth', in *Astronomy* (April 2018): 24.

galaxy. If this hypothesis bears fruit, then it is an opportunity for a great collaboration of geologists an astronomers. The new geology promises to be cataclysmal, cyclical, and governed in part by astronomical forces. This is clearly a long way from the geology I was taught in school.

The discussion of extinction events can be used to challenge several claims in the theology of creation. If this explanation of the correlation between formation of comets/asteroid impacts and extinction events is accepted, how can these and other natural processes leading to a range of extinction events have the 'dignity' of causes? How can these natural processes be said to be the cause of good in other things and that this is a moral good? Finally, if the next major asteroid impact and associated extinction event happens in the next ~ 20 My wiping out life on earth how can that understood within my theology of creation?

Recall the 'dignity' of causes was taught by Aquinas in the thirteenth century who said that if natural processes did not have real powers, they would appear to have a pointless existence. I suggested that not having any powers would be an 'indignity' and supported this with the contrast between something being a participant in a context versus being a 'wall flower', which is to say having no power or agency of its own.

In section 2 and 3 of Chapter II it was argued that created things have their God-given value and therefore dignity as co-creators in a life producing universe. This dignity must also be reckoned in terms of God's purpose for all created things, to draw them into a loving and just relationship with God. According to Christian tradition (Chapter IV, section 1b.) the entrée to this relationship is through the divine Word become incarnate in human form, in Jesus of Nazareth, his life, death and bodily resurrection from the dead. The body of Jesus, like all human bodies, was composed of 'star dust', atoms produced in stellar furnaces from hydrogen and helium, produced by the Big Bang. In all embodied life, including human bodies and including the body of Jesus, atoms are regularly replaced in daily life. Jesus' bodily resurrection means that the atoms of his dead body were included in Jesus' resurrected state, transformed by divine action, an anticipation and promise of what will happen to the whole created universe.

Sections 2a., 2c., 2d. and section 3a. of Chapter III set out the dignity of created natural processes in terms of their origin in God's creative will, their value to God as co-creators having their part in bringing about God's life-producing universe, and their value to God shown in the divine purpose for all created things. One consequence is that no created thing gains its dignity *only* by its usefulness for human life or, more specifically, for helping realise human interests whatever they may be at a given time. Nor does it lose its value by blocking or simply failing to help realise those interests, nor by having no apparent relevance to human interests. Most importantly the dignity of creatures with real powers is not lost or contradicted if these creatures are involved in bringing about suffering and death. But is that claim still credible when the suffering and death is on a grand scale of an asteroid collision? I believe this is what motivates the second criticism which questions whether these natural processes are good and if so, is this a moral good, and if not, how can they have any dignity? If that 'dignity' is referred to God, then the criticism denies that such a God is wholly good.

This asks how an entirely possible event is consistent with my theology of creation and how that theology is a framework within which to outline an answer. In reply I first want to challenge an assumption I hear in many conversations about natural evil: a truly good God would not create a world in which terrible suffering and death occur and occur so widely and deeply as we see on this planet. A basic theological reason for thinking that assumption is wrong, is that the divine purpose in creation is to draw the whole creation into a loving and just relationship with God in which created persons are invited to choose to enter this relationship on their own behalf and on behalf of the creatures with which they are embodied and embedded in this universe. This freedom, while being good and meant for good, is open to being used otherwise, including dreadful violence, suffering and death, whether of each other or of other creatures without freedom. Here, with brutal brevity, I am availing myself of Plantinga's free will defense, mentioned in Chapter 1, section 1(a).

According to this theology of creation God chooses to create a universe which produces persons with such freedom. The alternative must be to think that God would not create a universe with the purpose articulated in section 3(a). This might be envisaged as God creating a universe like the students presented in Chapter 1, or creating a world without any creature exercising freedom, perhaps even a lifeless world. I have set aside these alternative types of creation as unworthy of the superlatively good God, preferring to think that such a God would choose the better type of creation, in which creatures are co-creators in a life-producing universe for the purpose indicated. In this theology of creation, the created universe would include creatures who misuse their freedom to achieve their own ends, by violently producing suffering and death. We must set aside the idea that a truly good God would not create a world in which such terrible suffering and death occur.

Such violent suffering and death are to be distinguished from the suffering and death embodied in the vast food chains by which all living creatures are sustained in their life cycles. Those food chains are not violent because predator and prey do not violate the form of their own lives. The extinction events produced by the impact of large asteroids is different from suffering and death intentionally produced by the misuse of freedom and these do not arise within any food chain. On the other hand, extinction events have led to the evolution of other forms of life in which some creatures come to the fore in the niches vacated by species that were extinguished, and new creatures are brought into existence. On this planet the extinction events eventually opened the way to human beings coming into existence.[16] This accords with the theology of creation and has attracted criticism that it was by a chance event and that it involved enormous waste[17] as does the whole evolutionary process.[18]

---

16. But see Simon Conway Morris saying mammals would have come to the fore even without a mass extinction, see the opening discussion in, 206 | Simon Conway Morris on Evolution, Convergence, and Theism—Sean Carroll (preposterousuniverse.com).
17. From my theology of creation, what we count as waste is the working out of the value to God of all creatures with their own real powers as co-creators, a value, the realisation of which I argued we should expect to be maximised God who is not a micro-manager. On an historical note, George Wright (1838–1921), was a Calvinist in theology, Pastor of the Congregational Church in New England, and leading scientific authority on the glacial geology of North America. Wright wrote a major article expounding and defending Darwin against his critics. Darwin commended his account of Darwinism and asked to see his other writings, e.g., on final causes and the relation between Calvinism and Darwinism. Commenting on Paley he says, 'The watch found lying on the heath, from which Paley inferred the existence of a watchmaker, 'reveals two things we are likely to confound, namely design and man's method of executing design' Wright judged this to 'incur the danger of encouraging conceptions of God which are too anthropomorphic, both as to the narrowness of the design contemplated and as to the means to attaining the end.' According to Wright, 'The truth is that the rose-coloured vies of many evolutionists, still more of the pietistic interpreters of natural theology, are built upon a very narrow basis of facts, to the exclusion of another class of facts which abound in startling number.' Darwinism accentuated this other class of fact. Wright G. F., *Studies in Science and Religion*, (Andover, Mass., W. F. Draper, 1882), pp. 175, 183, 185–6.
18. That chance has a role in the operation of the universe was not a problem for Aquinas with respect to divine providence, see, Thomas Aquinas, *Summa Contra Gentiles*, III, 74. See also, Conway-Morris illuminates this play of chance and

If in the next several million years an asteroid collision occurs how could that be consistent with God being the wholly good creator? This tests the conclusion that sets aside the idea that God would not create a universe with terrible suffering and death. Does the conclusion still hold for the mega-deaths of such a collision? Might we ironically conclude that indeed with God all things are possible? Instead, theologically, the asteroid collision is part of the natural processes leading to a life-producing universe of great value to God. That value has been realised here and possibly elsewhere in the universe, with the prospect of further exploration of what life will become in this life-producing universe. Furthermore, an asteroid collision does not contradict the realising of God's purpose in creation. The key event towards the realising of that purpose has already taken place in the life, death, and resurrection of Jesus. Again, the mega-deaths event may never happen if, beforehand. human beings develop their God-given powers to destroy or deflect such an asteroid or if God brings about the resurrection of the universe. An asteroid collision with its mega-deaths would be an unintended consequence of the natural processes God has created for producing life, and its moral character is completely different from a similar outcome from nuclear war between nations.

3. A contradiction within the theology of creation?

In public presentations of my argument, I am asked whether there is a contradiction for me as a Christian, between my theology wherein God values creatures as co-creators, which according to the argument shows up in an evolutionary account of nature. There, the strong thrive at the expense of the weak but in the Reign [Kingdom] of God, a contrary set of values is proclaimed. This is all supposed to

---

in arguing for evolutionary convergence by unrelated organisms, via different routes, on the same solutions e.g., the camera eye. Conway Morris, S., *Life's Solution: Inevitable Humans in a Lonely Universe* (Oxford, Oxford University Press, 2005), and *The Runes of Evolution: How the Universe Became Self-Aware*, (West Conshohocken, Pennsylvania: Templeton Press, 2015). For many examples of convergence, see Map of Life website, http://www.mapoflife.org/about/. See also Lonergan's argument that a world ordered by classical laws and statistical laws leads to the pervasive processes of emergent probability. Lonergan (1958), pp. 121–128, 132–134.

fit together under the theology of creation driven by the idea of God being wholly good. But how is that possible, given the contradiction? My reply recalls the larger resources offered by the further scientific thinking about evolution and by a closer look at this theology of creation to show there is no such contradiction.

First, there is more to evolution than competition and the predator-prey dynamic. Different forms of cooperation emerge within the evolutionary processes, (microbes, ants, bats) including a sense of fairness amongst monkeys[19] and a form of compassion and care, for example among dolphins[20] and even dolphins cooperating with fishermen.[21] As Darwin noted, it must not be forgotten that although a high standard of morality gives but a slight, or no, advantage to each individual man and his children over the other men of the same tribe, yet that an increase in the number of well-endowed men and an advancement in the standard of morality will certainly give an immense advantage to one tribe over another. A tribe including many members who, from possessing in a high degree the spirit of patriotism, fidelity, obedience, courage, and sympathy, were always ready to aid one another, and to sacrifice themselves for the common good, would be victorious over most other tribes; and this would be natural selection.[22] Leher comments, 'While acts of altruism can be costly for the individual, Darwin argued that they helped sustain the colony, which made individuals within the colony more likely to survive ... that human generosity might have evolved as an emergent property not of the individual but of the group."[23]

The theoretical explanation of the observed cooperation is contentious[24] but has been vigorously pursued using mathematics of

---

19. SF Brosnan, and FBM.de Waal, 'Fair Refusal by capuchin monkeys', in *Nature*, 428 (2004): 140.
20. R Lilley, 'Dolphins save stuck whales, guide them back to sea', in *National Geographic* (2008).
21. FG Daura-Jourge, M Cantor, SN Ingram, D Lusseau, PC Simoes-Lopes, 'The structure of Bottlenose Dolphin Society is coupled to a unique foraging cooperation with Artisinal Fishermen, *Biology Letters*, 8/5, (2012): 702–705.
22. Charles Darwin, 1871, *The Descent of Man: and selection in relation to sex*, London, J. Murray, 137.
23. Jonah Lehrer, in *The New Yorker* (New York), 88/3 (March 5 2012): 9.
24. The article in Lehrer, summarises the beginning of this contentiousness. See also, DS Wilson and EO Wilson, 'Rethinking the Theoretical Foundation of Sociobiology', in *The Quarterly Review of Biology*, Volume 82/2 (2007): 327–345.

game theory by Professor Martin Nowark and his team at Harvard University's Programme of Evolutionary Dynamics. A key insight is that within groups defectors overcome cooperators, but groups of cooperators overwhelm groups of defectors. Cooperation can evolve under particular conditions and is extremely successful strategy. Based on empirical observation, E.O. Wilson's earlier summary of sociobiology' new theoretical foundation is, "Selfishness beats altruism within groups. Altruistic groups beat selfish groups. Everything else is commentary."[25]

Theologian Sarah Coakley worked for three years as a member of Nowark's programme at Harvard. The fruits of this engagement can be found in Coakley's Gifford Lectures for 2012, her book following from the lectures[26] and a collection of essays edited by Nowark and Coakley.[27] Coakley's work covers a wide canvass from which I note one theme that cooperation in evolution opens the way to an account of altruism and so to a rational account of sacrifice, (not driven by Dawkins' 'selfish gene' theory), enabling a recovery of the idea of sacrifice as of both evolutionary and theological significance.[28] It is also welcomed as support for the theology of creation in this work, which drawing on themes from Aquinas has independently understood God to maximise the realisation of the value of creatures as co-creators with cooperation and conflict as a key part of the idea of a life-producing universe.

Second, observations used in stating the proposed contradiction are correct, but saying they are contradictory is not. Theology thinks that Jesus making present the Reign of God in his own time and place was highly contentious, leading to him sacrificing his life by remaining faithful to God under conditions of human violence. One

---

25. Wilson and Wilson, *The Quarterly Review of Biology*, 82/2 (007): 345.
26. Sarah Coakley, *Sacrifice Regained: Reconsidering the Rationality of Religious Belief* (Cambridge: Cambridge University Press, 2012).
27. Martin. Nowark and Sarah Coakley, (editors), *Evolution, Games and God: The Principle of Cooperation*, (Cambridge, Massachusetts: Harvard University Press, 2013.) For a review of that book see, Andrew Pinsent, in Reviews in *Theology and Religion*, 22/4 (October 2015): 360–364.
28. Coakley notes that the borrowing of anthropomorphic language by evolutionary theorists as an intuition pump for their explanations, is no straightforward matter. Coakley, Gifford Lectures 2012, Lecture 2. A similar point is made by J Turner and A Maryanski, 'The deep origins of society: An assessment of EO Wilson's *Genesis*, in *International Sociology of Reviews*, 34/5 (2019): 547–549.

may think of the resonance between the suffering of Jesus and the suffering of humankind subject to the same violent powers of their encompassing fictions. But against this claimed *resonance*, allegedly so profound, there may be heard what seems to be a deeper mocking *dissonance* between these human sufferings and the idea of the world being created from the excess of divine love exchanged between the persons of the Triune God. For many, this *dissonance* has eaten away, dissolved, and so made impossible any idea of this world being created with a purposeful love by a holy God.

Nevertheless, this supposed 'impossibility' is possible. The good news of God in Christ eventually leads us to understand that the world is created from the excess of divine love, and, for love's sake, does so by making things make themselves.[29] And while this 'making themselves' might take more than one form, in our world one form it has taken is the evolutionary process of natural selection, which has all the appearances of having so much waste, pain and suffering, and of being purposeless, futile. The fact that this process, with elements of cooperation as well as competition[30], eventually produces a multitude of beautiful and extraordinary creatures, including humankind, does not contradict these appearances. The fact that humankind, with its extraordinary powers, produces much that is good, true, and beautiful does not prevent many people finding the human history of power, violence, pain, and suffering, overwhelming, challenging, weakening, and even undermining belief about the world being created by a purposeful love.

Yet in the light of the good news, these appearances, for all their power to challenge belief in God, are neither the first nor the last word. The processes of 'making things make themselves' must run its course, for this love's sake. This 'making things make themselves' includes the evolutionary process involving the local, temporary, reversal of entropy and the bringing forth of humankind as the new reality of *persons* who can only really exist as persons in relations of love and justice. And then the human history of 'making things make themselves' must follow a long and ongoing bloody history of human

---

29. This idea of 'creation makes itself' was discussed in Chapter II 2(a) and is directly related to the theme of creatures as co-creators leading to a fully participatory, life-producing universe.
30. These are discussed in Chapter II 2(a) as a consequence of God maximising the realisation of the value of creatures as co-creators.

beings learning the way of love and justice, beyond the limits of kin and tribe and then of nation, as the only way in which persons in relation can flourish and be themselves with and from the differences of others.

The divine love by which the world and life on this planet is brought into being along so costly a path becomes incarnate, and is subject to the same costly path, and so the violent history of the world is visited on its Creator. Here God incarnate absorbs this visitation and suffers the cost of this long history of human violence, initiated by God creating and sustaining the world from the excess of divine love. Here God incarnate fully embodies the other way of 'making things make themselves', the way of love and justice. It turns out that this love proves stronger than death. From within the world, the death and resurrection of God incarnate opens the world to the only future that is coming from God—the world raised from death and decay and sharing in the divine life—now in anticipation, finally in glory. Justice then will finally be done for and by the love which initiated the creation of the world and proved to be its most passionate servant because justice will be done for the created world.

The alleged contradiction within the theology of creation arises from not taking account of theology's resources to articulate and hold together the different realities involved: (a) the different kinds of creatures being brought into existence, including persons, and what is needed for making different creatures make themselves; (b) the anticipation of the only future that is coming from God inaugurated by the life, death, and resurrection of Christ.

4. Colleagues' objections

1a. Superlative power of God must be moral not just functional

In lectures, my colleague, Dr Kristian Camilleri, raised this objection to my theology of creation, which I think voices many people's objections to the idea that this universe has been created by a wholly good God.

> If there are grounds to believe that God did employ a process of Darwinian evolution, then the process not just the end state must be subject to God's goodness. A God who wreaked havoc on the world (e.g., Noah's flood), or permitted pain and

suffering on a grand scale over evolutionary time, for some other purpose (perhaps, but not necessarily, in order that it may arrive at a 'good end state') would not be morally justified. The end would not justify the means. The theological concept of a good God must carefully define the notion of 'good' morally, not simply superlatively, e.g., not all senses of the good are moral; a good knife is sharp, a better knife is sharper.

Any response to the problem of natural evil has the burden of demonstrating that God could not possibly have avoided the pain and suffering in creating this world. In other words, it must be shown that there was no other way to create a good world, however you chose to define this, other than the way God chose. If there were another way, which minimized suffering, but which maximized its goodness, then an all-knowing, all-powerful, wholly good God should surely have chosen this way.

Given the idea of God as creator, the above argument offers grounds to expect this God to create a universe in which created things with their own real powers are co-creators in a process (which subsequently we see as concurring with Darwinian evolution) that brings life into existence on this planet, with life elsewhere in the universe being entirely consistent. Kristian says the 'theological concept of a good God must carefully define the notion of 'good' morally not simply superlatively'. This mistakes what I am saying about God being understood in superlative terms. My claim is not that God is superlative in knowledge and power while morally otherwise. God is superlative in knowledge, power and goodness and the goodness includes moral goodness.

Kristian makes the point that the process, not just the end state, must be subject to God's goodness. I completely agree. Furthermore, I think the argument already shows that to be the case. The maximizing of the realization of the value of creatures as co-creators (with their own real powers) is not a means to achieving God's purpose in creation.[31] The realization of the value begins immediately things are brought into existence. The resulting physical and chemical complexification and evolutionary processes (throughout the universe) is an expression of this value. Is the realization of this value subject to God's goodness?

---

31. Other means are used to realize God's purpose for this universe, all to do with the special revelation of God.

Many people might well doubt that an all-powerful, all-knowing, and perfectly good God, would choose to create such a universe in which the maximizing of 'creatures as co-creators' involved so much suffering and death, along with all the good it produced. All this would be known in detail to the mind of God and, as we saw at the start of Chapter 1, we cannot think of God intervening into the ordinary operation of such a created universe, on pain of taking God to be deeply irrational, since God is its creator.

The moral character of God creating things with their own real powers is shown in the following points. From the above discussion of what kind of universe we should expect a perfectly good God to create, the things created:

(i) have the dignity of being causes rather than the indignity of not being causes;
(ii) are not only good in themselves but also the cause of good in other things;
(iii) by their own powers working together, they are co-creators, bringing new things into existence, penultimately living things, including intelligent life.

The question is whether (i), (ii) and (iii) represent a moral good? In (i), is the dignity of creatures at all levels to participate as co-creators a moral good as well as a functional good? Kristian simply says he does not regard this view of the dignity creatures as a measure of moral goodness. I think it is a moral good, for exclusion from participation devalues the non-participant, as the term 'wall flower' indicates, or as a dictatorship devalues the people so ruled.

In (ii) and (iii), the 'good of others' eventually includes producing life. Do living things represent a moral good? Do they have intrinsic worth? Do they have instrumental worth as means to some other moral good? I would answer 'yes' to all three questions. They have intrinsic worth because as co-creators they are like the living God, who brings into existence a life-producing universe *ex nihilo* and because the whole creation is to participate in the fulfilment of God's purpose in creating the universe. They have instrumental worth that includes life-forms being part of a great food chain by which life is sustained and new life forms generated.[32] The intrinsic worth of living things is irreducible to their instrumental worth.

---

32. See Ps 104:21: 'The young lions roar for their prey, seeking their food from God.'

1b. The 'only way' argument

For Kristian, any response to the problem of natural evil 'has the burden of demonstrating that God could not possibly have avoided the pain and suffering in creating this world.' In other words, it must be shown 'that there was no other way to create a "good" world, however you chose to define this, other than the way God chose.'

In my argument it is not a matter of 'demonstrating that God could not possibly have avoided . . .' Rather, the argument is that God *chooses* to maximally realize the value of creatures as co-creators in a life-producing universe, which, because of God's purpose, includes bringing forth persons. If I understand the spirit of Kristian's objection to my argument, it is saying surely such a God would give weight to compassion for suffering creatures and therefore (a) not maximize the realization of the value of creatures as co-creators in the first place, and (b) act in the world to relieve suffering.

As an example of (a), there would be less suffering, pain, and death in the world if such a God were to create all species in one act of 'special creation', along the lines envisaged by William Paley in his 1802, *Natural Theology*,[33] and so delete the long process of evolution. There would still be a great deal of life being (re)produced, so that it would be a life—producing universe. There would still be a great deal of suffering, but much less, with all the suffering of the evolutionary process eliminated. Why wouldn't a truly good God create such a world? Alternatively, why is maximizing the realization of the value of creatures as co-creators so important to God, or, more carefully, on this account of God?

The argument has been that God chooses what is 'better', morally, and functionally, (as per (i), (ii) and (iii) above), regarding the *type* of creation that,

- realises the *value* of creatures as co-creators with their own real powers, as good in themselves and good for others, in a life-producing universe;
- is informed by the freely chosen divine *purpose* of drawing the whole creation into a loving and just relationship with God.

---

33. William Paley (1743–1805), *Natural Theology, or Evidence of the Existence and Attributes of the Deity, Collected from the Appearances of Nature*, edited by Matthew D Eddy and David Knight (Oxford: Oxford University Press, 2006).

For God to maximize the realisation of this *value* means the maximizing of the realisation of the better type of creation—creatures as co-creators in a life-producing universe. It is a 'better' type of creation because it is more like the life-giving God than any other type of creation, such as an inert, chaotic, purely mechanical types of universes, which are not life-producing. This is the type of creation we should expect of a wholly good God. You may recall that the 'maximizing' expectation proceeded from the claim that God is that than which none greater can be conceived. Thus, God is superlative, and it is therefore fitting not to ascribe to God a lesser good. The maximizing expresses God's excellence. Creating a Paley-type universe would be a lesser good than the better type of creation. If you wonder whether this maximizing type of creation is overall better than a Paley-type creation, remember this follows from the argument just summarised. The 'better' claim is not reached by weighing the cost/benefit analysis of the disvalues/values in each type of creation. It is based on God being that good of which there is none greater and that a life-producing universe is more like the life-giving God than alternatives. Furthermore, I return to asking who is in a position to weigh the costs and benefits of the values and disvalues? Only God. Is God trustworthy?

1c. A good God indistinguishable from an evil God

An objection from Kristian to all theological answers, mine included, is that they all work with a notion of the good "that is conceived in such a way to make it empirically indistinguishable from evil or indifference. If one cannot tell a good from an indifferent, or even an evil, creator, what sense is there in calling it good? This would not hold up ordinarily.

> This ultimately rests on an act of faith in a *good* God." Kristian continues, Stephen's 'Good God' could have produced any number of universes like our with *even more* natural suffering, pain and death in the world—and still be called 'good'. Indeed, the extinction of the *human race* by means of an asteroid colliding with the earth (something which might well happen) would be perfectly consistent with Stephen's notion of an Omniscient, Omnipotent, Omnibenevolent God. (Provided it met a few other conditions—life-producing, etc.) As long

as they have the 'dignity of being causes' and maximize co-creation, the divine value of 'goodness' is upheld. By the definition Stephen produces, there is *no limit to the suffering* that could be produced and be declared 'good'. This is because the suffering of living creatures does not enter the notion of goodness.

Before concluding this section on my colleagues' objections, I will present an irrefutable mark of the goodness of God, that cannot be confused with evil or indifference. But let us approach that point by beginning with the second objection. To have unlimited suffering, it would need to be perpetual, pointless suffering, of each living creature. This might count as defining Hell. The life-producing universe with its food-chain produces values and disvalues, but the disvalues are not unlimited, for they arise on the road to viable life forms in abundance, with all participating in a food chain that sustains life. Kristian's objection may be more that there is an extraordinary amount of suffering and death in the life-producing universe, and it strongly tests the plausibility of the claim that all this is the creation of a wholly good God. Much depends on the kind of world such a God might be expected to create. If the expected world were represented by the hymn, 'All things bright and beautiful' then the actual world would certainly contradict such an expectation and render implausible the claim that the actual world is created by a wholly good God. But why take that hymn as a basis for what to expect of God? No more than one should accept its verse (now deleted!), *'The rich man in his castle / the poor man at his gate/ God made them high and lowly / and ordered their estate.'* Mary, the mother of Jesus, obviously thought of God very differently (Lk 1:46–55).

Kristian thinks the idea of the good that I am using is, 'empirically indistinguishable from evil or indifference. Then naturally if one cannot tell a good from an indifferent, or even an evil creator, what sense is there in calling it good? This would not hold up ordinarily. This ultimately rests on an act of faith in a *good* God.'[34] It is important

---

34. The idea of the evil God is supported, for example, see William Law, 2010, 'Evil God challenge', in *Religious Studies*, September 46/3 (2010): 353–373, and criticised, for example, Why not believe in an evil God? Pragmatic encroachment and some implications for philosophy of religion | Religious Studies | Cambridge Core; The 'Evil god' Objection | Reasonable Faith . Both accessed in September 2022.

to note that the idea of a good God is not based on an empirical survey of what happens in the world, either the natural world or the human world. In the Appendix, section 3(a), I refer to Aquinas agreeing with Anselm's idea of God as that than which none greater can be conceived. I accept this understanding of God. I would not knowingly worship a lesser God. This idea of God has traditionally been elaborated as God being all powerful, all knowing and all good. Challenges to the coherence of this articulation of the idea of God, and my response, is discussed in section 4(a). This is not the challenge Kristian presents. Retrieving my understanding of faith, this belief is analogous to an abductive inference and is tested in a similar way, of which this book is an example.

Support for this idea of God is drawn from the view that there are acts that are unconditionally morally wrong. As an example, I tell students of Robin Williams[35] once giving a lecture where he read a passage from a book called *The Rape of the Congo* about how a man was forced to watch his wife being raped by a gang, and how his wife then had to watch her man being tortured and killed. Williams asked where was God in this incident and countless many like it. Williams then said that the only reason God did not intervene is because God does not exist. I explain to students that I feel revulsion at such violence, a revulsion fed by everything about the incident that violates the man and the woman, their bodies, their relationship, their lives, and includes the realisation that this is a terrible violation of the woman and the man's dignity as persons, a violation of their unconditional worth.

Now my impression is that students are attentive, many heads are nodding. Then I make two points. *If* that analysis is correct and *if* I take this recognition of unconditional worth as a clue to reality, then my worldview, my account of reality, cannot be that everything is conditioned by everything else. For then there would be nothing that is unconditioned. So, *if* my analysis of revulsion is accurate and *if* I take this recognition of unconditional worth as a clue to reality, then my worldview must include something that is beyond all the

---

35. Robin Williams is a science journalist and broadcaster who is the presenter of *The Science Show* and *Ockham's Razor* on the ABC, Australia's national broadcaster. His reference to *The Rape of the Congo* took place in a speech at the first global atheist conference in Melbourne in 2010, with 4000 participants. He joined Richard Dawkins, and Daniel Dennett among other keynote speakers.

conditioning, something transcendent, that is the ground of this unconditional worth and must itself be of unconditional worth. Furthermore, on this analysis, I am in touch with that transcendent something at the very point when I feel this revulsion and recognise the violation of the unconditional worth of those suffering the violence. I then say to students that traditionally this transcendent something is called 'God'. I also point out that these ideas can be easily resisted by denying one or both of the two '*if*' points.

Students respond with a range of comments, and I mention two. One is that I am only talking about empathy and that doesn't require any metaphysics. I agree that I am talking about empathy, without which there would be no revulsion. The claimed recognition of unconditional worth is conditional upon the development of empathy, but I am inviting them to consider what is so recognised. I am inviting them to reflect on their own experience of revulsion, if that is their response, and to consider whether the analysis of the revulsion is correct, accurate, true. The other student comment asked me to respond to Plato's famous Euthyphro dilemma, concerning the nature of goodness. Is a thing good because God says it is good, or does God say it's good because it is good? I replied that here the good is the recognition and response to the unconditional worth of human beings and this is implicitly or explicitly shown in compassion, love and justice done.[36] This is why the 'Good Samaritan' is 'good'. Likewise, evil is the violation of this unconditional worth. On this view God is the ground of this unconditional worth and so we may say God is good. The good is to know and do what is truly worthwhile, where, in the first place, God is the ground of unconditional worth, and so of the truly worthwhile, which God commands. I believe this avoids the Euthyphro dilemma.

Kristian's objection recalls Richard Dawkins cited earlier, that the universe we observe has precisely the properties we should expect if there, is at bottom, no design, no purpose, no evil, no good, nothing but blind pitiless indifference. I make two points in reply. First, notice that Dawkins says the observable universe is precisely what we should expect if at bottom there is at no design only blind pitiless

---

[36]. For further discussion of this claim about the unconditional worth of human beings see S Ames, *The value presupposed and given in person-centred dementia care*, OBM Geriatrics 3/3 (2019), doi:10.21926/obm.geriatr.1903068, 1–18.

indifference. Dawkins doesn't test this claim by considering what to expect if at bottom there is the omni-God. My argument presents a different account of what kind of universe we should expect from such a God. Secondly I say that "at bottom" for Dawkins is his naturalism, shown in his claim "any creative intelligence of sufficient complexity to design anything comes into existence only as the end product of an extended process of gradual evolution."[37] I have indicated in Chapter IV 1a why I think that naturalism is an inadequate account of what is at 'bottom' because it is logically unable to account for human inquirers that have come into existence on planet earth. Furthermore, I take human inquiry as indeed good, an epistemological and moral good, without extending that unqualified judgment to how its results are used. If we say that nature has produced life, such as we find in human inquirers, then we need a richer account of nature than what Dawkins thinks is at 'bottom'. My argument is that this richer view is a theologically articulated account of the natural world, such as I have presented in Chapters II, III and IV and defended here, that is consonant with the evolution of life, including human inquirers. For further support for this claim see S Ames (2022).

Where next?

Kristian thinks the notion of goodness that I am using does not attend to the suffering of living creatures. This recalls the above claim (b) that a truly good God would surely give weight to compassion for suffering creatures and therefore God would act in the world to relieve suffering. While no one has exactly made the following point, I can envisage students saying that the rationality of God not acting in such a universe and the rationality of God 'maximizing' creatures as co-creators simply leaves out compassion for suffering creatures. Such indifference, if attributed to an allegedly wholly good God is an unbearable contradiction, making it impossible to worship God—if such a God exists. In which case, we would simply hand back our

---

37. Richard Dawkins, *The God Delusion* (London: Bantam, 2006), 31. Note the encompassing reference to 'any' intelligence. However, I have argued that the intelligence shown in human inquiry cannot be included in the scope of this 'any'. The problem is not the story of the evolution of life climbing the long road up Mount Improbable, which is not in dispute. It is not any problem to do with methodological or epistemic naturalism. It is rather the philosophical setting of metaphysical naturalism.

ticket, preferring to live in the world as if such a God did not exist. The following objection takes us further into the thought that there is a want of compassion in God for suffering creatures.

1d. God is reckless and cruel in creating this universe

One year, in the lecture on the problem of natural evil, my atheist colleague Neil Thomason acknowledged that an all-powerful and all-knowing God might well be thought to create a universe that maximizes creatures as co-creators but asked if a truly good God would be so reckless, especially in view of the cost to creatures, which of course such a God would know in detail in the very idea of such a universe?[38] This voices a concern many share.

Would such a wholly good God be so reckless? I start by accepting the question and offering three reasons for saying 'yes'. Firstly, at this point in the lecture, I said that we appear to need a character reference for God as wholly good. Where can we find such a reference? As a Christian I offer the testimony that Jesus gives to the character of God in the story of the Prodigal Son.[39] This is one way of testing the question about God's character. I retell the story about a man with property, slaves, great wealth, and two sons. The younger son asks his father for half his inheritance. I emphasise how outrageous the young man's request is because it discloses his wish that his father was dead.[40] But I add that what is even more outrageous is that the boy's father gives him half the inheritance and lets him go! This might be thought of as a 'reckless' act for, among other things, there is no knowing what will happen to his son. I explain that the parable invites us to think of God like the father in the story.[41] Even if the father is thought to be reckless, can anyone say that he did not love his son?

---

38. It is important to see, at least from my argument, that God creating such a universe depends on the goodness of God, not just on God being all knowing and all powerful.
39. Lk 10:25–37. Since we are inquiring whether there is any understanding of God that can address the problem of evil, I refer to the tradition I know best, which testifies to the character of God. Again, this does not assume belief in God so understood or in any God. Students who do not stand in this tradition are encouraged to treat it as a thought experiment.
40. See, Kenneth E Bailey, *Poet and Peasant and Through Peasant Eyes, A Literary Cultural Approach to the Parables in Luke* (Grand Rapids MI: Eerdmans, 1983).
41. Long before Nietzsche's madman rushed into the market, the death of God had been anticipated.

At this point in the lecture Neil shouted out, 'Yes, the father is not only reckless, but also cruel!' The lecture theatre went very quiet. I said to students that here they are presented with two different views of the good. One says the father is reckless and loving and so too is God. The other, that the father is reckless and cruel and if God exists, so too is God. We allowed the difference to stand. I went on to say that the parable speaks of a truly good God in a way that supports the idea that this God, the creator of the universe, would be so reckless, even foolish, in liberally giving to created things real powers and therewith the dignity of being co-creators, indeed maximising this co-creating in a life-producing universe.

The second reason is that God is no less reckless and loving in the creation of human beings in the image and likeness of God, with personal freedom to exercise its extraordinary God-given power for good,[42] knowing that it could be used for other interests. All the ill-use of these powers in causing suffering to other human beings and other forms of life is perhaps as great (quantitatively) as the suffering produced by evolution. Qualitatively, it is a different, more dreadful kind of suffering due to it being the outcome of a deliberate action. Opposition to the idea of God creating and giving creatures real powers to be co-creators, displayed in using evolution to bring life into existence, ought to also oppose the idea of God giving human beings such power and freedom to use it. I have never heard anyone extend their objection to God based on natural evil, to an objection to human beings being created with power and freedom, including their own. This would be to argue that God should not have created this kind of universe, including human beings, including anyone raising this objection!

Neil remains unconvinced by this argument. At least two points are worth noting. The problem of natural evil presupposes that the actual world is different from the kind of world we should expect the omni-God to create, and such a world would not include evolution. But I have argued why this supposed contradiction is mistaken. Secondly, Neil and I work with different understandings of the good, indicated by our appeal to different 'moments' of parenting. Neil appeals to the parent with knowledge and power to save a child from disaster and, if I have understood him, claims that a loving parent would always

---

42. Recall the discussion in Chapter II on Gen 1:26–28 and Ps 8.

intervene. This is a great good, though that 'always' can be challenged. I appeal to the raising up of children to flourish and then letting them go, hoping for their good, with the risk that ill may befall them. It is a risk all parents know. But this 'letting go' is a great good, beginning with the cutting of the umbilical cord.

There is a third reason for thinking of a perfectly good God being so reckless as to give created things real powers. For Christian theology, these created powers are visited upon this God who submits to them, as the victim of human violence, in all their (dis)order, in order to limit, transform, and overcome their (dis)order, in the life and death of the incarnate Son of God and in his resurrection from the dead. For this to not be just an ad hoc 'fact' about God, this suffering of God would have to be integral to the realisation of God's purpose in creation. I briefly argue this is the case in, 'Christ the image of the invisible God', in Chapter IV, section 4b.

This idea of the recklessness or foolishness of God is found in the New Testament, in 1 Corinthians 1:18–25. God is presented as sending his divine Son to become incarnate, die, and be raised from the dead, and all this as the way to fulfil God's purpose in creation. Christians understand the incarnation of the Son as revealing the true nature of God as self-giving love. This also reveals the character of divine power.[43] Creatures are co-creators with God who co-suffers with creatures in the crucifixion of Jesus. Southgate invites us to think of God co-suffering with all the suffering of sentient creatures.[44]

The discussion allows us to address the criticism that compassion for suffering creatures has no place in this account of God maximizing creatures as co-creators and of God not intervening in such a universe to stop or limit the dreadful suffering due to the natural processes God has created. Such indifference, if attributed to an allegedly wholly good God, is found to be an unbearable contradiction, making it impossible to worship that God.

This Christian account of the all-knowing, all-powerful, wholly good God who creates *ex nihilo* the life-producing universe for the purpose of drawing all created things into a loving and just relationship with God, invites us to accept that the 'wholly good' attributed to

---

43. William. C Placher, *Narratives of a Vulnerable God* (Louisville: Westminster John Knox Press, 1994).
44. Southgate, *The Groaning of Creation*, 55–57.

God includes the reckless love presented by the father in the parable, the reckless risk-taking creator of humankind presented in Genesis and the suffering divine Son in the crucifixion of Jesus. This is an account of the extreme, reckless divine love and compassion for the whole creation that opens the way to the life of the Triune God. This is also a reason to reject the criticism that the goodness of God is indistinguishable from evil or indifference. The God I am speaking of is the God who created a world worth dying for. This is not the mark of evil or indifference.

For some this 'reckless love' is too extreme, too careless of consequences to be identified with love or with the good. Some might press for an account of why God is so extreme, so reckless. We meet this demand from a different angle in the next dramatic objection.

5. Stephen Fry's tirade against God

Stephen Fry gave an interview on Ireland's RTE Network,[45] in which he was asked, as an atheist, what he would say if he died and found out God was real. His response went viral. He has been nominated for the 'Interview of the Year' award by the Sanford St Martin Trust, a religious organization celebrating 'excellence in religious broadcasting'. There was a time when an interview like this would not have been given much airplay, let alone be up for an award from any organization, especially religious!'[46] Here is the transcript of Fry's reply to what he would say if he died and discovered God was real.

> I'd say, 'bone cancer in children? What's that about? How dare you. How dare you create a world in which there is such misery that is not our fault. It's not right, it's utterly, utterly evil. Why should I respect a capricious, mean-minded, stupid God who creates a world that is so full of injustice and pain?' That's what I would say . . . The God who created this universe, if it was created by God, is quite clearly a maniac, utter maniac. Totally selfish. We have to spend our life on our knees thanking him; what kind of God would do that?

Interviewer: 'Do you think you would get in?' Stephen Fry continues:

---
45. https://brewminate.com/stephen-frys-rebuke-of-god-nominated-for-award-by-religious-organization-video/. Over 8 million views as of 3 September 2019.
46. Posted at the above link by Matthew A McIntosh, 23 March 2016.

I wouldn't want to get in, not on his terms. They are wrong. If I died and it was Pluto, Hades and it was the twelve Greek gods then I would have more truck with it because the Greeks were . . . they didn't pretend not to be human in their appetites, in their capriciousness, in their unreasonableness. They didn't present themselves as being all things, all wise, all kind, all beneficent, because the god who created this universe, if it was created by God, is quite clearly a maniac, an utter maniac, totally selfish—we have to spend our lives on our knees thanking him! What kind of God would do that? Yes, the world is very splendid, but it also has in it insects whose whole life cycle is to burrow into the eyes of children and make them blind; they burrow outwards from the eyes. Why? Why did he do that to us? He could easily have made a creation in which that didn't exist. It is simply not acceptable So, you know, atheism is not just about not believing there is a God, but on the assumption that there is one, what kind of God is he? It is perfectly apparent that he is monstrous, utterly monstrous and deserves no respect whatsoever. The moment you banish him, life becomes simpler, purer, cleaner, more worth living in my opinion.

Fry's question, 'What kind of God is this?' is precisely the question to be asked! Fry infers an answer to the question by looking at the world supposedly created by God. Fry says the world created by God is full of misery and injustice not of human making. Yes, it is splendid in many respects, but it also has pain and suffering especially shown in children with bone cancer or children with parasites burrowing into their eyes and besides children, lambs suffering a similar agony, and besides lambs . . .

Fry's answer to 'what kind of God?' assumes God has the knowledge and power to have created a different kind of world without any of this suffering. God's choice to create our universe rather than such an alternative universe, shows God's character, as utterly monstrous, capricious, mean-minded, stupid, a maniac. This strongly contradicts God presenting himself (or being presented) as all-kind, all-beneficent. In addition, God is utterly selfish, demanding we spend our life on our knees thanking him. Unsurprisingly, Fry finds that life is so much better when that God is banished from one's life. Life is more worth living.

My first response to Fry is to ask him to say what kind of universe we should expect such a God to create. Please show us by arguing *from* that idea of God *to* what we should expect. Without this, 'anything goes', in the sense that any expectation (including Fry's) could be put onto God and found to be contradicted by the way the world is. But that would prove nothing about God. This applies to Fry whose indignation with God is fuelled at least in part by what to him is obvious, namely that if, supposedly, God is the all-powerful, all-benevolent creator, then God not only could have but should have created a different kind of universe. This is Fry's implicit theology in which he argues from the idea of God in that theology. I surmise that for Fry, when God is so obviously a monster, he does not need to pursue that task. Furthermore, Fry has found people 'cherry picking' the positive aspects of the world to argue *to* God while ignoring the misery that Fry highlights. Especially, the universe with all the pain and misery we find in the very production of life, which we now know, thanks to Darwin. Fry rightly dismisses that approach.[47]

I too reject 'cherry-picking'. I have argued *from* this idea of God *to* the kind of universe we should expect this God to create.[48] This is a theological exposition that is not formed *from* scientific knowledge. It argues that at least one thing that is of value to God is creatures as co-creators, and that God maximizes the realization of this value, leading to a life-producing universe. This is a better type of creation than other types of creation that are not life-producing. It is 'better' because it is more like God who is life-giving, than other possible types of creation. My argument then continues that we find a concurrence between this theologically-envisaged type of creation and the scientific account of the universe, including the evolution of life by natural selection. The theological understanding of the kind of universe we should expect God to create is furthered by reflecting on God's purpose in creation. I engage Fry's assertion that God should have chosen to create a different kind of universe by arguing instead that God chose to create this life-producing kind of universe as the better type of creation.

---

47. Recall, above, George Wright's earlier rejection of theologians with rose-coloured glasses building upon a very narrow basis of facts, to the exclusion of another class of facts which are in startling number, to which Darwinism draws attention.
48. In Ames, *Can we live in, but not of, the immanent frame?* and Ames *The value given and presuppose in person centered dementia care* I have also argued *from* the world *to* God, without the kind of cherry-picking arguments Fry rightly rejects.

It is entirely open to Fry to criticise my argument. I imagine Fry might still ask, 'What kind of God is this?' who creates a world full of injustice and pain that is not our fault. There are two claims here. One is that the world includes a vast amount of suffering and death in the production of life, which is unjust. The other is that this pain and suffering is not our fault.

The first parallels the claim that the world is full of natural evils, which contradicts belief in a wholly good God, who loves justice. This reruns Fry's implicit theology as noticed above, and which this book attempts to answer. How shall we take Fry's talk of injustices? He gives every impression of not referring to what he finds merely distasteful, something that could be dismissed as merely expressing his feelings and opinions, as somehow socially conditioned. If so, is it another *ad hominin* attack on the supposedly wholly good God who loves justice? This is perhaps the fairest way to hear Fry. Otherwise, I wonder what kind of world must be assumed in which there are things that are unconditionally unjust (or just). As argued above, it cannot be a world in which everything is conditioned by everything else. For then there would be nothing unconditional. It must be a world in which there is something that transcends all conditions. And any claim to see such injustice also presupposes that the claimant is minimally in touch with that transcendent 'something', even if it is *incognito*. A traditional name for this transcendent 'something' is 'God'. Is this the world we must assume when taking Stephen Fry seriously? If so, then Fry's question is exactly right, 'What kind of God is this?'

The second claim is that all the pain and suffering produced by natural processes 'is not our fault', allowing Fry to ask 'Why? Why did he do that to us?' I wondered about 'not our fault'. Is Fry really thinking that evolutionary pain and suffering could be explained or justified or at least understood, if it was 'our fault'? Surely not. The suffering produced by natural processes, which is the basis for his rejection of God, predates the evolution of human capacities for making choices that could count as their fault. Instead, might Fry be partially resurfacing a traditional theology (that Fry had culturally imbibed) which envisages an original perfection in creation, broken and stained by human sin leading to death entering the world as God's judgment. In that theology those at fault for this serious moral offence, come under judgment as a punishment (so Augustine,

Anselm, Luther, Calvin).[49] Is Fry declaring against that theology (per assumption, the one Fry imbibed) that all the pain and suffering due to created natural processes is 'not our fault'? If so, Fry would appear to be rejecting this theology and doing so on the basis that it is unjust. If my reflection on his claim about 'injustices' is correct, then without realising it, Fry is doing so based on his being in touch with God *incognito*. Other theological resources have always been available within Christianity for a different theological account of creation, (more latterly, including the evolution of life on planet earth), and God's response to the disorders of human life, due principally to our misplaced loyalties to 'lesser gods'.[50]

Fry asks, 'What kind of God is this?' He answers that the God who created this universe (if it was so created) is a maniac, is stupid, mean-minded, capricious, utterly monstrous (because for Fry God could have created a universe without such suffering), and totally selfish— 'we have to spend our lives on our knees thanking him!' Fry is reacting to an image of God as selfishly demanding that we grovel on our knees, as if nothing else in our lives, not even our neighbour, could be allowed to compete with God for our attention and energies. Is this Fry allowing his grievance against God to caricature the devotion God calls for or has he also imbibed this image of God and encountered this pattern of devotion? It is the image of a controlling God who shows no appreciation of our humanity, our passions, our

---

49. See John Haught, *Resting on the Future, Catholic Theology for an Unfinished Universe* (New York: *Bloomsbury*, 2015).

50. In Christian theology, especially shaped by Augustine and later by Anselm, the expiation of so great a human fault required the sacrificial suffering of Christ, not in order to placate an angry God, but to ensure the created cosmic order of things fittingly regained its balance by the payment of the price which on this theology such restoration justly requires. See Colin Gunton, *The Actuality of Atonement: A study of metaphor, rationality, and Christian tradition* (Grand Rapids MI: Eerdmans, 1989); John Haught, *Resting on the Future: Catholic Theology for an Unfinished Universe* (London: Bloomsbury, 2015), Chapter 7. Though deeply embedded in Western Christianity, Catholic and Protestant, it never was the only theology available, as shown in Irenaeus (130–202ce), and in the importance of 'divinisation' for understanding the work of Christ for Christians East and West. See also, Stephen Finlan, and Vladimir Kharlamov, *Theiosis: Deification in Christian Theology* (Eugene OR: Pickwick Publications, 2006). Cited by Haught, *Resting on the Future*. See also my locating the theology of creation (Chapter II, sections 2, 3) in Christian tradition, section 4(b) of Chapter II.

weaknesses, nor, so I would add, our many possibilities *for* the good amid the perceived ambiguities of life which I have sought to place within the theology of creation including our misplaced loyalty to lesser gods. From my standpoint, I think Fry is rejecting a caricature of God and if my reflection on his claim about 'injustices' is correct, he is possibly doing so based on standing in the shadow of God *incognito*. If this reading of Fry is correct, it would show another part of Fry's implicit theology. In the context of this book this reading of Fry is offered as an invitation for him to revisit his question, 'What kind of God is this?', and the answers in his implicit theology.

6. The evidential problem of natural evil (William Rowe)

In discussing Rowe's highly praised evidential argument[51] I am informed by Trakakis' 2007 book length review[52] of how Rowe has developed the argument over a thirty-year period, which Trakakis marks as early (1978–1986), middle (1988–1995) and late (1996-present). The development maintains significant continuity while introducing improvements to respond to various criticisms.[53]

Before presenting my different kind of response, I will set out Rowe's 1979 argument and briefly indicate the direction of his 1996 paper. Rowe is concerned with three questions. Firstly, 'Is there an argument for atheism based on the existence of evil in the world that may rationally justify someone in being an atheist?' Secondly: How can the theist best defend his position against the argument for atheism based on the existence of evil? Thirdly: What position should the informed atheist take concerning the rationality of theistic belief?[54] Rowe gives an affirmative answer to the first question and supports that claim with the following argument.[55]

---

51. William Rowe, 'IX. The Problem of Evil and Some Varieties of Atheism', in *American Philosophical Quarterly*, 16/4 (1979): 335–341.
52. Nick Trakakis, *The God Beyond Belief: In Defence of William Rowe's Evidential Argument from Evil* (Dordrecht: Springer, 2007).
53. William Rowe, 'The Evidential Argument—A Second Look', in Daniel Howard-Snyder, editor, *The Evidential Argument from Evil* (Bloomington IN: Indiana University Press, 1996), 262–282.
54. Rowe, 'IX. The Problem of Evil and Some Varieties of Atheism', 335.
55. Rowe, 'IX. The Problem of Evil and Some Varieties of Atheism', 337.

1. There exist instances of intense suffering which an omnipotent, omniscient being could have prevented without thereby losing some greater good or permitting some evil equally bad or worse.
2. An omniscient, wholly good being would prevent the occurrence of any intense suffering it could, unless it could not do so without thereby losing some greater good or permitting some evil equally bad or worse.

---

3. There does not exist an omnipotent, omniscient, wholly good being.

Rowe thinks (2) is held by many atheists and non-theists and 'accords with our basic moral principles, principles shared by both theists and nontheists.' If this valid argument is to be challenged, it must find fault with (1). In defence of (1) Rowe asks us to consider the following story.

> Suppose in some distant forest lightning strikes a dead tree, resulting in a forest fire. In the fire a fawn is trapped, horribly burned, and lies in terrible agony for several days before death relieves its suffering. Rowe say that so far as we can see there does not appear to be any greater good that the prevention of the fawn's suffering would require either the loss of that good or the occurrence of an evil equally bad or worse. Even theists would agree that an omnipotent, omniscient being could have prevented the fawn from being horribly burned or have relieved it of its suffering. Rowe thinks the fawn's suffering was both preventable and pointless. This doesn't prove (1). After all, while we cannot think of any familiar good outweighing the fawn's suffering to which that suffering is connected in a way we do not see. 'Furthermore. there may well be unfamiliar goods we haven't dreamed of, to which the fawn's suffering is inextricably connected. . . . So the case of the fawn's suffering does not allow us to *establish* the truth of (1).'[56]

On the other hand, it is another thing to have rational grounds for believing (1) to be true. Rowe's two main points here are that it is not reasonable to believe that there is some good intimately connected to that suffering that even an omnipotent, omniscient being could not have obtained that good without permitting that suffering or some

---

56. Rowe, 'IX. The Problem of Evil and Some Varieties of Atheism', 337.

evil at least as bad. Even if it was deemed reasonable to believe this in the case of the fawn is it reasonable to believe it with regard to all the instances of seemingly pointless human and animal suffering that occur daily in our world?[57] Rowe's answer is,

> In the light of our experience and knowledge of the variety and scale of human and animal suffering in our world, the idea that none of this suffering could have been prevented by an omnipotent and omniscient being without thereby losing a greater good or permitting an evil at least as bad seems an extraordinary absurd idea, quite beyond our belief. It seems that although we cannot *prove* that (1) is true, it is, nevertheless, altogether *reasonable* to believe that (1) is true, that (1) is a rational belief.[58]

Rowe's later argument[59] includes the suffering fawn trapped in the forest fire (E1) and the rape, beating and murder by strangulation of a 5year old girl (E2). The argument is now,

> P: No good we know of justifies an omnipotent, omniscient, perfectly good being in permitting E1 and E2; therefore,
> Q: no good at all justifies an omnipotent, omniscient, perfectly good being in permitting E1 and E2; therefore,
>
> not-G: there is no omnipotent, omniscient, perfectly good being.
>
> The first inference, from P to Q, is, of course, an inductive inference. My claim was that P makes Q probable. The second inference, from Q to not-G, is deductive.

Rowe's later argument attempts to defend the inference from P to Q against various criticisms. I will not follow the remainder of Rowe's 1996 paper nor the remainder of his 1979 paper, setting out his view of the best response the theist can make to this argument for atheism nor his 'friendly atheist' response to such a theist. This is because my argument is a different kind of criticism, what Row calls

---

57. Rowe, 'IX. The Problem of Evil and Some Varieties of Atheism', 337.
58. Rowe, 'IX. The Problem of Evil and Some Varieties of Atheism', 338.
59. Rowe, 'The Evidential Argument—A Second Look', 263.

a direct attack on (1), which he doubts can succeed.[60] Rowe rightly rejects two examples of such an attack: (i) that suffering leads to moral and spiritual development otherwise impossible, but counters that much suffering goes far beyond what is required for character development; and (ii) that some suffering results from free choices of human beings and might be preventable only by preventing some measure of human freedom, but rightly counters that much intense suffering occurs not as a result of human free choices. Rowe is clear that a direct attack faces two general difficulties. One is that the theist does not know what greater good might be served or evils prevented by each instance of intense human or animal suffering. The second is that the theists' own religious tradition usually maintains that in this life it is not given to us to know God's purpose in allowing particular instances of suffering. Hence Rowe concludes the direct attack on (1) cannot succeed.[61] For the same reasons, Rowe would conclude a direct attack on P cannot succeed.

I will present a possible contender for a direct attack on Q: no good at all justifies an omnipotent, omniscient, perfectly good being in permitting El and E2; therefore, not-G: there is no omnipotent, omniscient, perfectly good being. The contender is the theology of creation presented above in Chapter II. This theology was developed in response to the logical problem of natural evil[62] and it has immediate relevance to the evidential problem of natural evil. Here in a summary is the possible contender. This theology of creation proceeds from the idea of the omni-God who creates the world *ex nihilo* and sustains in existence for some purpose and goes on to say what kind of world we should therefore expect such a God to create. Starting from threads in the work of Aquinas, including the idea of the superlative character of the omni-God, we should prefer to think that God sustains in existence *ex nihilo*, the better type of creation, compared to any lifeless universe, (such as chaotic, static, mechanical

---

60. Rowe, 'IX. The Problem of Evil and Some Varieties of Atheism', 338. This is no reflection on other forms of criticism focused on the details of Rowe's argument, for example, Langtry, Chapter 8; Peter Van Inwagen, 2006, *The Problem of Evil* (Oxford: Oxford University Press, 2006), 99–100. Murray, (2008), pp. 19–33.
61. Rowe, 'IX. The Problem of Evil and Some Varieties of Atheism', 338, 339.
62. The need to clarify that expectation was required of anyone affirming or denying that natural events were natural evils that contradicted the idea the actual universe was created by such a God.

universes), because the life-producing universe is more like the life-giving God than the alternatives. On this theology, the created universe manifests, without exhausting, the superlative goodness of God. The created universe is the better type of creation which God prefers to create and sustain in existence. It is of value to God as a life-producing universe created with the purpose of being drawn into a loving and just relationship with God, and through the costly means by which God incarnate, crucified, and resurrected, is bringing that purpose to fulfilment. For these reasons I claim this is the good that God would not want to give up.

Would the idea of God intervening to save the fawn from the dreadful suffering in the forest fire or the abused and murdered child have the consequence of God giving up this good? As indicated in Chapter 1, if God were thought to intervene to prevent some terrible suffering, it would follow that we should expect God to intervene in the many natural processes that would lead to similar terrible suffering. Two objections follow. It would make God to be deeply irrational, by intervening into such processes that God has created in the first place.[63] It would contradict the idea that God is omniscient. Secondly, it would amount to God changing the whole created universe to a different type of creation, which would be a lesser good, which the superlative omni-God would not do.

Rowe's objection P is that no good we know of justifies God in permitting E1 and E2. Rowe takes pains to spell out what he means by 'we know' so here I check whether the good that I am proposing is something Rowe allows we can claim to know.

> What counts as a "good we know of"? I do not mean to limit us to goods that we know to have occurred. Nor do I mean to limit us to those goods and goods that we know will occur in the future. I mean to include goods that we have some grasp of, even though we have no knowledge at all that they have

---

63. This recalls Leibniz' criticism of Newton's idea that God would have to intervene to maintain the stability of the solar system. See Query 31 of the *Opticks*, which prompted a response from Leibniz, 'Sir Isaac Newton and his followers have also a very odd opinion concerning the work of God. According to their doctrine, God Almighty wants to wind up his watch from time to time: otherwise, it would cease to move. He had not, it seems, sufficient foresight to make it a perpetual motion.' GH Alexander, editor, *The Leibniz-Clarke Correspondence*, (Manchester, Manchester University Press, 1956), 11.

occurred or ever will occur. For example, consider the good of Sue's[64] experiencing complete felicity in the everlasting presence of God. Theists consider this an enormous personal good. I have no doubt that it is.

So, even though we don't have a very clear grasp of what this great good involves, and even though we don't know that such a good state of affairs will ever obtain, we do mean to include the good of Sue's experiencing complete felicity in the everlasting presence of God as among *the goods we know of*. Of course, if the good in question never does occur, then it is not a good that justifies God in permitting E1 or E2. So, if some good state of affairs we know of does justify God in permitting E1 or E2, that good state of affairs must become actual at some point in the future if it is not already actual.[65]

Given the idea of the omni-God[66], I have argued to the kind of universe we should expect God to create *ex nihilo* and sustain in existence as the better type of creation, a life-producing universe in which God maximises the realisation of the value of creatures as co-creators. This is the occurring good that God justifiably upholds though it involves permitting E1 and E2. This contender for a good that God would not give up by intervening to prevent E1 and E2, is further supported for Christians by the narrative of this God not intervening to prevent E3, the violent execution of the innocent Jesus of Nazareth, the divine Son incarnate. Jesus' resurrection from the dead is argued to be part of God realising the divine purpose for the whole creation. As discussed in section 5 above, this leads us to expect the dead fawn to be raised from the dead and an indication of how we might understand this raising of the dead fawn is given in section 4, p.19. I believe my account of the kind of universe we should expect God to create, and which God justifiably upholds in existence, can be included 'as among *the goods we know of*' according to Rowe's account of *the goods we know of*. This contradicts Rowe's Q: no good at all justifies an omnipotent, omniscient, perfectly good being

---

64. This is the name given to the child in E2.
65. Rowe, 'The Evidential Argument—A Second Look', 264
66. If P is false, it means God exists and we know of a good that justifies God in permitting E1 and E2. To show that P is false I must show that God exists, which I have made clear is not part of the argument in this book. I have, however, indicated that I argue *to* God in Ames (2022), (2019) and (2018).

in permitting E1 and E2; therefore, not-G: there is no omnipotent, omniscient, perfectly good being.

As noted, Rowe is clear that a direct attack of the kind I am proposing on (1) cannot succeed.[67] For the same reasons Rowe would conclude a direct attack on P cannot succeed. I believe that the Christian tradition in which I stand (as set out above, especially Chapter II, sections 2, 3 and 4b., allows me to voice a view of the kind of universe we should expect God to create, and there with the value to God of all creatures with their own real powers as co-creators in a life-producing universe, as the better type of creation, while the purpose for which all is created by God, is to draw all creatures into a loving and just relationship with God, while the means used to enable the realisation of this purpose includes the suffering of God incarnate in Jesus of Nazareth. We should prefer to affirm of God this type of created universe, as the better type of creation, with this value to God, sustained in existence for this purpose, to be realised by these means. This is that greater good which God justifiably upholds as the better type of creation, though it entails the suffering and painful death of many living creatures, which God does not prevent because it would be the lesser good.

This conclusion brings us near to MJ Murray's[68] three conditions (A), (B), and (C) for a morally sufficient reason for permitting an evil, introduced in Chapter I, footnnte 7. I would like to see how it might apply not only to a discussion of Rowe's Evidential argument, but to my solution to the logical problem of natural evil, in Chapters II, III, and IV.

I first state Murray's conditions and restate them (italics) for this present context. For reasons set out in Chapter II, instead of Murray considering some being permitting an evil for the sake of some greater good, I refer to God permitting the known suffering and death in creating our life-producing universe, and possibly worse suffering and death due to natural processes still operating, but with so far unknown consequences, for example the accelerating rate of expansion of the universe.

---

67. Rowe, 'IX. The Problem of Evil and Some Varieties of Atheism', 338, 339.
68. MJ Murray, *An Introduction to the Philosophy of Religion* (Cambridge: Cambridge University Press, 2008).

(A) The Necessity Condition: the good secured by the permission of the evil, E, could not have been secured without permitting either E or some other evils morally equivalent to or worse than E.

(A′) *The Necessary Condition: the good of the better type of creation is secured by the permission of the suffering and death of living things due to natural processes in our life-producing universe, could not be secured without permitting this suffering and death due to known natural processes or, even due to previously unknown natural processes created by God.*

Drawing on my discussion of Rowe's evidential argument, our life-producing universe is of the better type of creation, which God created for a purpose without which any created universe would be a lesser good, which God would not prefer.

(B) The Outweighing Condition: the good secured by the permission of evil is sufficiently outweighing.

(B′) *The Outweighing Condition: the good secured by the permission of the suffering and death in the better type of creation is sufficiently outweighing.*

The 'outweighing' is not understood as the outcome of a survey of all the values/disvalues that occur within a life-producing universe. It refers to a judgement that the life-producing universe is more in accord with the goodness of God than any type of creation that is not life-producing. But notice Murray sets the condition as 'sufficiently outweighing.' The force of 'sufficiently' is to rule out the case 'where the amount or severity of the evil that must be permitted is so great that the benefits of the greater good are simply too meagre.'[69] In the argument I have pursued could it be that the benefits or the good of the better type of creation are insufficient, or meagre compared to the severity of the suffering and death involved in the better type of creation? Of course, we need to ask insufficient compared to what? The answer is internal to this discussion. The good that is opened to the whole of this better type of creation is the purpose of God in creating the actual universe. This is for the whole creation to be drawn into a loving and just relation with God, in which the superlative goodness of God leads us to expect inexhaustible good of which there is none

---

69. Murray, *An Introduction to the Philosophy of Religion*, 14–16.

greater. For Christians this view is supported by Scripture, for example, Romans 8:18, Philippians 3:7–11, and the exchange between the father and his son in Luke 15:21–24.[70]

(C) The Rights Condition: it is within the rights of the one permitting evil to permit it.

(C/) *The Rights Condition: it is within the rights of the omni-God to sustain in existence the better type of creation which the actual universe is.*

The idea of God having rights to permit or withhold may seem obvious to some and despotic to others. In the light of the superlative goodness of God, God justifiably holds in existence the better type of creation.

I have been exploring the application of Murray's three conditions for some being having a morally sufficient reason for permitting evil to our thinking of God as having a morally sufficient justification for permitting suffering and death even in the better type of creation. It seems the application can be carried through. The justification is not by subjecting God to some moral standard external to God. The justification is in terms of the superlative goodness of God which has informed the whole discussion.

7. JL Schellenberg—The new logical problem of evil[71]

Schellenberg makes three claims about God and one about evil.[72] The claims about God are,

---

70. Also relevant here is Marilyn M Adams, *Horrendous Evil and the Goodness of God* (Melbourne: Melbourne University Press, 1999). Adams clearly has natural evils in view, and these are distinguished but not separated from moral evils because however evils are brought about, Adams is interested in 'horrendous evils' which have a devastating impact on individual persons. Adams sees such evils as issuing a challenge to divine goodness, which approaches in analytic philosophy to the problem of evil do not address. Adams' account of the challenge and her 'solution' is distinctive, and she brings to the fore resources from medieval theology and philosophy and philosophy of religion. According to Adams (p.26), 'horrendous evils' are 'evils, the participation in which (that is, the doing or suffering of which) constitutes prima facie reason to doubt whether the participant's life could (given their inclusion in it) be a great good to him/her on the whole.'
71. JL Schellenberg in his chapter 'A New Logical Problem of Evil', in Daniel Howard-Snyder and Justin P McBrayer, editors, *The Blackwell Companion to the Problem of Evil* (West Sussex: John Wiley and Sons, 2013), Chapter. 3
72. Schellenberg, 'A New Logical Problem of Evil', 35–36.

Unsurpassable Greatness God is the greatest possible being. This is the concept of God as a *person* who is the greatest possible being. This is not saying that the concept of God is the concept of the greatest possible person.

Ontological Independence. No world created by God (or any part thereof) is part of God.

Prior purity. Prior to creation (whether 'prior' be taken logically or temporally) there is no evil in God of any kind.

The fourth claim is about evil, which, in accord with philosophical usage, 'evil' is taken to 'cover all suffering and any unpleasantness'.[73]

Evil. There is evil in the world.

I take the second claim about God to be consistent with, and so does not block, my theistic assumption that God freely creates the world *ex nihilo* for some purpose. On that view there is an absolute distinction between Creator and creation. Theists would say that the created world is ontologically dependent on God, meaning the existence of the created world depends on God sustaining it in existence at its inception and thereafter. The existence of God does not depend on the world. It follows that no world created by God (or any part thereof) is part of God.

From these three claims about God, Schellenberg argues we should expect God to create a world that progresses in embodying more and more good, reflecting the infinite goodness of God, a world without evil. Given the three claims about God and the argument that follows, Schellenberg concludes, 'there is no limit to the richness of value assimilable, without evil, by finite persons in pursuit of the infinite.'[74] This is contradicted by evil in the world.

---

73. Schellenberg, 'A New Logical Problem of Evil', 36.
74. Schellenberg, 'A New Logical Problem of Evil', 40. This is where I see the students' argument that God would create the world in its perfect end state to realise God's purpose in creation could be enhanced by Schellenberg's idea of God creating a world that progressively embodies more good reflecting God's infinite goodness.

Schellenberg says traditional theism regards the claims about God as necessary truths.[75] From these claims he proceeds[76] to develop premises leading to the central point[77] in his proof,

(9) If any world with goods permitting or requiring evil is exceeded by a world modelling the corresponding pure goods in God and the existence of greater worlds can limitlessly be ensured by God, then for any world X that requires or permits evil, there is some world Y that models pure goodness in God such that God has no good reason to create X rather than Y.

Combining (9) with other premises not summarised here, he obtains,

(11) If for any world X that requires or permits evil there is some world Y that models pure goodness in God such that God has no good reason to create X rather than Y, then God has no good reason to permit evil in the world.

From the premises he develops, Schellenberg concludes,

(14) There is no evil in the world.

Schellenberg meets my requirement by arguing from the claims about God to the kind of world we should expect God to create, namely a world without evil. Thus the claims about God are inconsistent with evil in the world and according to Schellenberg should be set aside.

Schellenberg further develops the proof by 'The Motives Approach' in which he considers the theist's answer to the question *why* God "would create and would create a world with finite persons."[78] Three motives standardly ascribed to God are considered.

> God it may be said, creates to share the good with finite beings. Or, more specifically, God may be said to create finite beings to enter into a relationship of love with them and to facilitate their love for each other. Somewhat differently, it may be said that God's creation amounts to an overflowing or diffusion of the good that is in God (the motive here would presumably be something like a desire to expand the range of the good for its own sake), or that God creates to display the glory of God.

---

75. Schellenberg, 'A New Logical Problem of Evil', 36.
76. Schellenberg, 'A New Logical Problem of Evil', 36–42.
77. Schellenberg, 'A New Logical Problem of Evil', 40.
78. Schellenberg, 'A New Logical Problem of Evil', 43

> [A]n inclusive disjunction referring to them all will necessarily be true. For either God creates for its own sake, or the sake of the created things or for God, or else God is motivated in all these ways.

The point is that if we say for example that God creates to share the good, what good are we talking about? Given the nature of God, it is good without evil. The same conclusion holds for the other motives ascribed to God. They yield the conclusion of a world without evil created by a wholly good God. Worthy of special treatment is the question whether 'a God intending to facilitate for finite persons relationships of love gives those persons an evil-permitting brand of libertarian free will?'[79]

The central point[80] of Schellenberg's answer draws on the assumption of the prior purity of God to clarify "how an evil-permitting free will cannot be part of any good that God is motivated to share with finite persons in creation, and how the love of deepest value is and must be possible even so—or, at least, why theists are committed to accepting these views." Further, "if God is loving before creation (perhaps in the context of something like a Trinity) the love of God must be a love operating without any possibility of the evils of rejection. How then could the thought of building that possibility into finite love even arise?" The last point is especially challenging—how ever could the thought of an evil-permitting possibility even arise in such a God?

Before giving my answer, let us hear the answers from theologians that Schellenberg rejects and his replies.[81] Firstly, "that God nonetheless might make the choice you are trying to put out of reach *just because it is thought more interesting*?" Secondly, "that a love that comes with radical freedom and therefore the possibility of rejection and other evil possibilities has its own distinctive excellence—one that Divine love lacks." Thirdly, responding to Plantinga (2004), drawing on Christian ideas of Incarnation and Atonement. "He wants to make use of what he calls the incomparable good of God coming close to us in our humanity and taking upon himself our sin. Such a happening obviously presupposes that there is evil. Thus, God can be found in possible worlds containing evil."

---

79. Schellenberg, 'A New Logical Problem of Evil', 43.
80. Schellenberg, 'A New Logical Problem of Evil', 44.
81. Schellenberg, 'A New Logical Problem of Evil', 45–46.

Schellenberg replies to the first by noting how it has God "reaching outside what is most great and interesting and rich, capable of being more deeply experienced and developed by finite beings unlimitedly. How could it be other than arbitrary and perverse, and thus significantly unGodlike, to do so?"[82] His reply to the second answer about love and radical freedom acknowledges that Divine love lacks the possibility of rejection but this "does not imply that reality should include this possibility." (If this implication followed it would mean a created world would instantiate evil and undermine his main conclusion. Schellenberg explains why the implication does not follow.) The good in God far exceeds the good of this excellence and following his (11) above "we should be thinking about how those higher goods could continually and ever more deeply be reflected in a world."[83] The deeper point Schellenberg makes is how prejudiced we may be in favour of familiar goods involving evil in some way, which impress us more than the impressive good modelled on God. Schellenberg thinks our prejudice for familiar goods applies to Plantinga's argument where the familiar goods have been made familiar by Christian theology. Schellenberg accepts that the Christian story of God's self-humbling and self-sacrifice can be told in a way that is properly called beautiful. But such must be compared with a beauty that can exist without any evil. "Presumably Plantinga himself, good Anselmian that he is, would concede that in the depths of the Divine, realised without evil, are goods too stunning for any human being to behold."[84] Entirely consistent with his argument Schellenberg says that these goods can be approached by finite persons in worlds entirely lacking evil. He emphasises that "in a world without evil, we could even imagine an event of Incarnation taking place, as the personal God displays the Divine love for finite persons and facilitates new ways of being bonded with them. The Felix Culpa approach therefore is too weak and too human—all too human—to perform the task required of it here."[85]

Schellenberg's question is how then could the thought of building that possibility of rejection into finite love even arise? My answer attends to his next sentence. "Notice also that, given Unsurpassable

---

82. Schellenberg, 'A New Logical Problem of Evil', 45.
83. Schellenberg, 'A New Logical Problem of Evil', 46.
84. Schellenberg, 'A New Logical Problem of Evil', 46.
85. Schellenberg, 'A New Logical Problem of Evil', 46.

Greatness, *God's* love for *finite creatures* must be unremitting and incapable of failure."[86] I accept this claim about God's unfailing love and so about God's goodness. Let us hold this thought together with the idea of God freely creating *ex nihilo* the world and everything in it, including human persons. Finite creatures all. Can we be sure that human persons' love must be unremitting and incapable of failure? I think not. Schellenberg holds that *given* God's Unsurpassable Greatness, God's love *must* be unremitting and incapable of failure. But no such *given* applies to finite creatures who love, that is persons, who in loving, we may say following Schellenberg's usage, "model" God's love. Logically, we cannot say that their love *must* be unremitting and without failure. This conclusion follows in virtue of their being finite creatures. Their loving is vulnerable to failing. It is a metaphysical vulnerability, which is not itself evil, but inherent in the good of finite created persons.

Given God's Unsurpassable Greatness, I see that God's love must be unremitting and unfailing. I am sure therefore that prior to creation God would certainly understand this logical point that any finite created persons, not being Unsurpassably Great, are vulnerable to failing to love. In this way we may understand how even the thought of the possibility of such a creaturely failure of love arises in the mind of the wholly good God prior to creation. Created persons would necessarily have a metaphysical vulnerability to failing to love in virtue of being God's finite creation. Would they still be good? I judge so because this vulnerability to failure provides no argument that created persons must fail in love only that there are no grounds for thinking their love must be unfailing. It is part of their being finite creatures and cannot be treated as evil, for I have taken evil to mean whatever contradicts God's goodness. A finite creature as such is good since it comes into being *ex nihilo* from a wholly good God. The creation of persons with a vulnerability to such failure is not itself a failure on God's part, but rather a consequence of created persons not being God! There is no need to think of God having to have a good reason to introduce evil into a created world. Any created world with finite persons must have this metaphysical vulnerability. It is unsurprising that, subsequent to creation in any world created by God that includes finite persons, their love might actually fail. The

---

86. Schellenberg, 'A New Logical Problem of Evil', 44.

actual failure to love falls within Schellenberg's above understanding of evil as covering "all suffering and any unpleasantness". It is therefore understandable that any such world could in this way include evil, which is to say a failure to love.

Let us pause to consider whether we should think of Schellenberg's God creating any world with creatures who were vulnerable to failing to love simply in virtue of their being finite creatures? I think so, because all the motives for God creating that Schellenberg presents still hold. Also, the idea of such a metaphysically vulnerable creation follows from Schellenberg's three claims about God in his argument, *and* his attributing God's unremitting and unfailing love to God's Unsurpassable Greatness. Any created world, X or Y, with this metaphysical vulnerability is good and models God's goodness. Furthermore, we can affirm Schellenberg's view that "given Prior Purity together with Unlimited Greatness there is no limit to the richness of value assimilable, without evil, by finite persons in pursuit of the infinite."[87] His point was that we do not need to invoke evil to enhance God's great love. But we have seen that vulnerability to the failure to love is part of the good creation, with no necessity yet no surprise that love actually fails. Is there any way we can think of the Unsurpassable Greatness of God enabling the overcoming of evil as part of finite persons pursuing the infinite?

Schellenberg unintentionally provides a clue in his thought that in a world without evil we could even imagine an event of Incarnation taking place, as the personal God displays the Divine love for finite persons and facilitates new ways of being bonded with them.[88] I note that Schellenberg's 'clue' aligns well with the position independently set out in Chapter IV, section 1b. as part of situating my theology of creation in the context of Christian tradition. That account of the Incarnation is in terms of God's eternal purpose in creation, where the Incarnation would have taken place even if there had been no sin. This contrasts with the Felix Culpa, 'O happy fault' tradition which explains the Incarnation as the remedy for human sin. Rather, in a world containing evil the eternal purpose of God for the whole creation realised in the Incarnation continued to be enacted under these adverse conditions.

---

87. Schellenberg, 'A New Logical Problem of Evil', 40.
88. Schellenberger, 'A New Logical Problem of Evil', 46.

This suggested alignment between Schellenberg's 'clue' and the Christian account of Incarnation, faces at least one question: does including a metaphysical vulnerability to failing to love for created persons represent a problem for thinking of an event of Incarnation? I think not and support this view by drawing on the traditional Christian understanding of the Incarnation as the union of two natures (divine and human) in one person.[89] This 'hypostatic' union ensures the human nature of the incarnate God is vulnerable yet invincible: invincible because not metaphysically vulnerable to failing to love; vulnerable to suffering and death because living unfailing love under the adverse conditions of human violence that could not bear such love. The human nature of God incarnate is truly human since according to the purpose of God in creation (see Chapter IV, section 1b., The divine economy), unfailing in love is included in the end for which human beings are created. In our world there are many examples of human persons failing to love. There is evil in our world. This does not contradict claims that this world is created by God, as God is understood in Schellenberg's argument. This is my answer to the new logical problem of evil.

Before concluding this discussion, I note Schellenberg's call for us to take care not to limit our idea of Divine goodness to the familiar ideas of the good in our account of God. Compared to these familiar goods, made familiar by Christianity, he wants to return our thinking to what may (by contrast) fairly be called the strange goodness of the Unsurpassable Greatness of God. This recalls the atheist student's point mentioned at the start of Chapter 1, about the strange goodness of God, but with this difference. For Schellenberg it serves an argument concluding that such a God does not exist. For the student it served to mark a condition for the remote possibility of God's existence, which he does not embrace. I return to this point now.

8. Conclusion—The strange goodness of God

At the start of Chapter I, I recalled an atheist student who said, 'Looking around the world, both the natural world and the human world, and remembering that people say this world was created by a perfectly

---

89. See the discussion of the Trinitarian Understanding of God, in Chapter IV, section 1b.

good God, I think it would have to be a very strange goodness.' A colleague cautioned with the comment, 'If it is too strange, we might not want to call it 'good'.' On the one hand I want to ask what is it, compared to which, the strange goodness of God would not be good? On the other hand, I want to explain how I am approaching the idea of the strange goodness of God and then draw on two examples from the overall argument.

The explanation is drawn from Luke 10:25-37. A lawyer asked Jesus, what he had to do to inherit eternal life. When Jesus asks what he reads in the law the lawyer cites the two great commandments: to love God with all your heart and to love your neighbour as yourself. Jesus commends him saying, 'do this and you will live.' So far this represents familiar goods. Then the lawyer asks, 'who is my neighbour?' Jesus tells the story of a Jew going down from Jerusalem to Jericho who was wounded by robbers and left lying on the side of the road. After two Jews walk past the wounded man a passing Samaritan stops to care for him. In the story, this is indeed a strange goodness because of the enmity between Jews and Samaritans. *Would we still want to call it good?* Yes, at least because according to the story the lawyer agrees it was the compassionate Samaritan who was neighbour to the wounded man, by showing him mercy. Also, the story of the good Samaritan has deeply influenced our culture's understanding of the good. What is it compared to which the claimed goodness of God in my arguments would possibly be so strange? It must be some familiar good with which the claimed goodness of God would be compared. Here are two examples taken from the overall argument.

I begin with a quote from Chapter I. "The point is pressed, 'If *you* had the knowledge and power to help someone in terrible need, you would of course help them. Not to do so could also be said to fail to follow God's second commandment to love your neighbour as yourself.' Students make the point that by not intervening in the myriad of situations of terrible pain and suffering God fails to lead by example, by not keeping God's own commandment." The point being made by students is that such natural processes are rightly said to be 'evil' because they can and do blindly undermine the 'good' of life through an overwhelming pain and suffering, or premature death, which we as moral agents would ordinarily try to prevent in order to preserve this good.

The first example is from the above quote. The familiar good is the good of life and therefore the good demonstrated by compassionate aid for suffering people and animals. The objection wants to know why God does not act in this way. To claim God is good in the face of divine inactivity is to either be mistaken or to invoke a very strange goodness, compared to this familiar good. But this is a mistaken comparison between the familiar good and the goodness of God presented here. Recall that making the natural evil claim requires those who affirm and those who deny the claim, to proceed *from* the idea of God who freely creates the world *ex nihilo* for some purpose, *to* the kind of world we should expect such a God to create. This is a different starting point from that of seeing some familiar instance of human or animal suffering that could be prevented or ameliorated and deciding to act accordingly.

Proceeding from this different starting point, the theology of creation claims that the idea of the goodness of God presses us to think of the value to God of creatures as co-creators, and that God would maximise the realisation of this value in a life-producing universe. It would have been fine if I claimed this showed us God's power and knowledge. But I claimed it showed the goodness of God and this was in effect a 'strange goodness' for many people because (i) the context in which the claim is made is not that of the familiar good and (ii) the context required the unfamiliar effort to think *from* the idea of the omni-God *to* the kind of world we should expect such a God to create. The claimed goodness of God inevitably seems a strange goodness. *But would we still want to call it good?* Yes, because by (i) and (ii), we understand the reason it was not called good is mistaken, and by the same we can see that it brings into view the large good of the whole creation ordered to being a life-producing universe, destined to enter a loving and just relationship with God.

The second example below will again point to the familiar good demonstrated by compassionate aid for suffering people and animals. Compared to this good, the objection denies that a wholly good God would really be so reckless, so uncaring of the consequences for pain and suffering for so many creatures by giving every created thing real power and maximising the operation of those powers. By comparison, the objection would say if this is good it is a very strange goodness. I agree and seek to turn the objection by noticing it is the good of a better type of creation with creatures as co-creators in a life-producing universe. And it would be deeply irrational for God to intervene to prevent the outworking of the powers God continuously sustains in operation for the sake of the better type of creation. Such intervention would also transform the universe into an inferior type of creation compared to the better type of creation, in which God creates a whole universe *ex nihilo*, in which even the smallest part has a contribution to make—no wall flowers—both on its own terms and as part of an inclusive, participatory, life-producing universe. Compared to the familiar good, a strange goodness of God is being claimed. *But is it too strange to call it good?*

One reason not to call it good would be if God thereby showed no compassion. In reply, God's compassion is affirmed but in a surprising, and therefore strange way. I appealed to the parable of the prodigal son, my second example, with the father's stunning gift of half the inheritance to the son who in effect wants him dead, and to the Genesis story of the gift to humankind of extraordinary power and freedom. Both responses identify the reckless, extreme, love of God. Here scripture is found to support the idea of God giving all created things their own real powers and maximising their operation. However, we explicitly approach the objection about 'God's lack of compassion' by saying this extreme, reckless love of God is shown in the incarnate divine Son willingly suffering crucifixion, by allowing these powers to be violently visited upon him, with related suffering for the Father and the Spirit, in order to keep open, the opening into the divine life the incarnation makes possible, against all opposition. God has the last word. In the theology presented above, this divine suffering in Christ is central to the Triune God realising the divine purpose for the whole creation. It is the place where God's costly compassion for the whole creation is revealed. It invites us to extend this thinking to God choosing to suffer with created things, intimately sustained in existence by God, as they suffer through all the processes of the life-producing universe, on the way to the fulfilment of the divine purpose for the whole creation. Compared to the good of familiar forms of compassion, this is an unexpected, surprising compassion. Here God does not intervene to address each suffering creature for the reasons explained above. Rather, God suffering in Christ ensures that the purpose for which all things are created will be fulfilled in the resurrected life-producing universe, wherein God will be all in all. This ensures there is no pointless suffering, even for the fawn that nevertheless suffers hideously in the forest fire. This is a strange goodness. *But would we still want to call it good?* Yes, because it affirms the good of compassion and even more the compassion of costly suffering for the sake of another, which we commonly recognise as a great good. It is strange because here it unexpectedly holds for the omni-God, the creator of the whole universe, who chooses to be so vulnerable, yet finally proves so invincible, for the good of all.

Finally, compared to familiar goods, the goodness of God is found to be a strange goodness. The strangeness is due to three shifts. One is the well-known effect of viewing some event or situation or individual person from our standpoint and then shifting to another standpoint. The second is discovering how different, how surprising, how strange is that other standpoint, showing us something otherwise hidden from our own view. The third is choosing to embrace the difference. Life offers many examples of these three shifts. In this discussion, the other standpoint has been elaborated in terms of the God revealed in Christ. The strangeness of this standpoint brings to light what is hidden from us. It also meets us in our being commanded to love our enemies, not just love those who love us; in our finding that God values most what we commonly value least; in realising that God is reckless and extreme love, so vulnerable but invincible, from which and for which this universe exists. This is the strange goodness of God who has created a world worth dying for.[90] Is it too strange to be called good or too good to be true? What if it is true? Earlier I said, 'Let us see.'

Though I don't know what you now see, the book remains an invitation to readers to revisit the decision about God and the problem of natural evil by drawing on the theme of the strange goodness of God.

---

90. I know I saw the idea of God creating a world worth dying for, but cannot recall and so cannot give due credit.

Appendix
Clarification of the Idea of God in the Problem of Natural Evil

The (1999, 2000) BBC TV series of the *Scarlet Pimpernel*, starred Richard Grant as Sir Percy Blakeney, alias the Pimpernel, and Elizabeth McGovern as Lady Blakeney. In one scene Lady Blakeney is talking with Robespierre who, having outlined certain political realities in France, asks, 'Lady Blakeney do you understand what I am saying?' Lady Blakeney replies, 'Sir, I even understand what you are not saying'. Robespierre is greatly amused. If you sometimes wonder if I understand what I am saying, I commend you. If you understand what I am not saying, I salute you! This is because I am attempting to speak about God.

Colleagues and many students present the problem of natural evil as a strong reason to reject the idea of God as the all-powerful, all-knowing, and all-good creator of the world.[1] For some this covers all ideas of God, so, unqualified atheism. For others this sets them thinking about alternative ideas of God rather than the omni-God. In this book I hope to show that the problem of natural evil turns out not to be reason for rejecting the latter idea of God, though some will think there are other reasons. Students think of this idea of God as

---

1. The more traditional terms speak of God as omnipotent, omniscient, and omnibenevolent, which I also refer to as the 'omni-God'. I have simply translated the 'omnis' as all-powerful, all-knowing, and all-good. In one lecture I spoke of God as the 'Triple A' God, which went down very well with students and colleagues as a current way of expressing the highest 'credit rating' for God. It naturally invites questions as to whether God has an economy and the answer on at least one understanding of God is, yes. See, S Ames, Being, Wellbeing and Globalisation', in P Price, editor, *A World United or a World Exploited? Christian Perspectives on Globalisation* (Adelaide: ATF Theology, 2013). I will usually refer to this understanding of God as the 'omni-God'.

'traditional', and in scholarly contexts it is known as 'classical theism'. Students carry little understanding of this classical idea of God. In this appendix, I begin to clarify and elaborate this idea of God and to do so partly by way of responding to other criticisms of this idea besides the problem of natural evil and partly by way of briefly acknowledging that there are alternative concepts of God.

This clarification will also serve to illuminate the idea of God that I use in responding to the problem of natural evil. It is entirely possible to avoid the problem of natural evil by invoking a different idea of God, for example by not saying God is all powerful. I will not be following that path. I aim to show that the problem can be addressed, and I believe resolved, using classical theism as elaborated in what follows, while retaining the key features of God as omniscient, omnipotent, and omnibenevolent. The focus on 'God' is appropriate because I will be arguing that those who press the problem of natural evil to deny the existence of this God do so by presupposing a theological task that they (almost) never perform, that is, giving an account of the kind of world they should expect such a God to create, which they believe is contradicted by many natural processes, that is, the natural evils of the actual world. In lectures I am asked if there are any circumstances in which I might give up my belief in God. I respond by saying that this would be the case if I thought there was not a good answer to the problem of natural evil.

1. Clarifying a high-profile and widespread confusion about the idea of God

The need to clarify the idea of God under discussion is not confined to proponents of the omni-God. It is also shown in Richard Dawkins' *The God Delusion* in which he criticises and rejects all the standard arguments for God from reason and personal experience as well as arguments from the Bible.[2] In Chapter 4 of his book, 'Why almost certainly there is no God', Dawkins proposes and rejects 'The God Hypothesis', which says that God is, 'a superhuman, supernatural intelligence who designed and created the universe and everything in it, including us'.[3] For Dawkins, this is a competing theory to be

---

2. R Dawkins, *The God Delusion* (London: Bantam Press, 2006), Chapter 3.
3. Dawkins, *The God Delusion*, 31. Note, in *The God Delusion*, 108, Dawkins does not use the argument from natural evil to oppose belief in God. This is because

tested like any scientific theory. As an alternative view, he proposes: 'any creative intelligence of sufficient complexity to design anything comes into existence only as the end product of an extended process of *gradual evolution*.'[4] Dawkins presents 'the central argument' of his book, what he considers 'a very serious argument against the existence of God, and one to which I have yet to hear a theologian give a convincing answer despite numerous opportunities and invitations to do so. Dan Dennett is cited as rightly describing it as "an unrebuttable refutation".[5]

Dawkins frames the discussion of his 'God Hypothesis' in the following way:

> One of the greatest challenges to human intellect, over the centuries, has been to explain how the complex, improbable appearance of design in the universe arises. The natural temptation is to attribute the appearance of design to actual design itself. In the case of man-made artifact such as a watch, the designer really was an intelligent engineer. It is tempting to apply the same logic to an eye or a wing, a spider or a person. The temptation is a false one, because the designer hypothesis immediately raises the larger problem of who designed the designer.[6]

Dawkins is not just concerned with defeating belief in a good God, but any idea of God. Dawkins has indicated his view on natural evils as follows. 'In a universe of blind physical forces and genetic replication, some people are going to get hurt, other people are going to get lucky, and you won't find any rhyme or reason in it, nor any justice. The universe we observe has precisely the properties we should expect if there is, at bottom, no design, no purpose, no evil, no good, nothing but blind pitiless indifference.' R Dawkins, *River Out of Eden* (London: Weidenfeld and Nicolson, 1995), 133.

4. Dawkins, *The God Delusion*, 31. This is Dawkins' 'scientific naturalism', which is a philosophical position concerning 'any creative intelligence'. Apart from the difficulties of Dawkins making his own 'God hypothesis' fit into this naturalism, I discuss more difficulties with this naturalism in Ames, S., 'The Rise and Consequences of Scientific Naturalism', *Anthropos in the Antipodes*, edited by Robyn Horner, Patrick McArdle, and David Kirchhoffer (Melbourne: Mosaic Books, 2013). See also Chapter II section 4a. Dawkins shows no sign of problems for his naturalism.

5. Dawkins, *The God Delusion*, 157–158

6. It is also a false move because, as many have commented, while design entails a designer, the appearances of design do not entail a designer, for the appearances may have been brought about by other means.

Dawkins continues,

> The whole problem we started out with was the problem of explaining statistical improbability. It is obviously no solution to postulate something even more improbable. We need a 'crane' not a 'skyhook', for only a crane can do the business of working up gradually and plausibly from simplicity to otherwise improbable complexity.[7]

Dawkins' objection to the idea of God as designer is that God must be very complex to be able to design a universe and so this is no explanation of complexity. Why does Dawkins think that God must be very complex? It is on the basis of his alternative to the God Hypothesis, that is, 'any creative intelligence of sufficient complexity to design anything comes into existence only as the end product of an extended process of gradual evolution'. If we assume Dawkins' alternative view and so require God to conform to this view, that a designer must be highly complex, then of course God emerges from the long process of cosmic evolution. On such a view God is no explanation of complexity. But on Dawkins' own 'God hypothesis', that God, who creates all things, cannot be made to fit within Dawkins' alternative view, which would have God emerging from a long evolutionary process. It is crucial to see this change in the understanding of God that Dawkins uses halfway through the argument! Recall the 'God Hypothesis': God is, 'a superhuman, supernatural intelligence who designed and created the universe and everything in it, including us.' If God creates all things, there is nothing that is prior to God that could independently explain God, much less create God.[8] So, it is illogical (given his 'God Hypothesis') to ask who designed/created God. Furthermore, if God is the supernatural creator *of* the universe,

---

7. Dawkins, *The God Delusion*, 158.
8. Lawrence Krauss is clear on this point where he says that if God is the cause of all causes, then there is no regress as to what caused God. Debunking the idea of God may still be done but on this idea of God, not by asking 'what created God?', not that Krauss believes in such a God. The problem for him is that there is not one shred of evidence for this idea of God. L Krauss, *A Universe from Nothing, Why There Is Something Rather than Nothing*, with an Afterword by Richard Dawkins (New York: Simon and Schuster, 2010), 172.

then God cannot be the product of a long evolutionary process *within the universe*.[9]

Finally, it is also worth noting that according to classical theism, God is simple rather than complex, as I will discuss below. Of course, Dawkins might have claimed that the 'God Hypothesis' is false because it fails for want of a good argument and is denied by the evidence of evolution. But that is quite different from claiming any appeal to the idea of God still must explain who designed God. This further demand for explanation is simply inadmissible given Dawkins' 'God Hypothesis'. To claim otherwise shows that Dawkins doesn't take seriously the implications of the idea of God (that he is proposing and criticizing) as an *alternative* to his naturalistic worldview that 'any' creative intelligence capable of designing must have evolved. Dawkins' argument uncritically assumes that God must fit within his *alternative* view, even though this is impossible by definition, based on his 'God Hypothesis'. It also shows his uncritical naturalism. Dawkins does not present an un-rebuttable refutation of his 'God Hypothesis'.

2. Alternative Concepts of God

There is a substantial literature on alternative concepts of God which I can only mention here.[10] Here 'alternative' means an alternative to

---

9. Such an idea of God was proposed by Samuel Alexander (1859–1938) a polymath who argued that space-time is at the bottom of an ontological hierarchy. Alexander argued that the label 'pantheism' cannot be applied to his system 'because the quality of deity doesn't belong to the whole world as if every part of that world was permeated with deity, "as it must be on strict pantheism"'. Alexander's position cannot be labelled 'pantheism', which says that the world is in God, yet God transcends the world. Thomas summarises, 'Alexander doesn't hold that God contains the universe, but is not exhausted by it. Rather, the universe contains God and is not exhausted by God.' See E Thomas, 'Samuel Alexander', *Stanford Encyclopaedia of Philosophy (first published Monday June 2, 2014; substantive revision Monday January 8, 2018; accessed 18 September 2018.) Finally, Alexander's God is not the God of Dawkins' 'God Hypothesis'.*

10. AA Buckareff, and Y Nagasawa, *Alternative Concepts of God, Essays on the Metaphysics of the Divine*, (Oxford: Oxford University Press, 2016). WJ Wilderman, 'Ground of Being Theologies', in P Clayton, editor *The Oxford Handbook of Religion and Science* (Oxford: Oxford University Press, 2008), 612–632. K Ward, *A Guide for the Perplexed* (London: One World Publication, 2013). ES Meltzer, editor, *Three Faiths—One God: A Jewish, Christian, Muslim Encounter* (London: MacMillan, 1989).

classical theism or its near neighbours.[11] I hope the contrasts that do appear in the discussion will help readers (who want to) be clearer about their own ideas of God, whether accepted, rejected, 'on hold' or in process.[12]

Pre-modern philosophical theology was dominated by two main ways of speaking of God.[13] The first is associated with the name of Plotinus, and is known as 'Neoplatonism', about which I will only say a little. The second is best represented by Aquinas (1225–1274 CE) and is known as 'classical theism'. Both traditions agree that God is that of which none greater can be conceived. Both traditions think of God as infinite, eternal,[14] and self-existent (uncaused, necessary existence), and that upon which the universe depends for its existence. The two traditions disagree in basic ways. In the first, the universe[15] is a necessary emanation of God. The infinite God includes, but is not exhausted by, all that exists. According to the second view, represented by Aquinas, the universe is the free creation of the infinite personal God. The universe of all created things depends on God for its existence but is not included within God. (Dawkins' 'God Hypothesis' is a tiny echo of one thread of classical theism.)

The first tradition is traced to Plotinus (204–270 CE), born in Egypt.[16] Plotinus considered himself as inheriting 600 years of

---

11. Two examples, Keith Ward, *Rational Theology and the Creativity of God* (Oxford: Blackwell, 1982); JW Richards, *The Untamed God: A Philosophical Exploration of Divine Perfection, Simplicity and Immutability* (Downers Grove Ill: InterVarsity Press, 2003).
12. A book that might well prove of interest to some readers is by Rowan Williams, *The Edge of Words, God and the Habits of Language* (London: Bloomsbury, 2014).
13. Keith Ward, *Rational Theology and the Creativity of God*, 1–3, and especially, 55–67.
14. See below for a discussion of the distinction between God as 'eternal', meaning timeless, or God as 'everlasting', from eternity to eternity in time.
15. Here 'universe' means 'all that exists' in whatever ways things exist. It does not depend on a particular cosmology, whether ancient or modern.
16. J Bussanich, 'Plotinus's Metaphysics of the One', in LP Gerson, *The Cambridge Companion to Plotinus* (Cambridge: Cambridge University Press, 1996); DJ O'Meara, 'The Hierarchical Ordering of Reality in Plotinus', Gerson, *The Cambridge Companion to Plotinus*. See also, LP Gerson, 'Plotinus', in Stanford Encyclopaedia of Philosophy, first published 2003, substantially revised 2018. E Moore, 'Plotinus', *International Encyclopedia of Philosophy*, a peer reviewed academic source. Both encyclopaedias accessed 15 January 2019. SH Nasr, *Religion and the Order of Nature* (New York: Oxford University Press, 1996), 90–93.

philosophical reflection on Plato. Plotinus expounded and defended Plato, while introducing his own innovations, known from the eighteenth century as 'Neoplatonism'. His major work *Enneads* was a compilation of his writings by his follower Porphyry (234–305 CE). Plotinus' metaphysics has three fundamental principles: the One (or the Good), Intellect, and Soul. God is the One, beyond being and non-being. From the One emanates the Intellect; from the Intellect emanates the Soul; from Soul emanates matter.[17] Jewish, Christian, and Islamic thought about God was influenced by Plotinus even while retaining the basic idea of a personal God as having freely created the universe *ex nihilo*, a mark of what is known as 'classical theism'.

Various scholars[18] have pointed out that with the rise of the new natural philosophy in the 15th fifteenth to seventeenth centuries, there was a shift in the understanding of God, departing from what had prevailed before. For many of them, this change in the idea of God is part of their explanation of the rise of modern atheism. According to Hyman, 'the modern God was a "thing" quite different from the premodern God. Indeed, to say that the modern God was a "thing" in many ways captures the distinction; for premodern theology, God was not a "thing" at all.'[19] For premodern theology, God was transcendent, the creator *of* the world. Following Aquinas, language about God could only be used 'analogically' not 'univocally' (one way of speaking both for ordinary things in our life and for God).

Our language is fitted to the realities of our world, but for Aquinas, God is a different reality. Analogy acknowledges some similarities along with many differences when speaking of God, who

---

17. Gerson *The Cambridge Companion to Plotinus*, section 2, paragraph 1. Here emanation that happens necessarily because the One exists necessarily. Later I explain why, according to Aquinas, we can say that God exists necessarily and yet freely creates the world *ex nihilo*.
18. A Funkenstein, *Theology and the Scientific Imagination: From the Middle Ages to the Seventeenth Century* (Princeton: Princeton University Press, 1986); W Placher, *The Domestication of Transcendence: How Modern Thinking about God Went Wrong* (Louisville, Ky: Westminster John Knox Press, 1996); MJ Buckley, *At the Origins of Modern Atheism* (New Haven: Yale University Press, 1987); MJ Buckley, *Denying and Disclosing God, The Ambiguous Progress of Modern Atheism* (New Haven: Yale University Press, 2004); G Hyman, *The Evolution of Atheism, The Politics of a Modern Movement* (New York: Cambridge University Press, 2015).
19. Hyman, *The Evolution of Atheism*, 37.

is the ontologically transcendent mystery. Within modernity, this use of analogy vis-á-vis God came to be lost. Moves within medieval theology[20] may have contributed to this change, but more powerful was the stunning new natural philosophy which privileged precise 'clear and distinct ideas',[21] including the language used to speak of God. This new philosophy eventually led to a change in how God was conceived, for example in understanding God's being and transcendence. 'If language is used univocally of God and of things in the world, it implies that God is, in some sense, closer to things in the world, indeed to such an extent that God becomes a "thing" himself.' To maintain the idea of God's transcendence, modern thinkers came to stress 'God's quantitative difference from worldly things'.[22] Funkenstein comments on the theological meaning of Newton's idea of space and time; 'from early on, Newton maintained that space and time are explicatory predicates of God's omnipresence and eternity'.[23] Compared to the infinite mystery articulated by Aquinas, God became 'domesticated'—a tame God,[24] an idol.

Criticism of this modern god and classical theism led to several sophisticated, influential twentieth century philosophical and theological currents, which is in one sense 'postmodern theology'. These include Paul Tillich's, 'ground of being' theology[25], and A.N. Whitehead's[26] 'process philosophy' which was taken up by C

---

20. Peter John Olivi (1248–1298) and Duns Scotus (1266–1308) supported nominalism and the univocity of language used of God and ordinary things.
21. Funkenstein, *Theology and the Scientific Imagination*, 38.
22. Hyman, *The Evolution of Atheism*, 38.
23. Funkenstein, *Theology and the Scientific Imagination*, 96.
24. Placher, *The Domestication of Transcendence*. These contrasting themes are also signalled in a work discussed below, JW Richards, *The Untamed God, A Philosophical Exploration of Divine Perfection, Simplicity and Immutability* (Illinois: Intervarsity Press, 2003).
25. P Tillich, *Systematic Theology*, Volume 1 (Chicago Il: Chicago University Press, 1951), 64; P Tillich, *The Courage to Be* (New Haven: Yale University Press, 1953), 774. See also, RM Price, *Ground of Being, Neglected Essays of Paul Tillich* (Mindvendor, 2015); WJ Wildman, 'Ground of Being Theologies', in P Clayton and Z Simpson, Z, editors, *The Oxford Handbook of Religion and Science* (Oxford, Oxford University Press, 2006).
26. AN Whitehead, *Process and Reality: An Essay in Cosmology: Gifford Lectures, 1927–1928* (New York: Cambridge University Press, 1929); PA Schlipp, editor, *The Philosophy of Alfred North Whitehead*, (Evanston, Illinois: Northwestern University Press, 1941). DR Griffin, *Whitehead's Radically Different Postmodern Philosophy: An Argument for its Contemporary Relevance* (Albany: State University of New York Press, 2007).

Hartshorne as 'process theology'.[27] Both of these movements have affinities with the thought of Plotinus in blurring the Creator/creature distinction. Introductions to other forms of postmodern theology are given by various collections of essays edited by Graham Ward,[28] JD Caputo and MJ Scanlon,[29] Kevin J Vanhoozer,[30] and JP Manourssakis.[31]

For me, the most serious postmodern critique of the idea of God, specifically the position of Thomas Aquinas, is that it reduces God to an idol. The critique draws on M. Heidegger's The *Onto-theological Constitution of Metaphysics,* written in 1957.[32] Jean Luc-Marion examines Heidegger's account of onto-theology which he summarises as follows;[33]

> Thus onto-theology is defined according to some extremely precise characteristics, without which we would remain unable to identify any philosophical thought as metaphysical: (a) the 'God' must be inscribed explicitly in the metaphysical domain, that is to allow itself to be determined by the historical determinations of being, in as much as it is entity, perhaps beginning with the concept of entity; (b) it must establish there a causal foundation. . . of all the common entities for which it is the reason; (c) to achieve this, it must always assume the function and perhaps even the name of *causa sui*, that is of supreme founding entity, because it was supremely founded by itself.

---

27. C Hartshorne, *A Natural Theology for Our Time* (La Salle, Illinois: Open Court, 1967); C Hartshorne, *Omnipotence and Other Theological Mistakes* (Albany: State University of New York, 1984).
28. G Ward, editor, *The Postmodern God, A Theological Reader* (Malden Mass: Blackwell Publisher, 1998).
29. JD Caputo, and MJ Scanlon, *God, the Gift and Postmodernism* (Bloomington: IN, Indiana University Press, 1999).
30. KJ Vanhoozer, editor, *The Cambridge Companion to Postmodern Theology* (Cambridge: Cambridge University Press, 2003).
31. JP Manourssakis, *After God, Richard Kearney and the Religious Turn in Continental Philosophy* (New York: Fordham University Press, 2006).
32. M Heidegger, *Identity and Difference*, (Chicago, Illinois: Chicago University Press, 2002), translated and with introduction by Joan Stambaugh. This is a different argument but connected to the 'modern God' above, shaped by the power of the new natural philosophy.
33. Jean Luc-Marion, *God Without Being*, translated by TA Carlson (London: University of Chicago Press, 2012), 205.

Marion proceeds to a careful analysis of Aquinas' understanding of God concluding that 'Thomistic thought without a doubt rejects the three features of onto-theologic constitution of metaphysics.'[34] Here are a few of the quotations from Aquinas that Marion presents to support this claim:

- Just as the substance of God is unknown, so it is for His *esse*.[35]
- God is known through our ignorance, inasmuch as this is to know God, that we know that we do not know what He is.[36]
- With the exception of a revelation of grace we do not, in this life, know about God what he is, and therefore that we are united to him as unknown.[37]

Marion makes the point that, Aquinas does not describe God as self-caused:

> 'The foundation for entities and for their being (*esse commune*) in God depends without doubt on causality, but it has nothing that is reciprocal, so that being certainly does not ground (conceptually) God, whose *actus essendi* [act of being] escapes all concepts, that an act determines being in Him. . . . God denies for himself the metaphysical figure of self-foundation, for which *causa sui* designates the paradigm.'[38]

Finally, I note Marion's point that Aquinas' successors inverted Aquinas' radical theoretical decision that God does not belong to metaphysics.[39]

3. Classical Theism—A Common Core of Beliefs

3a. Historical Threads

Disagreements among Christians about their beliefs concerning God, Christ, the world, and moral questions are well known. What is not so well known is that for most of the 2,000 years of Church

---

34. Marion, *God Without Being*, 233.
35. *De Potentia*, question 7, answer 2, ad 1.
36. *In librum De divinis Nominibus* VII, 4.
37. *Summa Theologiae* Ia, q.12, a.13, ad 1.
38. Marion, *God Without Being*, 233.
39. Marion, *God Without Being*, 208.

history there has been agreement about some core ideas of God, often called 'classical theism', running from the early church fathers, to Augustine (fifth century), Anselm (eleventh century), Thomas Aquinas (thirteenth century), and to the Reformation[40] scholastics (seventeenth century), up to the present. 'Properly abstracted, this classical theism is also common among other religions of the book, namely Judaism and Islam.'[41] W. Stoeger synthesises insights about God by late Medieval Jewish, Christian, and Muslim scholars such as Maimonides (1135–1204), Aquinas (1225–1274), Averroes (1126–1198), and Avicenna (980–1037). God is understood to be the supremely perfect, free, transcendent, and sovereign creator, who freely creates the world and on whom the world depends for its existence.[42]

Aquinas' discussion of God's existence and attributes in his *Summa Theologica* is widely taken as the standard account of classical theism.[43] While a great deal is said about God, it is worth recalling that according to Aquinas we can know *that* God exists, but we cannot know *what* God is.[44] Aquinas agrees with Anselm's idea of God as that

---

40. The 'Reformation' here refers to the Protestant Reformation of the sixteenth century, a wholesale change in the European religious landscape precipitated by Martin Luther (1483–1546). Diverse groups were involved, amounting to several reformations. 'These included the Reformed Churches following John Calvin (1509–1564), the Anglicans, the Anabaptists, and other radical reformers. However, Luther and Calvin were the two leading architects of the Reformation.' Two of the key teachings of these Reformers were that salvation comes by faith alone (*sole fide*) as a gift of the sovereign God and that the plain sense of the Bible was a source of truth over tradition, reason, and experience. GB Ferngren, *Science and Religion, A Historical Introduction* (Baltimore: Johns Hopkins University Press, 2002), 118.
41. JW Richards, *The Untamed God*, 24. See also W Stoeger, 'God, physics and the Big Bang', in P Harrison, editor *The Cambridge Companion to Science and Religion* (Cambridge: Cambridge University Press, 2010), 180ff. See also the papers in DB Burrell, C Cogliati, JM Soskice, and WR Stoeger, editors, *Creation and the God of Abraham* (Cambridge: Cambridge University Press, 2010). See especially, DB Hart, *The Experience of God, Being, Consciousness, Bliss* (New Haven: Yale University Press, 2013), Chapter 3.
42. Lonergan derives twenty-six attributes of God from the idea of God as the unrestricted act of understanding that understands everything about everything. B Lonergan, *Insight, A Study of Human Understanding* (London: Darton Longman and Todd, 1958), 657–669.
43. Richards *The Untamed God*, 26.
44. A distinction first introduced by Plotinus with respect to The One.

which none greater can be conceived.[45] He disagrees with Anselm who tried to prove God's existence from the idea of God, known as the 'ontological argument', which is still debated today. Aquinas thought that the existence of God is not self-evident to us, as shown in his 'five proofs' from different aspects of the world, by drawing on three of the four Aristotelian causes: formal, efficient, and final. Aquinas also sets out the attributes of God individually: simplicity, perfection, goodness, infinity, omnipresence, immutability, eternity, and unity.

On Aquinas' view of God, creation is not a temporal event about when the universe began, but a relationship of ultimate dependence for the creation's existence.[46] It follows that the creator is always sustaining or conserving all that is in existence. An analogy would be the music we hear being sustained by musicians, but only so long as they are playing.[47] How long the musicians have been or will be playing is not an issue. Creation is *ex nihilo*, meaning 'out of nothing'. This is a way of saying that in creating, God is not working with pre-existing matter to *manufacture* a world. God is the 'primary cause', the necessary condition for all that exists. God is not the sufficient cause for all that happens, for what happens is due to the operation of 'secondary causes', things created with their own real God-given powers. Stoeger remarks that on this view, God is 'not a micro-manager.'[48]

With this view, wherever anything exists and functions, God is present, sustaining it in existence with its own real functioning powers. God is distinct but not remote from anything or anyone. God is said to be immanent. But the idea of divine immanence does not collapse the distinction between Creator and created. God remains transcendent, the uncreated, necessarily existing Creator of all that exists contingently. It is a mistake to think of God as remote simply based on having some understanding that created reality is different from but analogous to the uncreated reality of God.

---

45. Note, this does not say that God is that which none greater *in fact* exists, but that than which none greater can be *conceived*.
46. Stoeger, 'God, physics and the Big Bang', 181. This is setting out the meaning of '*creatio ex nihilo*' not the mechanics of how God creates *ex nihilo*.
47. Neil Ormerod, *Grace & Disgrace: A Theology of Self-Esteem, Society, and History* (Newtown: NSW: EJ Dwyer, 1992), 49–50.
48. Stoeger, 'God, physics and the Big Bang', 182. This is setting out the meaning of *creation ex nihilo*, not how it is accomplished.

The distinction between primary and secondary causes is the basis for Krauss' earlier reference to God as the 'cause of all causes'. God is the primary cause, creating a world of secondary causes. The natural sciences study the world of secondary causes and so offer explanations of what happens in the natural world by appealing to specific law-like causes, either in the form of classical laws, where physical states follow necessarily from prior physical states or statistical laws telling of the frequency of events.

In this sense they answer a question as to why something happened, which can be properly treated as a 'how' question.[49] If, however, the 'why' question, is 'why is there anything at all?', or, 'why does the whole universe exist, and why is it endowed with the order that it manifests?'[50], then scientific explanations are logically unable to answer because scientific explanations assume the existence of what is doing the explaining, whereas the question asks why what is doing the explaining exists and has the properties it does. Stoeger thinks of theological and scientific questions and answers as complementary rather than competing.

Possible responses to these ultimate 'why' questions may be to deny the questions are legitimate[51] or to turn the question against itself—'why ask 'why?'" and thereby invalidate metaphysics[52], or to say we don't know, or that the universe just is, a 'brute fact' without

---

49. As a boy in high school recently fascinated with physics, I was one evening helping my mother Rose wash up after the evening meal. She asked, 'why is that cupboard door open?' The cupboard was above the kitchen sink. My answer was, 'well Mother, the sum of the forces acting on it are keeping it there.' This earned me a clip across the ears. My mother was asking a purposive 'why' question whereas I gave a recently learned scientific answer as to how come the cupboard door was open. Rose had never studied physics but was adept at dealing with smart alecs, as was shown later in her working life as an independent trade union official! This was a case of inappropriately treating a 'why' question as a 'how' question.
50. Stoeger, 'God, physics and the Big Bang', 181.
51. See the exchange between Lord Bertrand Russell and Father Copleston, broadcast in 1948 on the Third Programme of the BBC. Transcript reprinted in Bertrand Russell, *Why I Am Not A Christian* (London: Allen &Unwin, 1957), 155. Cited in Davies, *The Goldilocks Enigma*, 295.
52. Jean-Luc Marion, 'Metaphysics and Phenomenology: A Summary for Theologians', in G Ward, editor, *The Post Modern God, A Theological Reader* (Oxford: Blackwell, 1997), 285.

explanation[53], perhaps ultimately a universe in a multiverse[54], or that it was created by God. Depending on one's idea of 'God' you may ask, 'what created God?' and keep on asking, leading to an infinite regress. However, as already noted, if your idea of God is that God is the 'cause of all causes' the regress is blocked.

I should make clear that all of this and more that Aquinas said about God was based on ordinary human reasoning. This was followed by yet more he said about God based on the revelation of God in Christ and the testimony to this in the Bible as curated by the church and its creeds. This is especially the understanding of God as Trinity—Father, Son, and Holy Spirit.[55] This 'two-steps' approach has been the near universal one among Christian theologians until the Protestant theologian Karl Barth[56] and Catholic theologian Karl Rahner[57] in the twentieth century initiated a revival of Trinitarian thinking and this as the place to *begin* Christian theology without any preceding 'first step' of philosophy or natural theology.[58] For Christians, this Triune God is *the* pre-modern understanding of God that was articulated in the fourth and fifth centuries in the creeds coming from the Councils of Nicaea (325), Constantinople (381), and Chalcedon (450).[59]

This mention of the understanding of the Triune God in Christian history and theology will remain in the background at this stage of my

---

53. See the preceding footnote. Also see 'The Absurd Universe', P Davies, *The Goldilocks Enigma, Why is the Universe Just Right for Life?* (London: Allen Lane, 2006), 295.
54. GF Lewis, and, LA Barnes, *A Fortunate Universe, Life in a Finely Tuned Cosmos* (Cambridge: Cambridge University Press, 2016); P Davies, *The Goldilocks Enigma*.
55. ST 1, q. 27.
56. Karl Barth, *Church Dogmatics*, Volume 1, G Bromiley, and T Torrance, editors (London: T&T Clark, 2009).
57. K Rahner, *The Trinity* (The Crossroad Publishing Company, 1970).
58. A helpful introduction to Barth's theology is C Gunton, 'Becoming and Being', *The Doctrine of God in Charles Hartshorne and Karl Barth* (London: SCM Press, 2001). There are many excellent books on the Trinity. To those already mentioned, I add Catherine La Cugna, *God for Us, The Trinity and Christian Life*, (San Francisco: Harper, 1993); K Giles, *The Trinity and subordinationism: The Doctrine of God and the Contemporary Gender Debate* (Downers Grove Illinois: InterVarsity Press, 2002); PA Rolnick, *Person, Grace and God* (Grand Rapids: Eerdmans, 2007)
59. A good introduction to these councils is, M Edwards, *Catholicity and Heresy in the Early Church* (London: Routledge, 2009).

exposition of classical theism. One reason is that in this appendix I am mainly wanting to clarify the idea of God that atheist students and colleagues bring to the problem of natural evil. I prefer to proceed to the point where this discussion of the problem on natural evil calls for the distinctively Christian[60] understanding of God to be introduced into the *argument* from this starting point in philosophy or natural theology. Recall that Chapter III starts from the idea of the omni-God who creates the universe *ex nihilo* for some purpose. It is the discussion of divine purpose that leads to the expectation of God revealing God to creatures capable of receiving this revelation and inviting them into a loving and just relationship with God. Of course, the revelation of God is expected to inform and so transform the understanding of God as the omni-God, operative in the discussion up to that point.

3b. More on Motivation

What motivates this idea of God and what kind of support has been offered for it? As noted, one motivation is seeking an explanation of why there is anything at all. This is one of several 'big questions' familiar to most people at some point in their lives. We can usefully compare the different responses of two eminent theologians Richard Swinburne[61], and Keith Ward.[62] Swinburne identifies three different types of explanations: the complete, the ultimate, and the absolute. Firstly, a 'complete explanation' appealing to the existence of God, with a reference to God's intentions and abilities which might necessitate the existence of a universe like ours. Secondly, Swinburne considers an 'ultimate explanation' which he defines as a 'complete explanation' with the additional point that the ultimate terms of the explanation cannot themselves be explained at all. Rather, they are 'ultimate brute facts'.[63]

---

60. Both Jews and Muslims think Christians have gone astray in their trinitarian thinking which they believe is about three gods, rather than the belief in one God. Christians will respectfully differ having worked their way through a long debate (First Councils of Nicaea, 325) about a similar rejection of the Trinitarian account of God by Arius (265–336 CE) a Christian priest from Libya, who attracted wide support in the Church. See Chapter II, 4(b).
61. R Swinburne, *The Existence of God* (Oxford: Oxford University Press, 1979).
62. K Ward, *Rational Theology and the Creativity of God* (Oxford: Blackwell, 1982).
63. Swinburne, *The Existence of God*, 75.

Ward doesn't follow Swinburne here because such explanations would always come to an end with 'ultimate brute facts' claimed about God, for which ultimately there is no explanation. Ward agrees that God, understood as the 'ultimate brute fact', differs from the universe, which is capable of further explanation in terms of God's purpose. But Swinburne's idea of God is not Ward's and so it will help to see what is driving Ward's argument. It is driven by the demand for the rational intelligibility of the world to be satisfied. Ward explains this demand,

> As one reflects on the nature of the world, one seeks general rational principles which can explain why it is as it is. This search for general explanation is a deep-propensity of the human mind; man, as a rational being, is by nature oriented toward a quest for intelligibility. The search may be successful or not; but the orientation itself is not inferred from any other basic principle. The supposition is something we have to presuppose to get any explanation in the first place. It has the status of an ultimate postulate or conjecture, though of course repeated success in discovering explanations will increase our confidence in it.[64]

This 'ultimate postulate' is not something inferred from experience, but rather it is a supposition that gets inquiry going.[65] Ward rules out 'ultimate brute facts' as a form of explanation that contradicts human inquiry's supposition of the intelligibility of the world. Ward says the question from which we must begin is this: 'what would it be like for the world to be fully intelligible?' What sort of object would satisfy this demand? Ward argues that 'one would have to conceive of a being whose sheer nature explains its existence, as well as the existence of everything else. Seeing what it is, one would see that it must be as it is and could not be otherwise.'[66]

---

64. Ward, *Rational Theology*, 4. This philosophical approach to theology starts with a 'turn to the subject', the inquiring human subject, rather than starting from the features of the natural world. For a helpful introduction to this change see, Elizabeth Johnson, *Quest for the Living God, Mapping Frontiers in the Theology of God* (New York: Continuum, 2007), 25–38. The same direction of thought presented by Ward, only on a much larger scale, is Karl Rahner's, *Foundations of Christian Faith* (New York: Seabury, 1978), and the work of Bernard Lonergan (see below).
65. Ward, *Rational Theology*, 4, points out that this is what Popper calls a metaphysical conjecture, see K Popper, *The Logic of Scientific Discovery* (London: Hutchinson, 1959), 438.
66. Ward, *Rational Theology*, 6.

This is an example of what Swinburne calls an 'absolute explanation'[67] in which its ultimate terms are not 'brute facts' and are not further explainable in other yet more ultimate terms. Rather, according to Ward, they are self-explanatory or logically necessary. Swinburne rejects such an 'absolute explanation' for two reasons. One is that the idea of a self-explanatory being is incoherent or vacuous. The other is that the logically necessary cannot explain the logically contingent. A logically necessary being cannot explain a contingent world.[68]

Ward agrees that 'the idea of a self-explanatory being is not something we can comprehend but his point is that God as self-explanatory is not incomprehensible to himself. Being self-explanatory, however, does not entail that anyone else can understand the explanation, only that it exists.' Furthermore, he thinks the idea is not vacuous since he can identify some of the properties of such a being. Nor does he think the idea is self-contradictory.[69]

Regarding the second problem, Ward entirely agrees that the necessary cannot entail the contingent, however he considers that a common mistake among theologians is to think of God 'as either necessary in all respects or contingent in all respects—just the ultimate contingent fact.' Ward argues that we can have necessity and contingency in God.[70] He sums up his view, 'so, I think the notion of a self-explanatory being is coherent, is the most complete form of explanation and is the only adequate foundation of the intelligibility of the universe.'[71] Recall that for Ward, the 'intelligibility of the universe' means the universe is 'fully intelligible', which he claims as the supposition driving human inquiry and the driver of his position. This is not simply the same motivation as asking, 'why is there anything at all?' Rather, it appeals to the practice of human inquiry daily manifested in a myriad of ways and brings to light what Ward takes as a presupposition of inquiry, 'the universe is fully intelligible'.

---

67. Ward, *Rational Theology*, 76.
68. Ward, *Rational Theology*, 76.
69. Ward, *Rational Theology*, 8. On the nature of God, Ward says, 'seeing what it is, one would see that it must be as it is and could not be otherwise.' Thus, the idea of God as *causa sui* (self-caused) is to be set aside as self-contradictory.
70. Ward, *Rational Theology*, 8. I will discuss this in the next section dealing with some of the criticisms of this idea of God, where I will introduce the idea of the divine will. This is a point of difference to the idea of necessary emanations from God, of Intellect, Soul, Matter.
71. Ward, *Rational Theology*, 8.

A fuller story of human inquiry is told by Lonergan which allows him to argue that 'the real is completely intelligible'.[72] In the flow of experience we engage in three cognitive acts: being attentive to experience, being intelligent by seeking understanding of experience through the questions we ask, being critically intelligent by asking whether the understanding is true or probably so. A fourth cognitive act is making decisions in the light of what is judged to be a true understanding.[73] We engage in these acts often without noticing what we are doing. We carry out these actions because of the imperatives at the foundation of our consciousness: be attentive, be intelligent, be rational, be responsible.[74] Lonergan says human beings have a detached, disinterested, unrestricted desire to know.[75]

The evidence for these claims is the continuing eruption of the different kinds of questions we ask, an eruption that cannot finally be suppressed either by the emotional and other attachments within inquirers, or the religious and secular interests of societies and institutions in which they live. Furthermore, whatever the immanent content of our knowing, we can always ask if there is anything beyond. This reveals the intention of the desire to know is without restriction. Lonergan's point is that the objective of this desire to know is being, 'what there is'.[76] On this view of our cognitive operations, any affirmation of what there is entails that what is affirmed is intelligible.[77]

---

72. B Lonergan, 'The General Character of the Natural Theology of Insight', in *Collected Works of Bernard Lonergan*, Volume 17, edited by RC Crocken and RM Doran (Toronto: University of Toronto Press, 2004), 3-9. B Lonergan, *Insight, A Study of Human Understanding* (New York: Philosophical Library, 1970), 636-638. B Lonergan, 'Cognitional Structures', *Collection*, edited by FE Crowe (New York: Herderand Herder, 1967). A helpful introduction to Lonergan is provided by JF Haught, *Is Nature Enough? Meaning and Truth in the Age of Science* (Cambridge: Cambridge University Press, 2006), 32-54.
73. Well summarised in Haught, *Is Nature Enough?*, 33; see also 'Cognitional Structures', Lonergan, 'Cognitional Structures'.
74. B Lonergan, 'The Dialectic of Authority', *A Third Collection of Papers by Bernard J.F. Lonergan*, edited by FE Crowe (New York: Paulist Press, 1985), 7.
75. Lonergan, 'Cognitional Structures', 636.
76. Lonergan, 'Cognitional Structures', 227-231. This is a second order definition of being as the objective of this unrestricted desire to know enacted through the cognitive operations. Having this desire does not mean we have its objective! Haught, *Is Nature Enough?*, 42f, identifies five fields of meaning through which 'the [unrestricted] desire to know must travel if it is to encounter the rich texture of the world's being. These avenues: are affectivity, intersubjectivity, narrativity, beauty, and theory.'
77. Neither Lonergan nor Ward are saying human beings have grasped the full intelligibility of all there is. Such a full understanding of everything about everything belongs to God. Ward, mindful of the chequered career of metaphysics,

Kraus admits the idea of God as the cause of all causes blocks an infinite regress of explanations, but he says there is no evidence to support it.[78] What kind of evidence might support such a view of God? Ward supports this idea of God as the self-explanatory being by appealing to the supposition of human inquiry that reality is fully intelligible, and 'so the most one can do is show the coherence of such an object, to draw consequences from its posited existence and to ask whether these square with the world of one's experience.'[79] This is one kind of support for this idea of God.[80]

---

is sceptical of our arriving at a final systematic truth about the ultimate nature of things. This is not to abandon reason, but rather leads Ward not to neglect other considerations deeply rooted in human nature that a rationalist model is too systematic to fit reality as we experience it—evil, freedom, creative purpose, love, faith, and the dilemmas of choice. (Ward, *Rational Theology and the Creativity of God*, 69). Lonergan in, *Insight, A Study of Human Understanding*, has a richer idea of 'intelligibility'—for example, see his account of the patterns of experience in the subjective field of common sense: the biological, aesthetic, intellectual, and dramatic patterns of experience (181–206); see also his account of individual, group, and general human bias (218–244).

78. L Krauss, *A Universe from Nothing, Why There Is Something Rather Than Nothing* (New York: Free Press, 2012), 173.
79. Ward, *Rational Theology and the Creativity of God*, 5. This is very close to P. Medawar's discussion of the limits of science, which include critical comments on metaphysics that ask fundamental 'why' questions. The answers can be a fraud or like anxious children asking their mothers 'why' questions, receive palliative answers. See P Medway, *The Limits of Science* (Oxford: Oxford University Press, 1985), 91, 92. Also, to be noticed is his point that, 'metaphysics is not nonsense, and it is not bunk, for it can be and has been the source of scientific inspiration and of fruitful scientific ideas' (Medway, *The Limits of Science* 90). That being so, it is possible that such fruitful scientific ideas could be tested empirically, and if positive results followed this, would support (not prove) the metaphysics. This would be a form of 'abductive inference'. W Stoeger (2010, p. 185) proposes such an approach as offering a way to test multi-universe ideas, where direct testing is not possible.
80. A fuller discussion is provided by Lonergan, *Insight*, Chapter XIX on General Transcendent Knowledge where he discusses the idea of God and the affirmation of God. Lonergan presents the idea of God as unrestricted understanding and works out the implication of that claim in twenty-five considerations (657–666). There follows (669–677) the affirmation of God in which Lonergan claims 'the existence of God is known as the conclusion of an argument and, while such arguments are many, all of them, I believe, are included in the following form. If the real is completely intelligible, God exists. But the real is completely intelligible. Therefore, God exists.' Lonergan then discusses the minor and major premises of this argument. This argument is unknown to Krauss and different from the argument used by Ward. For my arguments *to* God, see S Ames 'From Physics to Metaphysics, A New Way', *Christian Perspectives on Science and Technology, New Series*, Volume

Ward sees the supposition as having strength even for someone like Steven Weinberg[81] who has no interest in a theological position. Weinberg would prefer scientific explanations not to stop at the ultimate initial state of the universe. 'We would prefer a greater sense of logical inevitability in the theory.'[82] In a later work, Ward comments that some physicists 'are unhappy with this ultimate non-rationality and have sought some sense of quasi-logical necessity which would dissolve away the last recess of arbitrariness.'[83] In support of this claim about 'some physicists', he cites Steven Weinberg's just stated preference. In Ward's view this is to 'resort to the principle of sufficient reason, which would make all things the necessary implications of some initial state which is itself necessarily existent.'[84] Ward comments that while this approach eliminates arbitrariness from the universe, 'it also seems to reduce the phenomena of freedom and creativity, of value realisation to relative insignificance.' This criticism of Weinberg's view is similar to one standard criticism of the traditional idea of God already noted: how can God existing necessarily create a contingent world? For Ward, however, a 'main advantage of introducing the concept of God according to which we can think of necessity and contingency in God, is that it enables the aspects of necessity and creativity to be held together in a coherent, non-arbitrary, and non-deterministic form of explanation.'[85] I return to this point below.

4. Clarifications in the light of Criticisms

The traditional idea of God as that than which none greater can be conceived, represented in Christian tradition by Anselm and elaborated

---

1, (2022): 46–71; S Ames, 'The Value Given and Presupposed in Person-Centered Dementia Care', *OBM Geriatrics*, 3/3 (2019) doi:10.21926/obm.geriatr.1903068.

81. Steven Weinberg is an American theoretical physicist and Nobel laureate in Physics (1979) for his contributions with Abdus Salam and Sheldon Glashow to the unification of the weak force and electromagnetic interaction between elementary particles.

82. S Weinberg, *The First Three Minutes* (New York: Basic Books, 1977), 17.

83. K Ward, 'God as a Principle of Cosmological Explanation', in RJ Russell, N Murphy, and CJ Isham, *Quantum Cosmology and The Laws of Nature, Scientific Perspectives on Divine Action* (Vatican City State: Vatican Observatory Publications and Berkeley California, The Centre for Theology and the Natural Sciences, 2nd edition, 1999), 255.

84. Ward, 'God as a Principle of Cosmological Explanation', 255.

85. Ward, 'God as a Principle of Cosmological Explanation', 255, 256.

by many others, has continued to attract critical discussion. The dust has not settled on these discussions. This section gives an indication of some of the 'dust' in motion! There is no claim to be comprehensive.

One set of criticisms argues for various forms of *philosophical incoherence* of this idea of God.[86] Another line of criticism is that the traditional idea of God is *too one-sided*, for example the emphasis on the transcendence of God, totally other than the world. According to this criticism, we need a dialectical approach to speaking about the transcendence *and* immanence of God. Here are two more examples of alleged 'one-sidedness'; the idea of the necessary existence of God, making impossible the freedom of God in creation; and the idea that God is immutable and so is unaffected by the world He has created and thus, the idea that God cannot suffer. The criticism is that this 'dialectical' approach applies to all that is traditionally said about God, leading to a less inadequate understanding of God and speech about God.[87] A third type of criticism is based on there being *evil in the world*. In this book, I am especially concerned with the problem of natural evil and pursue this criticism in Chapters II, III and IV.

4a. Philosophical incoherence

Y Nagasawa[88] classifies the many distinct arguments against Anselm's idea of God (which is effectively a version of classical theism) into three types. One is that each of the three 'omni' attributes are inconsistent in itself, the second is that the three 'omni' attributes are an incoherent set and the third is that there is an inconsistency between the three divine attributes and some contingent actual fact — in particular, evil in the world. Here we look at the first two arguments against Anselm's idea of God.

On the first type of criticism, consider divine 'omnipotence'. Is God able to create a stone that is too heavy for God to lift or is God unable to create such a stone? Either way, God is not omnipotent. The second type of criticism is that the three attributes represent an incoherent

---

86. For references to the many examples of these criticisms, see Y Nagasawa, 'A New Defence of Anselmian Theism', in *The Philosophical Quarterly*, 58/233 (2008): 580–581.
87. J Macquarrie, *In Search of Deity, An Essay in Dialectical Theism* (London: SCM Press, 1984).
88. Y Nagasawa, 'A New Defence of Anselmian Theism', in *The Philosophical Quarterly*, 58/233 (2008): 577–596.

set. For example, consider God's omnipotence and omnibenevolence. If God is omnibenevolent then is God not able to sin? If so, God is not omnipotent. There are many of these criticisms which supporters of 'Anselmian' or 'classical theism' rebut and so the exchanges escalate to refined technical debates. Here is how B Leftow presents Anselm's response to the supposed tension between God's omnibenevolence and God's omnipotence:

> A perfect being desires to do no wrong. If so, any ability to do wrong would be one to fail to do what it wants and do something it does not want to do. But one fails to do what one wants . . . by a simple lack of power, by lack of appropriate knowledge, by being in a circumstance that forces one to act against one's desires, and so on. So, given what a perfect being can be presumed to want, ability to do evil would be or rest on some deeper inability.[89]

For Anselm, being able to sin is understood to be due to a lack of power. However, being unable to sin is not a contradiction of being omnipotent. Another criticism of the incoherence of divine omnipotence and divine omnibenevolence is from Process Theology, the claim that since God has almighty power, God must be a tyrant. Process Theology, therefore, denies that divine power is omnipotent. Power, even unlimited power, however, does not logically entail a tyrannous use of power.[90]

Nagasawa offers a way to counter all objections by arguing for philosophical incoherence. First, he distinguishes between Anselm's basic idea of God and how that idea was elaborated. Nagasawa presents the following ideas:

> *Anselmian Thesis*: God is that than which none greater can be conceived."

Its elaboration is the following,

---

89. Following B Leftow, 'Anselm's Perfect-Being Theology' in B Davies, and B Leftow, editors, *The Cambridge Companion to Anselm*, (Cambridge: Cambridge University Press, 2004), 150.
90. See Adams' critique of process theologian D Griffin on this point in MM Adams, *Horrendous Evils and The Goodness of God* (Carlton: Melbourne University Press, 1999), 74–75.

Anselmian OmniGod Thesis: God is omniscient, omnipotent, omnibenevolent.[91]

It is usually assumed that if you hold to the first you are necessarily committed to the second. He sets out what he finds is the common structure to the 'incoherence' criticisms.[92]

1. If Anselmian theism is true, then the Anselmian thesis is true.
2. If Anselmian theism is true, then the omniGod thesis is true.
3. If the omniGod thesis is true, then God is an omnipotent perfect being.
4. There cannot be an omniperfect being.
5. Therefore, the omniGod thesis is false.
6. Therefore, the Anselmian thesis is false.
7. Therefore, Anselmian theism is false.

This is a valid argument and so undermining (7) requires at least one of the premises to be set aside. Nagasawa's point is that an array of arguments aiming to establish (4) may in turn be criticised. In a fitting Anselmian move, his aim is to provide one argument that disarms all the criticisms. He points out that proponents and opponents, without argument, assume (2) that the Anselmian thesis entails the omniGod thesis. He knows of 'no compelling philosophical argument to support the entailment' and 'the entailment lacks support from the religious canon. The Bible... no-where says that God is omnipotent.'[93] Nagasawa replaces the omni-God thesis with the following thesis:

The MaximalGod Thesis: God is the being that has the maximal consistent set of knowledge, power and benevolence.

Nagasawa considers and rebuts several objections to his proposal. He concludes that supporters of the *Anselmian Thesis* 'should be open to the possibility that God is not an omniscient, omnipotent, omnibenevolent being.'[94] He concludes that one might still wonder about evil in the actual world. 'However, formulating the argument

---

91. Nagasawa, 'A New Defence of Anselmian Theism', 577.
92. Nagasawa, 'A New Defence of Anselmian Theism', 585.
93. Nagasawa, 'A New Defence of Anselmian Theism', 586. But see Genesis 18:14 and Jeremiah 32:27 — both ask whether there is anything too wonderful or too powerful for God and expect a negative answer.
94. Nagasawa, 'A New Defence of Anselmian Theism', 591.

from evil ... by referring to a non-omniperfect God [not omnipotent and not omnibenevolent] is significantly more difficult than formulating such an argument by referring to an omni-perfect God.'[95]

For some readers this may resolve the problem of natural evil, in so far as it depends on God being the *Anselmian Omni-God*. Others will be left wondering about God and evil in the world, as Nagasawa noted. I will continue the discussion assuming the *Anselmian Thesis* articulated by the *Anselmian Omni-God* thesis. I am not (yet) embracing the *Maximal God* as I believe it is possible to answer some of the criticisms of the 'omni-God' including a resolution of the problem of natural evil. Were I led to embrace the *Maximal God* thesis, I am confident that much of what I offer by way of solution to the problem of natural evil would still be of value.

4b. Is God complex or simple?

I return to Richard Dawkins' claim that if God is able to design the universe, God must be very complex and God must therefore have been 'designed' by a long, slow, evolutionary climb up Mount Improbable. God must have emerged from the universe. As noted, this follows from Dawkins clearly stated evolutionary naturalism. In lectures, students have been surprised and sceptical of the claim that theological tradition says that God is simple. Initially, their preference has been (remarkably) to take Dawkins as an authority in theology as well as biology, and so an authority on how to understand God. On the other hand, Aquinas made 'simplicity' the first of God's attributes or perfections, from which the others can be derived.[96]

According to Richards, Christian theology has given several different senses to the idea of 'simplicity',[97] of which I mention three. One sense is that all divine properties are possessed by the same self-identical God. 'In this sense simplicity is more or less synonymous with God's unity and expresses the monotheistic conviction common to Judaism, Christianity and Islam.'[98]

---

95. Nagasawa, 'A New Defence of Anselmian Theism', 596.
96. Richards, *The Untamed God*, 213.
97. Richards, *The Untamed God*, 217.
98. Richards, *The Untamed God*, 218. For Christians, 'monotheism' and 'simplicity' have a trinitarian form.

Another sense of 'simplicity' is that God is not composite in the sense that God is not made-up of elements, properties, or parts more fundamental than God and God has no external causes, such as Platonic Forms. Were these ideas not excluded, they would contradict the idea that God is uncaused, meaning that God does not depend on anything external to God. Richards points out 'this seems to be the main reason why Aquinas insists that we cannot predicate properties to God and creatures in the same way (univocally) but only analogically.'[99]

A third sense of 'simplicity' draws on the distinction: Socrates' existence is essential *to* him, but his existence as such is contingent. Moreover, there could have been humans, that is, human nature or essence could have been instantiated, even if Socrates had never existed. In God's case there is no such distinction. . . We cannot get daylight between God's essence and existence as we can with finite creatures.[100]

In Aquinas' understanding, God does not have any nature or essence distinct from His act of existing for if a thing has an essence distinct from its being, it must have an existential cause which sustains it in existence. But God, as the Uncaused First Cause, cannot have a cause, and therefore His nature must be identical with His existence. God's nature is to be 'subsistent being itself.' Therefore, in contrast to finite creatures God is simple.

R Spitzer has an extensive discussion of divine simplicity. He helpfully begins with the idea of simplicity: 'the simpler a reality is, the fewer intrinsic and/or extrinsic boundaries it has.' He clarifies this idea with some examples. One is that the boundaries of a square exclude the boundaries of a circle so that one cannot have a 'square-circle' of the same area in the same respect at the same place and time, and this holds irrespective of the substance in which they inhere. As the creator of all, God is the unique unconditioned reality that fulfils the conditions for existence of all conditioned realities. Therefore, nothing that exists can be excluded from the unconditioned reality of God and we must therefore say that God is absolutely simple.[101]

---

99. Richards, *The Untamed God*, 214. See also, E Stump, and N Kretzmann, 'Absolute Simplicity', in *Faith and Philosophy*, 2/4, (1985): 353.
100. Richards, *The Untamed God*, 222.
101. This discussion is a mere snippet of the discussion in RJ Spitzer, *New Proofs for the Existence of God: Contributions of Contemporary Physics and Philosophy* (Grand Rapids, MI: Eerdmans, 2010), Chapter 3, 'A Metaphysical Argument for God's Existence'.

4c. Criticisms of God existing necessarily

One question is whether there is one or are many necessary existents. A second criticism focuses on the incoherence of the idea of God existing necessarily, yet supposedly freely creating a contingent universe.

Are there many necessary existents?

The question is discussed in some detail by RJ Spitzer[102] who shows there can only be one necessary existent. Spitzer summarises his argument by appealing to Aquinas as follows,

> [I]t has been shown that God is absolutely perfect, lacking no perfection. If, then, there are many gods, there must be many such perfect beings. But this is impossible. For, if none of these perfect beings lack some perfection, and does not have any mixture of imperfection, which is demanded for absolutely perfect being, nothing will be given in which to distinguish the perfect beings from one another. It is impossible, therefore, that there are many gods.[103]

Necessary divinity and contingent creation. Is this incoherent?

Here is Paul Davies'[104] criticism of the idea of God as a necessary being:

> Christians, like all monotheists, believe in *one* God. So, they need to show not only that God exists necessarily, but that this being is necessarily unique—otherwise there could be countless necessary beings making countless universes. Even if this can be all sorted out, we are still confronted with the problem that, in spite of God's necessary existence and nature, God did not necessarily create the universe as it is, but instead merely *chose* to do so. But now the alarm bells ring. Can a necessary being act in a manner that is not necessary? Does that make sense? On the face of it, it doesn't. If God is

---

102. Spitzer, *New Proofs for the Existence of God*, 132–134.
103. Spitzer, *New Proofs for the Existence of God*, 135; from Aquinas, *Summa Contra Gentiles*, Book One, Ch 42, paragraph 3.
104. P Davies, *The Goldilocks Enigma, Why is the Universe Just Right for Life?* (London: Allen and Lane, 2006), 231.

necessarily as God is, then God's choices are necessarily as they are, and the freedom of choice evaporates. Nevertheless, there is a long history of attempts to get around this obstacle and to reconcile a necessary God with a contingent universe.

I regard this issue as a major point needing clarification. Broadly, many authors who value human freedom want a way to hold together necessity and contingency in God. Options include dismissing classical theism because it cannot hold these together[105] and proposing a different idea of God[106], or developing the idea of the omni-God from classical theism to enable holding together necessity and contingency in God,[107] or pursuing a critical reading of Aquinas to show how this may be done.[108] In this already long appendix, I will pursue the last option.

Let's return to Augustine's question as to what God was doing before creation. His answer was that God was not doing anything before creation for God created space and time and everything else in one act. There was no 'before' creation. On this view, God must exist completely outside of time. God creates the whole of time from beginning to end. The whole is created by God 'in one and the same act'. It follows that 'when it is 1000 CE, God does not have to wait to see what is going to happen in 1001 CE. God created 1001 at the same moment as 1000. In fact, God makes every time at the same time—or, technically in the same non-temporal act . . . It is as if God sees the whole of time spread out in one "timeless present".'[109]

Thus, God apprehends each successive temporal event in the eternal now. As such all contingent events are fully known by God

---

105. As with Davies above.
106. For very different examples see Whitehead, *Process and Reality*, Hartshorne, *Omnipotence and Other Theological Mistakes,* and Jean Luc-Marion, *God Without Being.*
107. I have two examples, Richards (*The Untamed God*), Ward (*Rational Theology and the Creativity of God*, 1999, 2010). It is worth noting that in the last chapter of his 1982, Ward provides an extended account how he holds together necessity and contingency in God. While criticising Ward on this point Davies makes no reference to Ward's last chapter.
108. P Laughlin, 'Divine Necessity and Created Contingence in Aquinas', in *The Heythrop Journal,* (2009): 653.
109. K Ward, *God, A Guide for the Perplexed* (London: One World Publication pbk 2013), 134.

because God sees them all at once. God sees the whole of time and space in this world and any other worlds God has possibly created. We are invited to understand that wherever we are in our world with its temporal flow and the choices we make, is all before God in one 'timeless present'. If, for example, our choices had been different, then God's knowledge of them would be different as well. On this account God is thought to be 'eternal' rather than 'everlasting'.

This view of God's relation to created time is relevant to seeing how many from Augustine to Aquinas could coherently hold that creaturely contingency is a real possibility even with the necessity of divine existence, and of the unchanging character of divine knowledge. So far, we have considered 'if there are contingents, does God's knowledge of them deny their ability to be contingent?'.[110] It does not, but this set up of the problem still assumes that the necessary God can create contingents. Let's examine this assumption which seems to many to be self-contradictory.

A key point is what kind of 'necessity' is meant when God is said to be necessary. For example, did Aquinas intend 'logical necessity' when he spoke of God being necessary? If so, this would mean anything that followed from God would follow necessarily. There would be no possibility for contingent creation, creation would have to flow or emanate necessarily from God. If Aquinas did mean logical necessity, then the denial of the existence of God would involve a logical contradiction, rather like denying that the sum of all angles in a triangle is the sum of two right angles. But this denial cannot be what Aquinas intended. Laughlin points out that for Aquinas, the mark of contingency is transience or temporal finitude. By contrast, God's necessary being does not have a beginning or end in time, nor does God change or undergo change. God, according to this account, must be thought of as 'eternal' rather than 'everlasting'. Furthermore, one reason for positing a necessary God as opposed to a contingent God is the requirement to explain the existence of contingents. The opposition between divine necessity and contingent creation assumes that:

> For any contingent event C, the fact which explains it cannot be a necessary fact otherwise C would not be contingent.[111]

---

110. Laughlin, 'Divine Necessity and Created Contingence in Aquinas', 653.
111. Laughlin, 'Divine Necessity and Created Contingence in Aquinas', 654.

The problem we are discussing comes from assuming that if God is the first and necessary cause, then what follows from that cause will itself be necessary. From a necessary cause there can be no contingent proximate causes and *ipso facto* there are no contingencies. The assumption is that whatever comes from or is brought about by a necessary being proceeds necessarily (so Neoplatonism).

This assumption is not a problem for Aquinas who argues that creation is not logically necessary since the proposition 'God does not create' does not by itself entail a contradiction. (This would follow if divine necessity were thought to be logical necessity.) 'Indeed, creation is not required by some ineluctable logic or by the nature of deity so that God could not have willed not to create.' Rather, if it is open to God to choose between creating and not creating, having created then it is no longer open to God not to create. 'Whatever God wills in the act of willing cannot be changed but God's will remains free to choose what it is that God will in fact will. The acts of God's will are conditionally necessary, not absolutely necessary.'[112] Aquinas concludes, 'from the divine will, therefore, an absolute necessity cannot be inferred. But only this excludes contingency.'[113]

Since God existing necessarily is not a logical necessity, there is no logical contradiction in assuming it is open to God to choose to create contingents. But why make that assumption about God? There are several answers. One is Anselm's thesis about God, as that than which none greater can be conceived *and* the thought that compared to an idea of God without freedom there is a greater idea of God as having freedom. Admittedly, this depends on valuing human freedom as far better than lacking freedom and this valuing is supported by acknowledging that for human love to be truly love it must be freely given and received. A second answer is that attempts to give a complete account (explanation) of human persons in terms of impersonal factors (philosophically or scientifically) fail[114] and

---

112. Laughlin, 'Divine Necessity and Created Contingence in Aquinas', 654.
113. Laughlin, 'Divine Necessity and Created Contingence in Aquinas', 655; Aquinas, *Summa Contra Gentiles*, 1.85.
114. See the critiques of scientific naturalism in Cunningham, Connor, 'Naturalizing Naturalism: Materialism's Ghosts', *Darwin's Pious Ideas: Why the Ultra-Darwinists and the Creationists Both Get it Wrong*, (Grand Rapids, MI: Eerdmans, 2010), 265–369. J Haught, *Is Nature Enough?* (Cambridge University Press: Cambridge, 2006). S Ames 'The Rise and Consequences of Scientific

similarly, Buckley's critique of the use of the early modern natural philosophy making an inference from impersonal facts about the natural world to a personal God.[115] A similar failure holds for attempts to account for human persons from an idea of God as impersonal and as existing necessarily.[116] A third answer is that this explanatory failure would undermine the role of God's necessary existence as explaining contingent existence. Finally, the Hebrew Bible, the Christian Bible, and the Quran for Muslims, testify to God's agency as fundamentally personal, that is acting (analogously) by thought and will.

There remain many questions for clarification, some of which can be answered. Two that can be answered will be addressed later: what kind of world should we expect the omni-God to create? and since God creates freely, why would God create any universe? We will see what answers are provided by drawing on Aquinas.

What does it mean to say that God exists necessarily if the necessity is not 'logical necessity'? It at least means it is impossible for God not to exist. This is not the same as saying God is 'a brute fact', that God just is. Because of the aim of explaining the full intelligibility of the universe presupposed in human inquiry, we need to think of a fundamental reality that is self-explanatory and the explanation of the existence of everything else. Yet, because 'everything else' includes human beings with the capacity for free creative acts, we need to think of that fundamental reality as not only necessary but also freely creating the world. How might it be possible to hold together necessity and freedom in God? I take this up in the next section.

4d. Is God immutable?

Classical theism holds that God is the omnipotent, omniscient, omnibenevolent creator, who creates and sustains in existence all there is, *ex nihilo*. Many ideas about God are said to follow from this

---

Naturalism', in *Anthropos in the Antipodes*, Robyn Horner, Patrick McArdle, and David Kirchhoffer, editors (Melbourne: Mosaic Books, 2013). I stress that a critique of the philosophy of scientific naturalism is not a critique of the natural sciences.

115. M Buckley, 'A Dialectical Pattern in the Emergence of Atheism' in, *Denying and Disclosing God, the Ambiguous Progress of Modern Atheism* (Yale University Press: New Haven, 2004), 36–37.

116. See Ward (1999).

understanding of God, such as perfection and immutability, which entails God does not change. Christian tradition had drawn support for this idea of God from the Bible. Exodus 3:14, 'I am who I am'; Numbers 23:19, 'God is not man that he should lie, or a son of man that he should repent'; Malachi 3.6, 'For I the Lord do not change'; James 1.17, 'Every generous act of giving, every perfect gift, is from above, coming down from the Father of lights, with whom there is no variation or shadow due to change;' Hebrews 13.8, 'Jesus Christ is the same yesterday, today and forever'; Revelation 1:4, 'Grace to you and peace from him who is and who was and who is to come.'

After quoting Malachi and noting that God is pure Act with no potentiality to be actualised, Aquinas says, 'it is impossible for God to be in any way changeable.'[117] We can see this idea of God as immutable also deriving from the idea that God is perfect and divine simplicity—any change would suggest a composition of potentiality to change with some actuality. Any change would be a lessening of God. I now discuss three questions arising from classical theism's idea of God as immutable. One question is whether God is eternal rather than everlasting? Another is whether God as immutable is static rather than dynamic? A third asks whether God can suffer (typically referred to as God being 'passable' and its denial as God being 'impassable')

Is God 'eternal' or 'everlasting'?

The idea of God as 'eternal' is that God is beyond time, beyond the temporal sequence of past, present and future. The idea of God as 'everlasting' is that God is of infinite duration in time in both directions — God is from 'everlasting to everlasting'. The 'God is eternal' view has been criticised as a mistake made by the vast majority of theologians in the West and the East.[118] Clearly, classical theism holds to the idea of God as 'eternal' rather than as 'everlasting'. But is it a mistake? The answer, either way, is contested and the literature is immense. I will consider three criticisms of the idea of God as eternal.

The first criticism affirms what it takes to be the plain meaning of the Bible, including those texts just cited, to uphold the idea of God

---

117. ST 1 Q. 9. A1. Richards (2003), p. 196.
118. For example, J Hoffman, and GS Rosenkrantz, *The Divine Attributes* (Oxford: Blackwell, 2002), Chapter.5. See also RT Mullens, *The End of the Timeless God* (Oxford: Oxford University Press, 2016), Chapter 3.

as everlasting.[119] After surveying the Biblical data on divine eternity, A. Padgett concludes 'the Bible knows nothing of a timeless divine eternity in the traditional sense.'[120] W.L. Craig thinks this is too swift as a conclusion as there are indications of the timeless eternity in passages such as Genesis 1 and Proverbs 8:22-23[121] and such New Testament texts[122] as Jude 25, 'to the only God, our Saviour through Jesus Christ our Lord, be glory, majesty, dominion, and authority, *before all time* and *now* and *forever.*' (Emphasis added.) 2 Timothy 1.9 says 'God's purpose and grace, which were given to us in Christ Jesus before age-long time but now manifested by the appearing of our Saviour Christ Jesus.' In 1 Corinthians 2.7, Paul speaks of a secret, hidden wisdom of God 'which God decreed before the ages for our glorification.' Such expressions are in line with the Septuagint, which describes God as 'the one who exists before the ages' (LXX Ps 54.20 [Ps 55.19]). These and other passages speak of the beginning of time but says Craig, 'since God did not begin to exist at the moment of creation, it therefore followed that He existed "before" the beginning of time. God, at least "before" creation, must therefore be atemporal.'[123]

Craig thinks the Biblical evidence is not clear, and that we seem forced to conclude with Barr that 'if such a thing as a Christian doctrine of time has to be developed, the work of discussing it and developing it must belong not to biblical but to philosophical theology.'[124]

---

119. Mullens, *The End of the Timeless*, 199–204; O Cullman, *Christ and Time* (London: SCM Press, 1962).
120. AG Padgett, *God, Eternity and the Nature of Time* (New York: St. Martin's, 1992), p. 33.
121. WL Craig, *God, Time and Eternity: The Coherence of Theism II—Eternity* (Dordrecht, Springer Netherlands: 2001), 5. See also P Copan, and WL Craig, *Creation out of Nothing, A Biblical, Philosophical and Scientific Exploration* (Grand Rapids MI: Blackwell's Academic, 2004), Chapter. 1. For an alternative view of the Biblical tradition concerning God from process theology see DR Griffin, *God, Power and Evil, A Process Theodicy* (Louisville: John Knox Press, 2004), 31 –37.
122. Craig, *God, Time and Eternity*, 6–7.
123. Craig, *God, Time and Eternity*, 7.
124. J Barr, *Biblical Words for Time* (London: SCM Press, 1962), 149. I am inclined to agree with Barr but require the working out to also refer to the natural sciences. My inclination is informed by a possible parallel provided by the 'Galileo Affair' (see later) which showed that after all it was not possible to use a collection of explicit Biblical texts, to settle the view that the earth was fixed at the centre of the universe with the Sun, the moon, seven planets and the fixed stars all moving around the earth. Both philosophy and the new natural sciences were needed to eventually arrive at the heliocentric universe.

Craig reviews fifteen arguments for the timelessness of God collected by Brian Leftow in *God and Eternity*[125] and concludes that only one of them is 'promising'.

> Drawing on Boethius's characterization of eternity as complete possession all at once of interminable life, Leftow[126] points out that a temporal being is unable to enjoy what is past or future for it. The past is gone forever, and the future is yet to come. The passage of time renders it impossible for any temporal being to possess all its life at once. Even God, if He is temporal, cannot reclaim the past. By contrast a timeless God lives all His life at once and suffers no loss. So, if God is the most perfect being, He is timeless. Here, I think we do have an argument for divine timelessness that is really promising.[127]

Craig's extended discussion of various themes to do with divine timelessness concludes that much depends on whether a tensed or tenseless theory of time is preferred. If the latter, Craig finds the idea of divine timelessness can go through.[128]

A second criticism of God as atemporally eternal comes from Hoffman and Rosencrantz who make the following argument[129]:

1. If God exists, then he performs actions.
2. Necessarily, any action is an event.
3. Necessarily, any event occurs in time.
4. Necessarily, if God's actions occur in time, then he is in time.

Therefore, if God exists, then he is in time.

The argument could as easily apply to a human agent. Thus, the argument assumes we can simply speak about God as we do about human agents. It assumes God is in time, as are human agents. If so, their conclusion follows immediately. Is the assumption correct or does the alternative of speaking of God as atemporally eternal still allow us to speak of God acting? In the next section I will argue for an affirmative answer.

---

125. B Leftow, *Time and Eternity* (Ithica, NY: Cornell University Press, 1991), Chapter 12.
126. Leftow, *Time and Eternity*, 278.
127. Craig, *God, Time and Eternity*, 32–33.
128. Craig, *God, Time and Eternity*, 133.
129. Hoffman and Rosencrantz, *The Divine Attributes*, 104,

We have been considering whether a God who exists necessarily can create contingently. An affirmative answer follows on the understanding that, if it is open to God to choose between creating and not creating, having created, then it is no longer open to God not to create. 'Whatever God wills in the act of willing cannot be changed but God's will remains free to choose what it is that God will in fact will. The acts of God's will are conditionally necessary not absolutely necessary.'[130] But as Aquinas argued only absolute necessity excludes contingency. Thus, we may think of the God who exists necessarily beyond all time, choosing to create a contingent world with its temporal order. It would be no small matter for this idea of God, which would include the eternal God electing to create a contingent world, which act of willing cannot be changed — by God. It would thus express the idea of the nature of God as including the God who creates contingently. Classical theism has resources to allow us to think of the immutable God, transcending all time, freely electing beyond all time to create the contingent universe.

Is God static or dynamic?

The standpoint of the eternal 'timeless present', beyond time, in which God sees all contingent events in time and space, is a standpoint only God can occupy. I can form a notion of that standpoint, but I cannot possibly understand God *from* that standpoint as if that standpoint was also mine or even available to me. It is not. If I try to imagine myself in relation to that standpoint, then God is at most an unchanging, unyielding, unavailable, incomprehensible silence. From the idea of God's eternal 'timeless present', many conclude that we must think of God as the static, ultimate reality.[131] I think this inference to God being static is mistaken.

---

130. Laughlin, 'Divine Necessity and Created Contingence in Aquinas', 654.
131. In one parish where I served as a priest, people told me that life was becoming too fast, with too much change (1973) and that there needed to be a still point, an unchanging point. They believed that God was that unchanging still point. I noticed a difference between the life of this parish and their homes with them getting on with life. Parish life was virtually unchanged since it was founded 20 years before. Further listening to people brought to light the role their idea of God contributed to this static form of parish life.

A rough analogy of the difficulty is provided by the following artist's view (Fig.1) of the 13.7-billion-year-old universe.[132] The standpoint assumed by the artist is not a standpoint anyone including the artist can occupy.

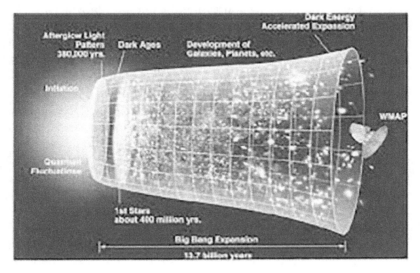

Fig. 1

Both us and the artist are somewhere inside the expanding universe, near its pictured 'open end'. Likewise, theologically, we stand within the created universe, which in all its detail and immensity, with all its dynamisms, is sustained in existence by God moment by moment in our past, present, and future. We are each the beneficiaries of God's action sustaining us in existence and opening us to our relationship with God. As mentioned earlier, another analogy to this idea of creation would be the music we hear being sustained by musicians, but only so long as they are playing. The whole universe would cease to exist if God were not sustaining it in existence. Now let us extend the analogy to us being among the 'notes' God as musician is playing or singing into existence. So close is God to each creature, albeit largely *incognito*.[133]

---

132. https://en.wikipedia.org/wiki/Big_Bang, accessed 27 January, 2020.
133. I say 'largely' because I think there are moments, in which we may become aware both of the sheer contingency of our existence as persons and the precious, unconditional worth of our existence. I recall such a moment a

As God creates contingently, so we may ask if God acts contingently in the world. Nothing in the understanding of God pursued here blocks the idea of God acting in the world. Drawing on the idea of the 'omni' God I have in Chapter III pursue one way into speaking about God acting in the world by addressing the question of why God has created this world, specifically asking about God's purpose in creating. From the idea of God that we are considering and, with more help from Aquinas, I will argue to what is the purpose of God in creation. This theological understanding of God and creation therefore places each of us, along with all created things, as standing before God, each in our own time and place, possible recipients of any action God may freely take. Though each is a speck of dust in a vast creation, yet to each God as creator is so close, albeit *incognito*. So, should we think of God acting in the world, and if so, is that action also *incognito* or does that action have witnesses, even recipients? The subsequent discussion of divine purpose in creation and of divine action to fulfil that purpose entails the idea of God acting in the world (see Chapter III). This is one way towards thinking of God as dynamic, not static.[134]

Many of the great religious traditions make claims about divine actions in the world; epiphanies, a call to some task, miracles, revelations, inspiring texts, mystical experience, guidance, bringing into existence a community, judgement against individuals and communities. Any claim that God acts in the world would need to

---

few weeks after the birth of my son. Holding this little 'bundle', I felt such an awareness both with respect to my son and myself, that I was awed at this gift of life. There are many testimonies to such experiences, in very different contexts. I regard the combined awareness of the contingency and of unconditional worth of our existence to be an intimation of God's presence and of life as a gift. I come to that understanding by taking seriously my experience of such worth and asking what kind of world would have a place for such worth. A world in which everything was conditioned by everything else would mean there was nothing unconditional. It would have to be a world in which there was something that transcends all conditions and that I am in some way in touch with that transcendent 'something' in the experience of unconditional worth just mentioned. I take such moments as a 'signal' of transcendence but the 'signal to noise' ratio in contemporary life is greatly in favour of noise via the 'weapons of mass distraction'. Such moments continue happening in our secular culture, but mostly without being recognised as intimations of God, for while many are aware of such moments, they are often already certain there is no God.

134. I have barely grazed the surface of the extensive discussion of divine timelessness and divine action. As one example of the complexity of discussions, see Craig, W.L. (2001).

be tested in some way, and for those immersed in a culture saturated by science and technology, a good example of that testing is the five volume series *Scientific Perspectives on Divine Action*.[135] Also, any claim for divine action in the world, especially made in a political context, needs to be tested lest God be misrepresented and people led astray.[136]

Does God suffer or is God beyond all suffering?

Much effort has been put into maintaining the view that God is impassable; that God does not suffer. The Christian gospel presents Jesus Christ as the divine Logos incarnate[137], the Son of the Father incarnate, whose life, death and resurrection brings salvation and the fulfilment of God's purpose in creation. Given Christians worship Christ crucified as God incarnate, theologian J. Moltmann asks why the idea of God being impassable took hold? Moltmann[138] suggest two reasons:

- It was his essential incapacity for suffering that distinguished God from man and other non-divine beings, all of whom are alike subjected to suffering as well as to transience and death.
- If God gives man salvation by giving him a share in his eternal life, then this salvation also confers immortality, non-transience and hence impassability too.

The options are either an essential incapacity for suffering or subjection to suffering leading to death, which cannot apply to God. Moltmann distinguishes between passive suffering to which one

---

135. See the magnificent five volume, series *Scientific Perspectives on Divine Action*, General Editor, Robert J Russell(Vatican City and The Centre for Theology and the Natural Sciences, Berkeley, California)
136. One example of such a claim is the powerful support from the Churches for the ANZAC invasion, in World War I, calling for the nation to support the war, for the British Empire and thus for God. Those involved in the actual experience of war came to a very different view. It seems the Churches supporting the war never recovered from the loss of credibility on their claims about the God of Empire. See, J Mose, 'Was there an ANZAC Theology?', *Colloquium*, 35/1 (2003): 3–13.
137. See John 1:1-14. This is one of many texts in the New Testament drawn into the sometimes-fierce debate within the first few centuries of the early church concerning the understanding of God, leading to the idea of the triune God set out by the Council of Nicaea (392), in what came to be known as the 'Nicene Creed'.
138. J Moltmann, *The Trinity and the Kingdom of God*, translated by M Kohl (London: SCM Press, 1981), 23.

is subjected, and active suffering voluntarily undertaken.[139] If our understanding of God excludes the former, — that created things can inflict suffering on God — does it exclude the latter? The clearest motivation for thinking it does not is the claim that 'God is love'. It seems impossible to affirm this of God and yet deny that God is capable of suffering. Among early Christian theologians however, only Origen takes up the theme of God suffering through love for the world. Moltmann takes us through various accounts of God suffering in Jewish rabbinic and kabbalist traditions about the divine Shekinah, Spanish mysticism of the 'pain of God', Anglican theology of the 'sacrifice of eternal love', and a Russian-Orthodox philosophy of religion as the 'divine tragedy'.[140] I won't pursue the details here of these and other discussion of the suffering of God[141], in order to press on with focus on whether the understanding of God in classical theism blocks all thought of God voluntarily suffering.

This question is parallel to asking whether the God who exists necessarily can create contingently. There, a key point was 'whatever God wills in the act of willing cannot be changed, but God's will remains free to choose what it is that God will in fact will.' Are we to think that God wills to suffer voluntarily in response to the suffering of creatures? Nothing in classical theism's idea of God so far discussed allows us to answer affirmatively, but nor does it entail God not so choosing. (As Moltmann indicated, the latter has for other reasons been presupposed in Jewish and Christian traditions as the more fitting for God.) It is a matter contingent on God's will and so not open to being derived from classical theism's idea of God. An answer would have to be shown us by God. It would have to be revealed and Christians acclaim that revelation is done in Christ, who is the divine Logos incarnate, who was crucified.

One of the implications of the idea of God being discussed is that 'whatever God wills in the act of willing cannot be changed.' Thus, we might think it would be the God who exists necessarily choosing to create a contingent world and therewith choosing to voluntarily suffer

---

139. Moltmann, *The Trinity and the Kingdom of God*, 23.
140. Moltmann, *The Trinity and the Kingdom of God*, 23-47.
141. For example, Dorothy Soelle, *Suffering* (Philadelphia: Fortress, 1975); Johann Baptist Metz, *A Passion for God: The Mystical Political Dimension of Christianity*, (New York: Paulist, 1998); Marilyn McCord Adams, *Horrendous Evils and the Goodness of God* (Carlton: Melbourne University Press, 1999), 168-174.

with the suffering of creatures, a choice that could never be changed. It would be no small matter for this idea of God, which would include God electing from all eternity to create a contingent world and to voluntarily suffer with the suffering of creatures. Again, it seems classical theism has resources to allow us to think of the suffering of the immutable God.[142] But should we think of God in this way?

The idea of the God who suffers has revived in the twentieth and twenty first centuries, in part because of the enormous suffering in the First World War and the Second World War, especially the holocaust, and the challenge all this made to religious sensibilities nurtured in the previous century by the powerful myths of empire promoted across Europe, the United Kingdom, and Australia, and the idea of progress in the United States of America and the Western world. It was also due to recognition of the relevance of the biblical prophetic testimonies of the Hebrew Bible to the suffering of God with the people of Israel[143] and the New Testament accounts of the suffering of God, incarnate in Christ[144] and the concise assertion that 'God is love' (1 John 4:8). Classical theism has the resources to allow us to think of the suffering of the immutable God, and that is the understanding of God that I draw on in the discussion of the problem of natural evil.

---

142. For a powerful rejection of the idea of God suffering see, D Hart, 'No Shadow of Turning: On Divine Impassibility', *Pro Ecclesia*, 11/ 2 (2002).
143. A Heschel., *The Prophets* (New York: Harper & Row, 1962).
144. J Moltmann, *The Crucified God: The Cross of Christ as the Foundation and Criticism of Christian Theology*, translated by RA Wilson and J Bowden (London: SCM, 1974); PS Fiddes, *The Creative Suffering of God* (Clarendon Press, 1988); P Gavrilyuk, *The Suffering of the Impassible God: The Dialectics of Patristic Thought* (Oxford: Oxford University Press, 2004); J Keating, *Divine Impassibility and the Mystery of Human Suffering* (Grand Rapids, MI: Eerdmans, 2009), For a discussion of divine impassibility and divine passibility in recent theology, see C Mostert, 'God's Transcendence and Compassion', *Pacifica*, 24/2, June 2011.

Bibliography

Adams, MM, 1999, *Horrendous Evil and the Goodness of God*, (Melbourne: Melbourne University Press).

Alexander, D, 2008, *Creation or Evolution, Do we have to Choose?* (Oxford: Monarch Books).

Allison, J, 1998, *The Joy of Being Wrong: Original Sin Through Easter Eyes* (New York: Crossroads).

Alvarez LW, Alvarez, W, Asaro, F, HV Michel, 1980, 'Extraterrestial cause for the Cretaceous-Tertiary extinction', *Science*, 208/4448: 1095–1108.

Ames, S, 2004, 'Resonance and Dissonance between Church and Society' in Francis Sullivan, F, and Lippert, S, eds., 2004.

Ames, S, 2010, 'Why would God use evolution?', in J Arnould, ed. 2010, *Darwin and Evolution, Interfaith Perspectives* (Adelaide: ATF Press, 2010).

Ames, S, 2013, 'The Rise, Critiques and Consequences of Scientific Naturalism', in R Horner, R, McArdle, P, and Kirchhoffer, D, eds., *Being Human, Groundwork For A Theological Anthropology For The 21st Century*, (Preston, Mosaic Press).

Ames, S, 2014, 'Being, Wellbeing and Globalisation' in Price, P, ed., 2014.

Ames, S, 2019, 'The Value Given and Presupposed in Person-Centred Dementia Care', *OBM Geriatrics*, volume 3, issue 3, Treatment of Dementia.

Ames, S, 2021, 'Critique of Daniel Dennett's, From Bacteria to Bach and Back, the Evolution of Minds', in *Journal of Biomedical Engineering and Innovations*, 3/1.

Ames, S, 2022, 'From Physics to Metaphysics, a New Way', in, Christian Perspectives on Science and Technology, New Series, 1.

Aquinas, T., 1975, *Summa Theologiae [ST], Volume 14, Divine Government*, translated by TC Obrien (Spottiswoode: Blackfriars).

Arnould, J, ed. 2010, *Darwin and Evolution, Interfaith Perspectives* (Adelaide: ATF Press).

Atran, S, 2004, *In Gods We Trust: The Evolutionary Landscape of Religion*, (Oxford: Oxford University Press).

Barr, J, 1962, *Biblical Words for Time*, (London: SCM Press).

Barrett, CK, 1962, *From First Adam to Last: A study in Pauline Theology*, (London Adam & Charles Black).

Bailey, KE, 1983, *Poet and Peasant and Through Peasant Eyes, A Literary Cultural Approach to the Parables in Luke*,(Grand Rapids MI: Eerdmans).

Barrow, J, 1988, *The World Within the World*, (Oxford: Clarendon Press).

Bath, K, 2009, *Church Dogmatics, Volume 1*, G Bromiley, G, and Torrance, TF, eds., (London: T&T Clark).

Barton, CS, and Wilkinson D, 2009, *Reading Genesis After Darwin*, (Oxford: Oxford University Press).

Biagioli, M, 1990, Galileo's System of Patronage, 28 *History of Science*.

Biagioli, M, 1993, *Galileo, Courtier: The Practice of Science in the Culture of Absolutism (Science and Its Conceptual Foundations)*, (Chicago, University of Chicago Press).

Blackwell, R, 1991, *Galileo, Bellarmine, and the Bible: Including a Translation of Foscarini's Letter on the Motion of the Earth* (Notre Dame IN: Notre Dame University Press).

Blackwell, RJ, 2002, 'Galileo, Galilei', Chapter 8, in Ferngren, GB, 2002.

Birch, C, 1998, 'Neo-Darwinism, Self-Organisation and Divine Action in Evolution', in, Russell, RJ, Stoeger SJ, WR, and Ayala F, eds., 1998.

Boyer, P, 2002, *Religion Explained: The Evolutionary Origins of Religious Thought*, (London: Vintage, 2002).

Brosnan, SF, de Waal, FBM, 2004, 'Fair Refusal by capuchin monkeys', *Nature*, 428: 140. 18.

Brown, R, 1968, *The Semitic Background to the Term 'Mystery' in the New Testament*, (Philadelphia: Fortress).

Buckareff, AA, and Nagasawa, Y, 2016, *Alternative Concepts of God, Essays on the Metaphysics of the Divine*, (Oxford: Oxford University Press).

Buckley, MJ, 1987, *At the Origins of Modern Atheism*, (New Haven: Yale University Press).

Buckley, MJ, 2004, *Denying and Disclosing God, The Ambiguous Progress of Modern Atheism*, (New Haven: Yale University Press).

Bussanich, J, 1996, 'Plotinus's Metaphysics of the One', in Gerson, LP, 1996.

Burrell, DB, Cogliati, C, Soskice, JM, and Stoeger, WR, 2010, eds., *Creation and the God of Abraham*, (Cambridge: Cambridge University Press).

Caputo, JD, and Scanlon, MJ, 1999, *God, the Gift and Postmodernism*, (Bloomington: IN, Indiana University Press).

Carroll, S, Mindscape, https:// www.youtube.com/watch?v=bWowIh6Zjzo.

Chadwick, H, 2008, trans, Augustine, Confessions, (Oxford: Oxford University Press).

Christias, D, 2019, 'Towards a Reformed Liberal and Scientific Naturalism', in *Dialectica*, 73/4.

Clarke, KJ, ed., 2016, *A Blackwell Companion to Naturalism* (Malden MA, USA: John Wiley and Sons Inc).

Clayton P, and Simpson, Z, eds.2008, *The Oxford Handbook of Religion and Science*, (Oxford, Oxford University Press).

Coakley, S, 2012, *Sacrifice Regained: Reconsidering the Rationality of Religious Belief* (Cambridge: Cambridge University Press, 2012).

Conway Morris, S, (2005), *Life's Solution: Inevitable Humans in a Lonely Universe* (Oxford, Oxford University Press).

Conway Morris, S, (2015), *The Runes of Evolution: How the Universe Became Self-Aware*, (West Conshohocken, Pennsylvania: Templeton Press).

Conway Morris, S, 2022, *From Extra-terrestrials to Animal Minds to Six Myths of Evolution*, (Templeton Press).

Copan, P, and Craig, WL, 2004, *Creation out of Nothing, A Biblical, Philosophical and Scientific Exploration*, (Grand Rapids MI: Blackwell's Academic).

Cox, H, 2016, 'How the Market Became Divine', *Dialogue: A Journal of Theology*, 5/11.

Craig, WL, 2001, *God, Time and Eternity: The Coherence of Theism II—Eternity* (Dordrecht, Springer Netherlands).

Craig, WL, 2001, *God, Time and Eternity: The Coherence of Theism II—Eternity* (Dordrecht, Springer Netherlands).

Crick, F, 1970, *Nature*, 227/ 5258.

Cunningham, C, 2010, *Darwin's Pious Idea, Why the Ultradarwinists and Creationists Both get it Wrong*, Grand Rapids Mich Eerdmans).

Cusa, N, 1954, *Of Learned Ignorance*, trans. Germain Heron, (Routledge & Kegan Paul).

Darwin, CR, 1859, (1st edition), *On the origin of species by means of natural selection, or the preservation of favoured races in the struggle for life*, (London, John Murray).

Darwin, C, 1871, *The Descent of Man: and selection in relation to sex*, (London, J. Murray).

Daura-Jourge, FG, Cantor, M, Ingram, N, Lusseau, D, Simoes-Lopes, PC, 2012, 'The structure of Bottlenose Dolphin Society is coupled to a unique foraging cooperation with Artisinal Fishermen, Biology Letters, 8/5, 702–705.

Dawkins, R., 1996, *River Out of Eden: A Darwinian View of Life* (London, Phoenix).

Dawkins, R, 1986, *The Blind Watchmaker* (Harlow: Scientific and Technical).

Dawkins, R, 2006, *The God Delusion*, (London: Bantam).

Davies, P, 2006, *The Goldilocks Enigma, Why Is the Universe Just Right for Life?* (London: Allan Lane).

Davies, B, and Leftow, B, eds. 2004. *The Cambridge Companion to Anselm*, (Cambridge: Cambridge University Press).

Davies, P., 2010, 'Universe from bit', in Davies, P, and Gregersen, N, *Information and the Nature of Reality: From Physics to Metaphysics* (Cambridge: Cambridge University Press).

Davies, P, and Gregersen, N, (2010), Information and the Nature of Reality: From Physics to Metaphysics (Cambridge: Cambridge University Press).

Deason, GB, 1986, 'Reformation Theology and the Mechanistic Conception of Nature', in Lindberg DL, and Numbers RL, 1986.

DeCaro, M, and Macarthur, D, eds., 2004, *Naturalism in Question*, (Harvard University Press).

de La Mettrie, JO, 1996, *Machine Man and Other Writings*, trans. and ed., Thomson, A. (Cambridge: Cambridge University Press).

Dennett, D, 2006, Breaking the Spell: *Religion as a Natural Phenomenon* (New York: Viking).

Dodds, MJ, 2012, *Unlocking Divine Action, Contemporary Science and Thomas Aquinas* (Washington DC: Catholic University of America Press).

Drake, S, 1957, *Discoveries and Opinions of Galileo* (New York: Doubleday, 1957).

Edwards, D., 1999, *The God of Evolution, A Trinitarian Theology*, (New York, Paulist Press).

Edwards, D, *How God Acts, Creation, Redemption, and Special Divine Action* (Hindmarsh: ATF Press).

Edward, B, and Collins, R, 2002, 'Scientific Naturalism' in Ferngren, GB, 2002.

Edwards, M, 2009, Catholicity and Heresy in the Early Church (London: Routledge).

Eagleton, T, 2015, *Hope Without Optimism* (New Haven: Yale University Press).

Eldred. M, 2008, *Social Ontology, Recasting Political Philosophy through the Phenomenology of Whoness*, (Frankfurt, ontos/verlag).

Ellis, B, 1988, *Truth and Objectivity*, (Oxford: Blackwell).

Esposito, J, 2000, ed., *The Oxford History of Islam* (Oxford: Oxford).

Eric Mascall, E, 1966, *Existence and analogy: a sequel to 'He who is'*, London: Darton, Longman & Todd.

Farrer, A, 1943, *Finite and Infinite, A Philosophical Essay*, (Westminster: Dacre Press).

Farrer, A, 1962, *Love almighty and ills unlimited: an essay on providence and evil containing the Nathaniel Taylor lectures for 1961*, (London: Collins).

Feigl, H, and Scriven, M, eds., 1956. *The Foundations of Science and the Concepts of Psychology and Psychoanalysis*, (University of Minnesota Press).

Ferngren, GB, 2002, *Science and Religion, A Historical Introduction* (Baltimore: Johns Hopkins University Press).

Fiddes, PS, 1988, *The Creative Suffering of God* (Clarendon Press).

Finlan, S, and Vladimir Kharlamov, V, 2006, *Theiosis: Deification in Christian Theology* (Eugene OR: Pickwick Publications).

Finocchiaro, M, 1989, translator and editor, *The Galileo Affair, A Documentary History* (Berkley: University of California Press).

Francis Sullivan, F, and Lippert, S, eds., 2004. *Church and Civil Society* (Adelaide, ATF Press).

Galileo, G, 1957, 'The Letter to the Grand Duchess Christina', in Drake 1957, *Discoveries and Opinions of Galileo* (New York: Doubleday, 1957).

Funkenstein, A. 1986, *Theology and the Scientific Imagination: From the Middle Ages to the Seventeenth Century*, (Princeton: Princeton University Press).

Garner, S, 2002, 'Image bearing Cyborgs?' in Garner, S, ed. 2002.

Garner, S, ed. 2002, *Theology and the Body*, (Adelaide: ATF Press, 2002).

Gavrilyuk, P, 2004, *The Suffering of the Impassible God: The Dialectics of Patristic Thought*, (Oxford: Oxford University Press).

Gerson, LP, 2018, 'Plotinus', in *Stanford Encyclopaedia of Philosophy*. Accessed, 15 January 2019.

Gerson, LP, 1996. *The Cambridge Companion to Plotinus* (Cambridge: Cambridge University Press).

Giles, K, 2002, *The Trinity and subordinationism: The Doctrine of God and the Contemporary Gender Debate*, (Downers Grove Illinois: InterVarsity Press).

Gingerich, O, 'The Copernican Revolution', in Ferngren GB, 2002.

Green, J, and Palmer, S, eds., 2005, *In Search of the Soul: Four Views of the Mind Body Problem* (Illinois: Intervarsity Press).

Griffin, DR, 1977, *Evil Revisited: Responses and Reconsiderations* (Albany, NY: State University of New York Press).

Griffin, DR, 2004, *God, Power and Evil, A Process Theodicy*, (Louisville: John Knox Press).

Griffin, DR, 2007, *Whitehead's Radically Different Postmodern Philosophy: An Argument for its Contemporary Relevance*, (Albany: State University of New York Press).

Gunton, C, 1988, *The Triune Creator, A Historical and Systematic Study* (Grand Rapids: Eerdmans).

Gunton, C, 1989, *The Actuality of Atonement: A study of metaphor, rationality, and Christian tradition*, (Grand Rapids MI: Eerdmans).

Gunton, C, 1991, *The Promise of Trinitarian Theology*, (Edinburgh, T&T Clark).

Gunton, 2001, *'Becoming and Being', The Doctrine of God in Charles Hartshorne and Karl Barth*, (London: SCM Press).

Gunton, C, 2003, *Father, Son & Holy Spirit: Toward A Fully Trinitarian Theology*, (Edinburgh: T&T Clark).

Hamilton, S, and Kells, S, 2019, *Sold Down the River, How Robber Barons and Wall Street Traders Cornered*, (Text Publishing, Melbourne Australia).

Harari, YN, 2016, *Homo Deus, A Brief History of Tomorrow* (London: Harvill Secker).

Harrison, P, 2007, *The Fall of Man and the Foundations of Science* (Cambridge: Cambridge University Press).

Harrison, P, ed. 2010, *The Cambridge Companion to Science and Religion*, (Cambridge: Cambridge University Press).

Hart, DB, 2002, 'No Shadow of Turning: On Divine Impassibility', *Pro Ecclesia*, 11/ 2.

Hart, DB, 2013, *The Experience of God, Being, Consciousness, Bliss* (New Haven: Yale University Press).

Hartshorne, C, 1967, *A Natural Theology for Our Time*, (La Salle, Illinois: Open Court).

Hartshorne, C, 1984, *Omnipotence and Other Theological Mistakes*, (Albany: State University of New York).

Haught, JF, 2006, *Is Nature Enough? Meaning and Truth in the Age of Science*, (Cambridge: Cambridge University Press).

Haught, J, 2008, God After Darwin, A Theology of Evolution (Boulder, CO: Westview Press).

Haught, JF, 2006, *Is Nature Enough? Meaning and Truth in the Age of Science*, (Cambridge: Cambridge University Press).

Haught, J, 2015, *Resting on the Future, A Catholic Theology for an Unfinished Universe*, (New York: Bloomsbury Academic).

Havel, V, 1987, 'The Power of the Powerless' (English translation by P Wilson), in Vladislav, J, 1987.

Helminiak, DA, 2015, *Brains, Consciousness and God, A Lonerganian Integration*, (Albany, State University of New York Press).

Hempel, C, 1969, 'Reduction: Ontological and Linguistic Facets', in Morgenbesser S, Suppes, P, and White, M, eds, (1969).

Hick, J, 1966, *Evil and The Love of God* (London: MacMillan).

Heidegger, M, 2002, *Identity and Difference*, (Chicago, Illinois: Chicago University Press), trans. with intro. by Stambaugh, J.

Heschel, A, 1962, *The Prophets*, (New York: Harper & Row).

Hildebrand, AR, Penfield, GT, et al, 1991,'Chicxulub crater: a possible Cretaceous/ Tertiary boundary impact crater on the Yucatán peninsula, Mexico', *Geology*, 19/9: 867–871.

Hoffman, J, and rosenkrantz, GS, 2002, *The Divine Attributes* (Oxford: Blackwell).

Holmes R, III, 2012, *The Emergence of Everything: How the world became complex: Matter-Energy, Life, Mind* (New York: Columbia University Press).

Howard-Snyder, D, and McBrayer, P, eds., 2013, *The Blackwell Companion to the Problem of Evil* (West Sussex: John Wiley and Sons).

Hull M Pincelli, HM, Andrea Bornemann, A, Donald. Penman, E, 2020, 'On impact and volcanism across the Cetacous-Paleogene boundary, *Science*, 367/6475: 266–272.

Hyman, G, 2015, *The Evolution of Atheism, The Politics of a Modern Movement*, (New York: Cambridge University Press).

Jablonski, D, and Chaloner, WG, 'Extinctions in the fossil record (and discussion)', *Philosophical Transactions of the Royal Society of London B*, 344/1307 (1994): 11–17. 12.

Johnson, E, 2007, *Quest for the Living God, Mapping Frontiers in the Theology of God*, (New York: Continuum).

Johnson, E, 2014, *Ask The Beasts: Darwin and The God of Love* (London: Bloomsbury).

Keating, J, 2009, *Divine Impassibility and the Mystery of Human Suffering*, (Grand Rapids, MI: Eerdmans).

Kittel G, and Friedrich G. eds., 1973, Bromley, GW, trans., *Theological Dictionary of the New Testament* (Grand Rapids, MI: Eerdmans, Third Edition), Volume VI.

Koperski, J, 2015, *The Physics of Theism, God, Physics and the Philosophy of Science*, (West Sussex, UK: Wiley Blackwell).

Kingsley, C, 1863, *The Water Babies* (London: Hodder & Stoughton).

Kray, KJ, 2015, ed., *God and the Multiverse: Scientific, Philosophical and Theological Perspectives* (New York: Routledge).

Krauss, L, 2012, *A Universe from Nothing, Why There Is Something Rather than Nothing*, with an Afterword by Richard Dawkins (New York: Simon and Schuster).

Langtry, B, 2008, *God, The Best, And Evil* (Oxford: Oxford University Press).

Lehrer, J, 2012, *The New Yorker* (New York).. 88/3.

Lewis GF, and Barnes, LA, 2019, *A Fortunate Universe: Life in a Finely Tuned Cosmos* (Cambridge: Cambridge University Press).

Lilley, R, 2008, 'Dolphins save stuck whales, guide them back to sea', *National Geographic.*

Lindberg, D, 2002, 'Medieval Science and Religion', in Ferngren, GB, 2002.

Lindberg, D, and Numbers, L., 1986, eds., *God and Nature, Historical Essays on the Encounter between Christianity and Science* (Berkeley, University of California Press).

Lonergan, B, 1957, *Insight, A Study of Human Understanding*, (London: Darton, Longman and Todd).

Lonergan, B, 1967, 'Cognitional Structures', *Collection*, Crowe, FE, ed., (New York: Herder and Herder, 1967).

Lonergan, B, 1972, Method in Theology, Chapter 4 (London: Darton Longman and Todd.

Lonergan, B, 1985, 'The Dialectic of Authority', *A Third Collection of Papers by Bernard J.F. Lonergan*, edited by FE Crowe, FE, (New York: Paulist Press).

Lonergan, B, 2000, fifth edition of 1957, *Insight: A Study of Human Understanding*, Frederick E Crowe and Robert M Doran, editors (Toronto: Lonergan Research Institute of Regis College, University of Toronto Press). Collected Works of Bernard Lonergan, Volume 3.

Lonergan, B, 1972, Method in Theology, Chapter 4 (London: Darton Longman and Todd.

Lonergan, B, 1974, 'Theories of Inquiry', in Ryan WFJ SJ, and Tyrrell, BJ, SJ, eds, 1974.

Lonergan, B, 1985, 'Healing and Creating in History', in Crowe, F, ed., 1985.

La Cugna, C, 1993, God for Us, The Trinity and Christian Life (San Francisco: Harper).

Luc-Marion, J, 2012, God Without Being, translated by TA Carlson (London: University of Chicago Press).

Law, W, 2010, 'Evil God challenge', *Religious Studies*, September 46/3.

Leftow, B, 2004, 'Anselm's Perfect-Being Theology', in B Davies, B, and Leftow, B, eds. 2004.

Lycan, W, 1988, Judgment and Justification (Cambridge: Cambridge University Press).

Lycan, W, 1981, "Is' and 'Ought' in Cognitive Science', in *Behavioural and Brain Sciences*.

Lyotard, J, (1962) *The Postmodern Condition: A Report on Knowledge*, translated by G Bennington (Minneapolis, University of Minnesota Press, 1984.

MacMurray, J, 1961, *Persons in Relation*, (London: Faber & Faber).

Macquarie, J, 1984, *In Search of Deity, An Essay in Dialectical Theism*, (London: SCM Press).

McDowell, J, 2004, 'Naturalism in the Philosophy of Mind,' in DeCaro, M, and Macarthur, D, eds., 2004.

McGrath, A, 2010, *Science and Religion, A New Introduction*, 2nd edition (Malden MA: Wiley-Blackwell).

McGrath, A, 2011, 'A Wider Teleology' in A Mc Grath, *Darwinism and the Divine*.

McGrath, A, 2011, *Darwinism and the Divine, Evolutionary Thought and Natural Theology*, The 2009 Hulsean Lectures, University of Cambridge (Malden, Mass: Wiley-Blackwell).

Medway, P, 1985, *The Limits of Science* (Oxford: Oxford University Press).

Meltzer, ES, ed., 1989, *Three Faiths—One God: A Jewish, Christian, Muslim Encounter* (London: MacMillan).

Metz, JB, 1988, A *Passion for God: The Mystical Political Dimension of Christianity*, (New York: Paulist).

Milbank, J, 1990, *Theology and Social Theory: Beyond Secular Reason* (Oxford: Blackwell).

McLeish, T., 2014, *Faith and Wisdom in Science* (Oxford: Oxford University Press, 2014).

Milbank, J, 2014, *Beyond Secular Order: The Representation of Being and the Representation of People* (Chichester: Wiley-Blackwell).

Moltmann, J, 1974, *The Crucified God: The Cross of Christ as the Foundation and Criticism of Christian Theology*, trans, by Wilson RA, and Bowden, J, (London: SCM).

Moltmann, J, 1981, *The Trinity and the Kingdom of God*, trans. Kohl, M (London: SCM Press).

Moore, AL, 1898, *Science and the Faith* (London: Keagan Paul, Trench, and Co).

Moore, E., 2019, 'Plotinus', in *International Encyclopedia of Philosophy*. Accessed, 15 January 2019.

Morgenbesser S, Suppes, P, and White, M, eds, (1969) *Philosophy, science, and method; essays in Honor of Ernest Nagel* (New York: St Martin's Press).

Morowitz, HJ, 2002, *The Emergence of Everything: How the World Became Complex*, (New York: Oxford University Press).

Mose, J, 2003, 'Was there an ANZAC Theology?', *Colloquium*, 35/1.

Mostert, C, 2011, 'God's Transcendence and Compassion', in *Pacifica*, 24/2.

Mulherin, C, 2019, *Science and Christianity, The Conflict Myth* (Melbourne: Garratt Publishing).

Mullens, RT, 2016, *The End of the Timeless God* (Oxford: Oxford University Press).

Murphy, N, 2006, *Bodies and Souls, or Spirited Bodies* (Cambridge: Cambridge University Press).

Murphy, N, and Brown, WS, 2009, *Did My Neurons Make Me Do It?* (Oxford: Oxford University Press).

Murray, MJ, 2008, *Nature Red in Tooth and Claw* (Oxford, Oxford University Press).

Murray, MJ, 2008, *An Introduction to the Philosophy of Religion*, (Cambridge: Cambridge University Press).

Muzaffar Iqbal, 2000, 'Science, Medicine and Technology', in J Esposito.

Muzaffar Iqbal, 2002, *Islam and Science* (Ashgate, Hampshire: Ahmad Dallal).

Nagasawa, Y, 2008, 'A New Defence of Anselmian Theism', *The Philosophical Quarterly*, 58/233.

Nagel, T, 2012, *Mind and Cosmos: Why the materialist, neo-Darwinian Conception of Nature is Almost Certainly False*, (Oxford: Oxford University Press).

Nasr, SH, 1996, *Religion and the Order of Nature*, (New York: Oxford University Press).

Newton, I, 1704, *Opticks; or, a Treatise of the Reflections, Refractions, Inflections, and Colours of Light*, (London: printed for Sam. Smith, and Benj. Walford, Printers to the Royal Society, at the Prince's Arms in St. Paul's Church-Yard, MDCCIV).

Nowark, M, Coakley, S, eds., 2013, *Evolution, Games and God: The Principle of Cooperation*, (Cambridge, Massachusetts: Harvard University Press).

Numbers, RL, 1977, *Creation by Natural Law, Laplace's nebular hypothesis in American thought*, (London, University of Washington Press).

Nussbaum, M, 2000, *Upheavals of Thought*, (Cambridge: Cambridge University Press).

O'Meara, DJ, 1996, 'The Hierarchical Ordering of Reality in Plotinus', in Gerson, LP, 1996.

O'Meara, TF, 2012, The Vast Universe, Extraterrestrials and Christian Revelation (Collegeville: Liturgical Press).

Ormerod, N, 1992, *Grace & Disgrace: A Theology of Self-Esteem, Society, and History*, (Newtown: NSW: EJ Dwyer).

O'Shea, JR, 2010, 'Normativity and Scientific Naturalism in Sellars' 'Janus-Faced' Space of Reasons', in *International Journal of Philosophical Studies*, 18/3.

Padgett, AG, 1992, God, *Eternity and the Nature of Time* (New York: St. Martin's Press).

Paley, W, 1802, *Natural Theology: Or Evidence of the Existence and Attributes of the Deity. Collected from the Appearances of Nature* (London: R Faulder).

Papineau, D, 1999, 'Normativity and Judgement', *Aristotelian Society Supp*, 77.

Papineau, D, 2000, 'The Rise of Physicalism', in Stone, WF Marrtin, and Wolff, J, eds., 2000.

Papineau, D, 2015, 'Naturalism', in *Stanford Encyclopedia of Philosophy*.

Paul, R; Deino AL; Hilgen FJ; F Klaudia, F; Kuiper, F; Darren MF; Mitchell, W; Leah E Morgan; Roland; Jan Smit Mundil, 2013, 'Time Scales of Critical Events Around the Cretaceous-Paleogene Boundary', *Science*, 339/6120, 684–687.

Peacocke, A, 1983, *An Introduction to Physical Chemistry of Biological Systems*, (Oxford: Clarendon Press).

Peacocke, P., 2009, *Evolution, The Disguised Friend of Faith?*, (West Conshohocken: Templeton Press).

Pinsent, A, 2015, *Reviews in Theology and Religion*, 22/4.

Placher, WC, 1994, *Narratives of a Vulnerable God*, (Louisville: Westminster John Knox Press).

Placher, W, 1996, *The Domestication of Transcendence: How Modern Thinking about God Went Wrong*, (Louisville, Ky: Westminster John Knox Press).

Plantinga, A, 1965, 'The Free Will Defence', in Max Black, ed., *Philosophy in America* (Ithaca, NY: Cornell University Press.

Plantinga, A, 1977, *God, Freedom, and Evil*, (Grand Rapids, MI: Eerdmans).

Pope Francis, *Laudato Si*, http://w2. vatican. va/content/francesco/en/encyclicals/documents/papa-francesco_20150524_enciclica-laudato-si. Html.

Popper, K, 1959, *The Logic of Scientific Discovery*, (London: Hutchinson).

Price, P, ed., 2014, *Christian Perspectives on Globalisation, A World United or Divided*, (Adelaide: ATF Press).

Price, RM, 2015, *Ground of Being, Neglected Essays of Paul Tillich*, (Mindvendor).

Prigogine, I, 1980, *From Being to Becoming: Time and Complexity in the Physical Sciences*, (San Francisco: WH Freeman and Company).

Quine, WVO, 1948, 'What there is', *Metaphysical Review*, 2/s.

Rahner, K, 1978, *Foundations of Christian Faith*, (London: Darton Longman & Tod).

Rahner, K, 1978, 'Christology within an Evolutionary View of the World', in *Foundations of Christian Faith: An Introduction to the Idea of Christianity*, translated by William V Dych (New York: Crossroad).

Rahner, K, 1997, *The Trinity*, Joseph Donceel, J, trans., Laguna, C, index and glossary, (New York: Crossroad).

Rampino M, and Caldeira, K, 'Periodic impact cratering and extinction events over the last 260 million years', Monthly Notes of the Royal Astronomical Society, 454 (2015): 3480–3484.

Rampino, M, Caldeira, K, 'Comparison of the ages of large-body impacts, flood-basalt eruptions, ocean-anoxic events and extinctions over the last 260 million years: a statistical study', International Journal of Earth Sciences, 107 (2015): 601–606.

Rampino, M, 'Dark Matter's Shadowy Effect on Earth', Astronomy (April 2018): 24.

Rampino, M, 'Relationship between impact-crater size and severity of related extinction episodes', Earth Sciences Reviews, 102990 (2020): 201.

Reid, D, 2013, 'A Reading of Westcott's Gospel of Creation: An Early Venture into Ecological Theology?', *in Journal of Anglican Studies*.

Richards, JW, 2003, *The Untamed God: A Philosophical Exploration of Divine Perfection, Simplicity and Immutability*, (Downers Grove Ill: InterVarsity Press).

Rolnick, PA, 2007, Person, Grace, and God (Grand Rapids: Eerdmans).

Rovelli, C, 2021, *Helgoland*, translated by, E Segre, and, S Carnell (Dublin: Allen Lane).

Rowe, W, 1979, 'IX The Problems of Evil and Some Varieties of Atheism', in *American Philosophical Quarterly*, 16/4 (1979).

Rowe, W., 1996, 'The Evidential Argument from Evil: A Second Look', in D Howard-Snyder, *The Evidential Argument from Evil* (Indiana University Press, 1996).

Russell, B, 1957, *Why I Am Not A Christian* (London: Allen &Unwin).

Russell, RJ, Stoeger SJ, WR, and Ayala F, eds., 1998, *Evolutionary and Molecular Biology, Scientific Perspectives on Divine Action*, (Vatican City: Vatican Observatory and Berkeley: Centre for Theology and the Natural Sciences).

Russell, RJ, Murphy, N, and Isham, IJC, eds., 1999. *Quantum Cosmology and The Laws of Nature: Scientific Perspectives on Divine Action*, Vatican City State: Vatican Observatory Publications and Berkeley, CA: The Centre for Theology and the Natural Science).

Ryan WFJ SJ, and Tyrrell, BJ, SJ, eds, 1974. *A Second Collection*, (Toronto: Lonergan Research Institute of Regis College, Toronto, University, of Toronto Press).

Rysiew, P, 2020, 'Naturalism in Epistemology', in *Stanford Encyclopaedia of Philosophy*.

Schellenberger, JL, 2013, 'A New Logical Problem of Evil', in Howard-Snyder, D, and McBrayer, P, eds., 2013.

Schlipp, PA, ed., 1941, *The Philosophy of Alfred North Whitehead*, (Evanston, Illinois: Northwestern University Press).

Schweizer, E, (1973), πνευμα, πνευματικοσ. in Kittel G, and Friedrich G. eds., 1973.

Scullion, J, SJ, Genesis 1–11 (1984); Genesis 12–25 (1985); Genesis 26–37 (1986); (Minneapolis: Augsburg Publishing House).

Sellars, W, 1956, 'Empiricism and Philosophy of Mind', in, Feigl, H, and Scriven, M, eds., 1956.

Sellars, W, 1962, *Science, Perception and Reality*, (London: Routledge, and Kegan Paul).

Shanks, A, 2000, *God, and Modernity: A New and Better Way to Do Theology*, London: Routledge).

Smart, JJC, 1959, 'Sensations and Brain Processes', *Philosophical Review*.

Smolin, L, 1997, *The Life of the Cosmos*, (Oxford: Oxford University Press).

Smolin, L, 2006, *The Trouble With Physics: The Rise of String Theory, The Fall of a Science, and What Comes Next* (Boston: Houghton Mifflin Harcourt).

Spitzer SJ, R, 2015, *The Soul's Upward Yearning, Clues to Our Transcendent Nature from Experience and Reason* (San Francisco, Ignatius Press).

Sober E, and Wilson, DS, 1988, *Unto Others: The Evolution and Psychology of Unselfish Behaviour*, (Cambridge MA: Harvard University Press).

Soelle, D, *Suffering*, (Philadelphia: Fortress).

Southgate, C, 2008, *The groaning of creation: God, evolution, and the problem of evil*, (Louisville: Westminster John Knox Press).

Spaeman, R, 2006, *Persons: The difference between 'someone' and 'something'*, trans. O'Donovan, O, (Oxford, Oxford University Press).

Statement from the Heart, 2017, https://ulurustatement.org. Stoeger, W, 2010, 'God, physics and the Big Bang', in P Harrison, ed. 2010.

Stenger, V, 2006, *The Comprehensible Universe, Where Do the Laws of Physics Come From?*, (New York: Prometheus Books).

Stengers, I, 1984, *Order Out of Chaos: Man's New Dialogue with Nature*, (New York: Bantam Books).

Stoeger, SJ, W, 1999, 'Contemporary Physics and the Ontological Status of The Laws of Nature', in Russell R, Murphy N, and Isham, CIJ, eds., 1999.

Stoeger, SJ, W, 2010, 'God, physics and the Big Bang', in P Harrison, P, ed. 2010.

Stoeger SJ, W, 2013, *Theology and Science*, 11/1, Taylor & Francis.

Stoljar, D, 2015, 'Physicalism', in *Stanford Encyclopedia of Philosophy*.

Stone, WF Marrtin, and Wolff, J, eds., 2000, *The Proper Ambition of Science*, (London: Routledge).

Southgate, C, 2008, *The groaning of creation: God, evolution, and the problem of evil*, Louisville: Westminster John Knox Press.

Swinburne, R, 1979, The Existence of God (Oxford: Oxford University Press).

Taylor, C, 1994, *Sources of the Self: The Making of Modern Identity*, (Cambridge: Cambridge University Press).

Taylor, C, 2007, *A Secular Age*, (Cambridge, Mass., Belknap Press Harvard University Press).

Teilhard de Chardin SJ 1955, The Phenomenon of Man (New York: Harper and Rowe).

Tillich, P, 1951, *Systematic Theology, Volume 1*, (Chicago Il: Chicago University Press).

Tillich, P, 1953, *The Courage to Be*, (New Haven: Yale University Press).

Thomas, E, 2018, 'Samuel Alexander', Stanford Encyclopaedia of Philosophy.

Tooley, M., 2015 'Problem of Evil', in *Stanford Encyclopaedia of Philosophy*. Section 1.

Tooley, M., 1991, 'The Argument from Evil', in *Philosophical Perspectives*, 5: 89–134.

Torrance, A, 1996, *Persons in Communion: An essay in Trinitarian description and human participation, with special reference to volume one of Karl Barth's Church Dogmatics*, (Edinburgh: T&T Clark).

Trakakis, N, 2007, 'An Epistemically Distant God? A Critique of John Hick's Response to the Problem of Divine Hiddenness'. *Heythrop Journal* XLVIII.

Trakakis, N, 2007, *The God Beyond Belief: In Defence of William Rowe's Evidential Argument from Evil*, (Dordrecht: Springer).

Turner, J and Maryanski, A, 2019,'The deep origins of society: An assessment of EO Wilson's Genesis, in International Sociology of Reviews, 34/5 (2019).

Tyson, P, 2014, *Returning to Reality, Christian Platonism for Our Times* (Eugene OR: Cascade Books).

Tyson, P, 2017, De-fragmenting modernity, Reintegrating Knowledge with Wisdom, Belief with Truth, and Reality with Being (Eugene Oregon, Cascade Books).

Tyson, P, 2022, *A Christian Theology of Science, Reimagining A Theological Vision of Natural Knowledge* (Grand Rapids, MI: Baker Academic).

Vanhoozer, KJ, 2003.ed, *The Cambridge Companion to Postmodern Theology* (Cambridge: Cambridge University Press).

Vladislav, J, ed., 1987, *Living in Truth*, (London: Faber & Faber).

Ward, G. ed. 1998, *The Postmodern God, A Theological Reader*, (Malden Mass: Blackwell Publisher).

Ward, K, 1982, *Rational Theology and the Creativity of God*, (Oxford: Blackwell, 1982).

Ward, K, 1999, 'God as a Principle of Cosmological Explanation', in Russell RJ, Murphy, N, and Isham, CJ, *Quantum Cosmology and The Laws of Nature, Scientific Perspectives on Divine Action*, (Vatican City State: Vatican Observatory Publications and Berkeley California, The Centre for Theology and the Natural Sciences, 2nd edition).

Ward, K. 2013, *A Guide for the Perplexed*, (London: One World Publication).

Walker SI, and Davies, P, 2016, 'The Hard Problem of Life', *arXiv:1606.07184v1 [q-bio. OT]*.

Walton, J, 2011, *Genesis 1 as Ancient Cosmology* (Winona Lake, Indiana: Eisenbrauns).

Weinberg, S, 1977, *The First Three Minutes*, (New York: Basic Books).

Welker, M, 2014, ed., *The Depth of the Human Person: A multidisciplinary Approach,* (Grand Rapids, MI: Eerdmans).

Westcott, BF, 1886, 'The Gospel of Creation', an appendix in his 1886, *The Epistles of St John: the Greek Text with Notes and Essays*, (2nd edition. Cambridge & London: Macmillan).

Whitehead, AN, 1929, *Process and Reality: An Essay in Cosmology: Gifford Lectures, 1927-1928* (New York: Cambridge University Press).

Wildman, WJ, 'Ground of Being Theologies', in Clayton P, and Simpson, Z, eds.2008.

Williams, R, 2014, *The Edge of Words, God and the Habits of Language*, (London: Bloomsbury).

Wilson, EO, 1975, *Sociobiology: The New Synthesis*, (Cambridge MA: Harvard University Press).

Wilson, DS, and Wilson, EO, 2007, 'Rethinking the Theoretical Foundation of Sociobiology', in The *Quarterly Review of Biology*, Volume 82/2.

Wilson, DS, and Wilson, 2007, *The Quarterly Review of Biology*, 82/2.

Wright GF, (1882), *Studies in Science and Religion*, (Andover, Mass., WF, Draper, pp. 175, 183, 185-6.

Wright, NT, 2007, *Surprised by Hope*, (London: SPCK).

Wright, NT, 2003, *The Resurrection of the Son of God* (Minneapolis: Fortress Press).

Wright, NT, 2019, *History and Eschatology, Jesus, and the Promise of Natural Theology* (London: SPCK).

Young, N., 1974, *Creator, Creation and Faith*, (London: Collins).

Zizioulas, J, 2006, *Communion and Otherness: Further Studies in Personhood and the Church*, McParland, P, editor (New York: T&T Clark).